Client/Server

Programming

with **Microsoft® Visual Basic®**

Kenneth L. Spencer
Ken Miller

PUBLISHED BY
Microsoft Press
A Division of Microsoft Corporation
One Microsoft Way
Redmond, Washington 98052-6399

Library of Congress Cataloging-in-Publication Data
Spencer, Kenneth L., 1951–
    Client/server programming with Microsoft Visual Basic / Kenneth L.
  Spencer, Ken Miller.
      p.   cm.
    Includes index.
    ISBN 1-57231-232-7
     1. Client/server computing.   2. Microsoft Visual Basic.
  I. Miller, Ken (Kenneth)   II. Title.
  QA76.9.C55S74   1996
  005.2--dc20   96-13257
                                                  CIP

Printed and bound in the United States of America.

1 2 3 4 5 6 7 8 9 MLML 1 0 9 8 7 6

Distributed to the book trade in Canada by Macmillan of Canada, a division of Canada Publishing Corporation.

A CIP catalogue record for this book is available from the British Library.

Microsoft Press books are available through booksellers and distributors worldwide. For further information about international editions, contact your local Microsoft Corporation office. Or contact Microsoft Press International directly at fax (206) 936-7329.

Blue Sky is a registered trademark of Blue Sky Corporation. Borland, Borland International, dBASE, and Paradox are registered trademarks of Borland International, Inc. Btrieve is a registered trademark of Btrieve Technologies, Inc. PATHWORKS, VAX, and VMS are trademarks of Digital Equipment Corporation. Logic Works is a registered trademark and ERwin is a trademark of Logic Works, Inc. FoxPro, Microsoft, SourceSafe, Visual Basic, Win32, Windows, and Windows NT are registered trademarks and ActiveX is a trademark of Microsoft Corporation. ORACLE is a registered trademark of Oracle Corporation. InstallShield is a registered trademark of Stirling Technologies, Inc. Visio is a registered trademark of Visio Corporation.

Companies, names, and/or data used in screens and sample output are fictitious unless otherwise noted.

Acquisitions Editor: David Clark
Project Editor: Ron Lamb
Technical Editor: Linda Rose Ebenstein
Manuscript Editor: Averill Curdy

To my loving wife, Trisha Spencer.
We have had a wonderful life together
and shared many trials and victories.
You have been my inspiration,
always encouraging me to rise to my dreams.

Thanks, my dear, for a wonderful 25 years.
I hope the next are just as good and exciting.
Love does indeed grow better with time.

—Ken Spencer

To my wife, Madaline, and my son, Jeffrey.
Words cannot express how I feel for you both.

—Ken Miller

TABLE OF CONTENTS

ACKNOWLEDGMENTS

This book would not have been possible without the support of Jon Roskill, director of marketing for Visual Basic at Microsoft. Jon has supported our work with Visual Basic over the past few years in innumerable ways. He's one of those few people who get things done and get them done right NOW! Jon is also a terrific spokesman for Visual Basic and routinely gets the word out about our books as well. Thanks, Jon.

We would especially like to thank Linda Ebenstein, technical editor on this project. Linda ran every line of code in each sample application to help ensure that everything works as stated. Any remaining problems are solely our responsibility. Hats off to her tenacity despite the long days and nights necessary to meet the schedule.

Major thanks also go to David Clark, Ron Lamb, Averill Curdy, Deborah Long, and everyone else behind the scenes at Microsoft Press. This book is as much a result of their insights and work as our own. We feel that this work is the best we've ever done, and they are the ones who made the difference.

Closer to home, we'd like to thank Trisha Spencer, Ken Spencer, Jr., Jeff Spencer, Madaline Miller, and Jeffrey Miller. No matter how much support authors receive, the writing of a book is a significant intrusion on a family. Thanks to our wives and children for their moral support and understanding.

INTRODUCTION

For the past few years we've been developing client/server applications using Microsoft Visual Basic. What makes our experience different from many others' is the success rate we have attained. Unlike the horror stories we hear from many others and those we see in the trade press, our experiences with the applications with which we've been involved have been wholly successful. We'd like to show you how you can experience the same success.

The best way to learn a new approach is by doing it, and the best way for us to encourage you is by providing lots of sample code. Much of the code you are about to see will be new and useful and by itself will pay for this book. But we'd like to offer an even greater value.

There is an old saying: "Give a man a fish, and you feed him for a day. Teach a man to fish, and you feed him for life." We hope to do both. The sample code is a fish you can enjoy immediately. The assortment of techniques and methodologies we present are a pole, line, and hook. We sincerely hope you will eat well for the rest of your career.

Who Should Read This Book

To get the most out of this book, you should understand the syntax of Visual Basic and be able to build Visual Basic applications. You should also know how to create a relational database using Microsoft SQL Server. An understanding of OLE automation would also be helpful because it is one of the techniques we use to provide flexible implementations.

The ease of use provided by Visual Basic, the robust functionality of Microsoft Office, and the high performance afforded by SQL Server combine to create an excellent foundation on which to construct your applications. We encourage you to explore these products separately and in conjunction with this book and others. You'll be amazed at what you can do and how easy it is to do it.

What Is in This Book

Platforms Covered

Microsoft Windows 95, Microsoft Windows NT Workstation, and Microsoft Windows NT Server are the only development platforms used in this book. Why did we choose only these platforms? All of our clients who are doing serious database development are moving to 32-bit operating systems in the near future, so we felt it would be useful to focus on the 32-bit area.

The focus on 32-bit platforms allows us to limit our discussions to topics that are relevant to 32-bit applications. We did not have to dig through reams of materials on avoiding resource issues, differences in the Win16 and Win32 API, and so on. There is also plenty of information already available on 16-bit topics.

Structure of the Book

This book consists of lots of information on building client/server solutions using Visual Basic. We take a real-world approach to the development process, and this takes us into areas such as database design, object design, OLE automation, using third-party tools, and much more.

Each sample is designed to be short and to the point to make it easier for you to review. Chapter 1 includes the most complex application in the book. Chapter 12 is devoted to the Car Rental Demo application that Microsoft uses in many of its demonstrations of Visual Basic. We thought it would be useful for you to see this application because it has been demonstrated so often.

What Is on the Companion Disc

The companion CD contains code for all the samples in the book, as well as a fully functional application, which is in the Atx subdirectory. (The Atx program is not discussed in the book but is provided to demonstrate what a fully functional application looks like.) The code is provided on the companion CD in two ways: in the directories described in the book so that you can browse the CD and in a special Setup directory from which you install the files onto your hard disk.

The files are provided in these two ways because real-mode CD-ROM drivers under Windows 95 truncate long filenames. If you have such a driver, you will not be able to browse the directories or files on this disc (and you should contact your CD-ROM drive manufacturer for an updated Windows 95 driver). However, you can still install the files onto your hard disk.

To install the program files onto your hard disk, run Setup.exe, which you can find in the root directory of the companion CD, and then follow the on-screen instructions.

To be able to run most of the samples provided on the CD, you will need to set up your database by following the steps in "Building Your Database Schema in SQL Server" on page 84. Also, some applications depend on OLE servers, such as our splash screen OLE server. To use these applications, build the OLE server and run it so that it is registered in the Registry. Then resolve the reference to the OLE server in the application by choosing References from the Visual Basic Tools menu, build the application, and run it.

Many of the samples depend on our CSUtilities.dll OLE server, which you can find in the Utilities directory. Build this OLE server as described in "Sample Program: Client/Server Utilities" on page 140, and register it by running Regserver-32.exe with CSUtilities.dll as the single command-line parameter. (You can find Regserver32.exe in the clisvr subdirectory under the directory in which you installed Visual Basic.)

To run the samples on the companion CD, you will need Microsoft Windows NT Server version 3.51 or later running SQL Server version 6, at least one client running Microsoft Windows NT version 3.51 or later of Microsoft Windows 95, Microsoft Visual Basic version 4 Enterprise Edition, and Microsoft Access version 7 or later. Some of the samples also require third-party software.

Contacting the Authors

You can contact the authors at the following addresses:

Ken Spencer
Computer Technologies, Inc.
(910) 632-1430
CompuServe: 71551,2724
MSN: ken_spencer_cti

Ken Miller
Ken Miller, Inc.
(914) 648-2699
CompuServe: 73504,1240
MSN: KenMiller

1

Visual Basic and Client/Server Systems: The Basics

If you examine the way your organization is structured today and the way people perform their jobs, you will find many instances in which both the structure and the jobs were designed around the technology available at the time. Client/server technology has such sweeping implications that it's time to reevaluate the way organizations solve a number of problems.

In just the past few years, client/server systems have become common features of corporate computing. Because of the dropping prices of hardware and software, client/server systems provide increased performance at lower cost—an unbeatable combination. However, simply moving legacy applications from a mainframe to a client/server system might provide some cost savings, but they will be limited. Using the technology this way is like replacing a five-year-old VCR that works OK with the latest model and justifying the purchase because the new VCR has the most advanced features. If the only thing you do with your VCR is play the occasional rental movie, you wasted your money.

Instead, the organization must examine the way it functions and be willing to make changes so it can use the technology to become more competitive and take advantage of new opportunities. (It is often helpful to have a team focused on reorganization working closely with the client/server development staff during the process.)

Moving to a client/server architecture also requires that you reconsider the ways you build and support your applications. Changes to the architectural and design methodologies (covered more fully in Chapter 2) necessitate reconsidering everything from your network infrastructure to your development language, version management tools, database tools, and homegrown utilities. To fully exploit the technology, you not only need the new development tools, but you need to change the way your developers think about what they do, as well as the structure of the organization itself, to support a different style of development and to utilize the results of that development.

New technologies continue to emerge that make developing and deploying client/server systems not only desirable but necessary. By failing to move appropriate applications to client/server platforms, organizations ignore the benefits of an enabling technology that can help them stay competitive and keep their operations cost effective.

You'll find that the architecture and methodologies advocated by this book offer a number of benefits:

- Shorter development cycles

- Longer life cycles for applications

- Easier access to information for end users from standard tools such as Microsoft Office

- Automatic features based on Remote Automation in Microsoft Visual Basic 4

- Scalability, such as in the migration of Microsoft Access to Microsoft SQL Server

- Better control of development through version control and object libraries

- Increased performance by the distribution of CPU cycles and data over multiple systems

This chapter serves as an introduction to client/server systems and the advantages of using Visual Basic 4 and SQL Server 6.x, and it explains some of the concepts and models we've developed that are the foundation of many other discussions throughout the book.

What Is a Client/Server System?

A client/server system usually runs on at least two different systems—one acts as a client and the other as a server. However, it is possible that both client and server are housed on a single system. Usually one server provides services to several client systems, although there might be only one client. The server function is frequently performed by a file server, except when maximum performance is required and a specialized server is used. Often the client is a networked desktop system. Whenever the user wants to retrieve or store information, the client portion of the application issues a request, which is sent (usually over a network) to the server. The server executes the request and returns information to the client.

A database does not constitute a client/server system, although client/server systems frequently use a database to perform the server activity. Applications designed to use Access, Microsoft FoxPro, Paradox by Borland, or other desktop databases are not client/server systems, *even when those databases reside on a network server*. Those are examples of networked database applications because all processing is performed by the client.

How a Client/Server System Works

Client/server systems were originally developed in an effort to provide significantly greater performance, with only a modest increase in price, by moving some of the processing from the client to the server. This might improve performance, but it does little for cost. Here's how you can achieve a significant performance/price ratio: instead of buying 11 super PCs, sticking a very large disk drive in one of them, using it as the server, and running a networked database application on the 10 remaining clients, you buy 10 adequate PCs and one super-duper server PC. Build a client/server application that uses the super-duper server for most of the processing, and use the clients for making simple requests and presenting the information to the user.

Figure 1-1 on the next page shows how a typical client/server system is configured. In this diagram, the hub and wiring are shown only for clarity. Networks vary at the hardware level, so your components will definitely consist of more than a simple hub and some wires.

In Figure 1-1 the Microsoft Windows 95 client generates a SQL query (*Select LastName, FirstName from MyTable*). The query is sent over the network to the Microsoft Windows NT server running SQL Server. SQL Server then processes the query and returns the data to the Windows 95 client. The operation of the client/server system shown is different from a desktop database application in the manner in which the data is processed. Using a desktop database such as Access, the entire database table requested in the query would be sent to the client for processing. The client would process the data and then display the result set. A typical PC database is much less efficient at running on a network because of the amount of data sent over the network and because the application load is not split across the desktop PC and the server. The only work the server does in this case is to handle the standard file-serving chores by providing access to the database from the PC.

As soon as you start developing applications using Visual Basic 4, the model changes. The OLE automation and Remote Automation features of Visual Basic 4 change the way a client/server system can be built and utilized. Running

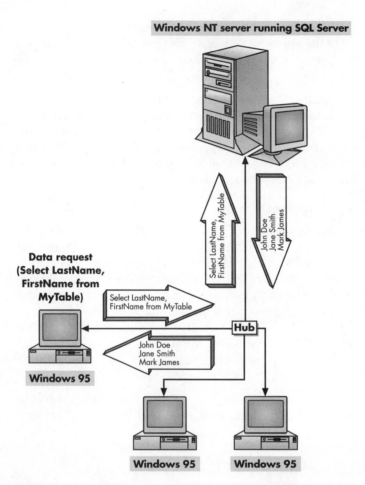

Figure 1-1. *Client/server systems typically request and receive data over a network.*

Visual Basic 4 applications on Windows 95 or Windows NT provides a powerful combination of features for your clients, complete with expanded resources, preemptive multitasking, a recoverable file system (Windows NT File System or NTFS), and more.

Improved features and functionality aren't the only differences between how client/server applications have been built in the recent past and how we propose building them. As you examine the suggested architecture of client/server systems using Visual Basic 4 (Figure 1-2), you will see a fundamental difference because the architecture we propose is actually multitiered.

Notice how Remote Automation can be used to keep an eye on inventory through an Executive Alarm System. Client A sends a request to the server to watch the amount of inventory. This triggers a periodic check of the total inventory value by a program on the server, requiring no further interaction by the client. The server sends an alert when the inventory value exceeds $2 million and also triggers a different Remote Automation program on the client, which displays the status of the inventory and requests action by a manager.

The request by Client B uses a different approach. Client B requests a listing of all inventory from the server. If this query were run interactively, it would bog down the server, the client, and the network while retrieving, waiting for, and transporting the data. Instead, Client B issues the request by calling a stored procedure in SQL Server. This stored procedure then uses MAPI to send the response to the client's Microsoft Mail account.

Of course, you can and should use the technique shown in Figure 1-1 for other parts of the system that don't require these special types of functionality.

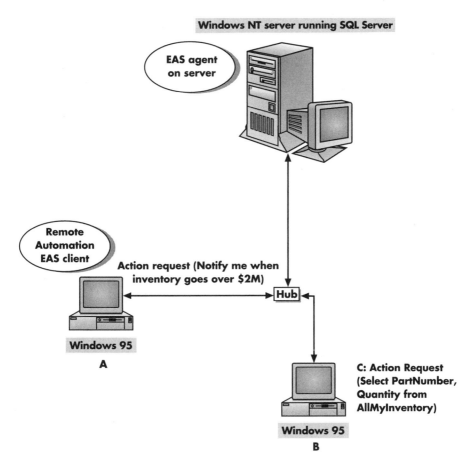

Figure 1-2. *The power of Remote Automation in an Executive Alarm System (EAS) application and of stored procedures in SQL Server.*

Our example is complicated by the consideration of what can be done with Access in a client/server environment. One of the best ways to build a client/server system that is compatible with Open Database Connectivity (ODBC) is to use a local Access database, with the server containing attached tables. One reason this works so well is that the Access database will contain the internal structures (fields and indexes) for the ODBC database—attached tables, reducing the amount of work that must be done each time a request to the database is processed.

Access understands the ODBC capabilities of the remote database and can pass all queries to the server for execution except when a query uses functions or features supported by Access but not by the back-end database.

The local Access database is also useful for storing relatively static data, such as a list of states used in shipping addresses. Because of the list's small size and the infrequency with which the list changes, it can be downloaded from the server when the application starts and a local copy referenced. One other method is to generate a time-stamped transaction file for the table in a shared folder on the server. Each client can pick up the transaction file and apply it at a specified interval and then notify the server that the table has been updated. Other approaches could also be used, such as having a server process connect to each local database and apply the update. You must use care when storing any data in a distributed manner because a well-designed architecture is essential for ensuring that no data is out of sync with the master copy.

Why Use Visual Basic 4 and SQL Server 6 for a Client/Server System?

Visual Basic has long been our tool of choice for creating client/server applications. The reasons are many, but they all stem from Visual Basic's powerful integration with other Microsoft Windows—based applications, its ease of use, and the awesome power it provides.

The object technology in Visual Basic 4 adds so much power that you can now use it to build incredible applications with a solid object foundation. Remote Automation, combined with standard OLE automation features, makes Visual Basic 4 a killer development environment. Entire books have been written about Visual Basic 4 database development alone. Remote Data Objects (RDO) and the RemoteData control also make Visual Basic 4 a powerful client/server development tool.

NOTE Visual Basic is what we term "object-centric." We use this term to avoid the sometimes heated debate over what makes a language object-oriented—one of the most-used and least-agreed-upon terms in software. One thing programming purists all agree on is that Visual Basic is not object-oriented, as it lacks polymorphism, inheritance, and encapsulation, which are the three characteristics everyone agrees are necessary. Discussion of these terms is beyond the scope of this book, but suffice it to say that Visual Basic, at best, only partially exhibits these characteristics.

Project management is now possible with Visual Basic because Microsoft Visual SourceSafe is tightly integrated into Visual Basic Enterprise Edition. SourceSafe can completely manage your source code, whether you have a small or a large development shop. Source-code management is the only way that you can effectively manage a large application and the thousands of lines of code it requires.

Another key feature of Visual Basic 4 is Visual Basic for Applications (VBA), the much-written-about language that is now part of Office and Microsoft Project as well. You can literally port most of the code from one of these applications to another, and the code will work.

Strategic Significance

Don't underestimate the strategic significance of using Visual Basic 4 running on a Microsoft Win32 client, and SQL Server 6.*x* running on Windows NT. These products are much more than just powerful, easy-to-use upgrades of their previous versions. They are Microsoft's premier offering when it comes to constructing client/server applications.

Visual Basic's new class modules provide the ability to quickly and easily build reusable component libraries. These libraries are easy to maintain and provide a simple one-stop shop for both applications and developers. The new Jet database engines (Jet 2.5 for 16-bit applications and Jet 3.0 for 32-bit applications) provide a more complete Data Access Object model, which affords Visual Basic applications the ability to fully manipulate and access a variety of data sources. The dream of running code on multiple PCs can finally be achieved through Visual Basic Remote Automation.

Like Visual Basic, the latest release of SQL Server provides a host of new features to make development and use easier. The SQL Enterprise Manager lets database administrators (DBAs) manage geographically distributed databases from their desktops. Built-in replication using the publish/subscribe metaphor makes controlled distribution and collection of data almost trivial. Exposure of the SQL Manager through OLE objects lets a programmer do anything from code that can be done from the DBA's desktop.

But choosing these tools based on their features alone would be a mistake. Client/server applications are like a football team: all the players must work together in order to reach the goal. Likewise, the easiest-to-use front-end tool or the highest-performance database is useless unless it works well with other applications. The beauty of the Visual Basic/SQL Server/Windows NT team is the ease with which their play can be coordinated.

Enabling technology

Visual Basic 4 and SQL Server 6 provide an enabling technology for many organizations. In other words, you can construct applications tailored to business needs that are not easily addressed by other technologies. For instance, the example in Figure 1-2 shows how the Executive Alarm System (EAS) notifies an executive when a certain business rule comes into play. Traditional methods for accomplishing the same task use one of the following techniques:

- Creating a polling application on the executive's desktop

- Using a polling application on the server and sending the results by electronic mail

- Using a polling application on the server and printing a report

- Giving a manager the task of monitoring the rule (the most likely option)

The problem with each of these options is the amount of overhead and the lack of verification. For example, people might not read the electronic mail notifying them of the results in a timely manner because they are out of town. Or someone might miss picking up the special report because the printer is out of paper or because it was turned off, flushing the buffer (and the report). The list goes on and on.

Visual Basic 4 allows a developer to be more creative and design a simpler solution that has built-in verification. How? Suppose that a polling application on the server monitors a company's inventory level (nothing new here). When the desired inventory level is exceeded, the application uses Remote Automation to fire up another application on an executive's desk. The remote application then returns a success value to indicate that it has displayed the information. The remote application could also require that the executive acknowledge the information within a certain time period. If the acknowledgment is not made, the remote application notifies the original application on the server, which then moves up on an escalation list to determine whom to notify next. It might generate an electronic mail message to the original executive and use Remote Automation to notify the next executive on the list. It could also trigger a process to use a pager to notify someone.

Another type of problem occurs when an organization must have good communications between groups of people. For instance, a company might have many people who talk to customers and answer their questions but only one order department that actually takes the order once the customer has his or her questions answered. How many times have you been ready to order after spending 15 minutes on the phone, only to be put on hold and transferred to an order desk? To the order desk, you must repeat all of your demographic information, what you want to order, and all the other details of the order.

How can we improve this process? The first step might be to try to reengineer the order function to allow anyone to take an order. Or we might use an application that allows the person talking with the customer to enter the demographic information, determine what the customer wants to buy, and then click the Order button, which uses Remote Automation to instantly notify the order-entry group. The order-entry group could check and approve the order while the customer is on the phone or click a Transfer button to indicate that the client should be transferred to a particular order-entry clerk. Imagine how the customer feels when the order-entry clerk picks up the phone and says, "Hi, Ms. Smith. I see that you have ordered the new SuperWidget."

There are literally hundreds of other problems that this new technology enables us to solve in a more elegant and simple fashion than before. Several sample applications are given in this book.

Expanding programming paradigms

Imagine you know nothing about computer programming. Your introduction to computers comes in the form of the Lotus 1-2-3 macro programming language, so you become a macro programming maniac. After automating all of your company's spreadsheets, you begin to look for new challenges.

Your search brings you to a mailing list problem: your company wants to maintain a list of existing customers for the occasional promotional mailing. Using your 1-2-3 prowess, you attack and solve the problem. The new application you create is a bit messy, but it works so well that it grows and grows until it becomes terribly slow.

A programmer friend suggests that programming in FoxPro is a more appropriate solution to your mailing list problem. You take the initiative and learn FoxPro. Wow! Now your mailing list application screams. Not only that, while reprogramming it you added all sorts of new capabilities that the FoxPro programming paradigm makes possible.

The next time a programming problem pops up, you have a new way of looking at it: you can now view it in terms of the database model, whereas originally you could view it only in terms of the spreadsheet model. This additional, different way of thinking about a problem sometimes takes a while to absorb. After a few applications, however, you learn what works and what doesn't, and pretty soon it all becomes second nature.

The tools presented in this book are like that. They provide not only new functionality but different ways of seeing problems, as suggested below:

- View the problem globally. For instance, when looking at an order-entry problem, don't just talk to order-entry clerks: look at the process from the customer's perspective, and see what other organizational actions affect, and are affected by, order entry.

- Make sure you understand the available technology. Learn and experiment with Remote Automation, OLE servers, and other features of Visual Basic 4. Keep an eye out for powerful tools that could help you solve future problems, even if those tools don't seem immediately useful.

- Look at the "big picture." Problems such as long hold times or inaccurate inventory counts are usually symptoms of a bigger problem. Solve the big problem, and the symptoms will disappear.

Data Access Techniques in Visual Basic

Visual Basic provides many ways of connecting to databases and working with data. Data Access Objects (DAO) and Open Database Connectivity (ODBC) are two of the most popular. Figure 1-3 shows where they fit into the overall picture of data access techniques. Notice that ODBC can be used in several different ways, including using it in conjunction with DAO.

DAO provides a convenient object model for working with data programmatically regardless of the source of that data. Because ODBC can be used in conjunction with DAO, virtually any database system can be used with an application written using DAO, without regard for the details of the database. This assumes that a minimum level of functionality is provided by both the database and its ODBC driver.

ODBC offers many benefits. Besides database independence, there is such an enormous amount of ongoing enhancement of ODBC drivers that their performance and features improve almost monthly. The ODBC standard is a boon for programmers. By learning the ODBC API, you can program applications for any database for which there is an ODBC driver. Talk about leverage!

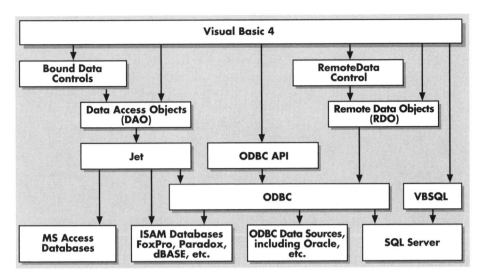

Figure 1-3. *The Visual Basic data access model contains many options.*

Multitiered Solutions Based on a Services Model

What is this hot new trend called "multitiered solutions," and does it really matter? This section addresses this issue and serves as an introduction to the concept. Throughout the book, we will occasionally return to this concept to show why placing services in different tiers is important to code reusability and the impact on the bottom line.

Tiers

A tier in the context of this book is simply a layer, usually consisting of a particular piece of software. For instance, in a typical client/server relationship, the client is one tier and the server is another tier. In reality, the tiers used in any business system will be more vague than a simple list and will likely bleed over from one tier to another. The introduction of OLE automation and Remote Automation in particular allows us to rethink the multitiered model. In a typical Visual Basic 4 client/server environment, the client might be running tier 1, which is the user interface, and tier 2, which is an OLE class library implemented as a dynamic link library (DLL), while the server system is running SQL Server as tier 3, with the possibility of another tier of agents, as shown in Figure 1-4 on the next page.

Multitiered client/server model

	Service Type	Location
User services	User interface	Client
Business services	Business rules	Client or server
Data services	Database procedures, triggers, etc.	Server

Figure 1-4. *The standard multitiered model that most people use. In the real world, services are often split into different parts as later examples illustrate.*

Services

Most people break the services model into several parts (usually three), with names such as user services, business services, and data services.

User services are typically used to enter, edit, and display information and can also be thought of as interface services. These activities define a large part of traditional software development in client/server implementations.

Business services are usually objects that perform some action such as register-ing a student for a class or processing a customer's order. These services are typically placed in the second or lower tier and are called from the interface services tier or some other tier. (Other objects that are placed in the business services tier are more generic and perform tasks such as graphic conversions, currency conversions, graphic display functions, generic format tasks, and so on. This wide variety of functions and associations leads us to call this support services instead of business services.)

Data services handle the interface to the database, other data sources such as the Internet, file sources on a file server or client system, and any other entity that provides data to a service user.

Other capabilities can be categorized into tiers as well. For example, Remote Automation and MAPI could make up their own tiers (4 and 5) or be part of tier 1 or 2. The ideas presented here lead to the following short list of service types:

- Interface services (tier 1)
- Support services (tier 2)
- Data services (tier 3)
- Remote access services (tier 4)

- MAPI services (tier 5)

- Graphics services (tier 6)

Implementation of Services in Visual Basic 4

Most proponents of the multitiered model suggest moving all business rules into the support tier (2). Everything that requires access to one of these rules then calls the service in tier 2. This logic would move validation of items such as order numbers or customer names from the database (triggers and stored procedures) into tier 2, using a language capable of generating small and fast code such as C or C++.

Using this logic we must carefully consider how Visual Basic 4 and its object design fit into this picture. We suggest you move objects into tier 2 when it makes sense, but consider the database another object layer for data-specific rules. For instance, you could move credit card validation to a Visual Basic object but leave order number and customer validation as triggers. Performance continues to be an issue in these applications, however. Perhaps as hardware capabilities improve so will our ability to utilize an implementation that more closely fits an ideal model.

Remember that a database such as SQL Server is designed to run extremely well using triggers and stored procedures. SQL code is actually precompiled for these types of procedures in most client/server databases to provide optimum performance.

Placing data-specific rules in a trigger has another advantage in that nobody can get to the data without going through the rule. A trigger encapsulates the rule within the data, preventing any access to the data without going through the rule—precisely what we want to do with a business rule.

Another way to approach this subject uses both techniques by combining triggers, stored procedures, and Visual Basic objects. Nothing says that a SQL Server trigger can't execute a Visual Basic object as part of its rule processing. For instance, the credit card validation rule might perform some checks in the database and then pass the data to the Visual Basic object VerifyCredit for completion. The VerifyCredit object would pass back the status (pass or fail) to the trigger.

Object Models in the New World

Visual Basic 4 provides the best means for good, solid object development. In particular, the OLE automation features of both EXEs and DLLs offer lots of ways of easing the programming task when developing projects. Figure 1-5 on the next page shows a simple view of the object model used in developing applications with Visual Basic 4.

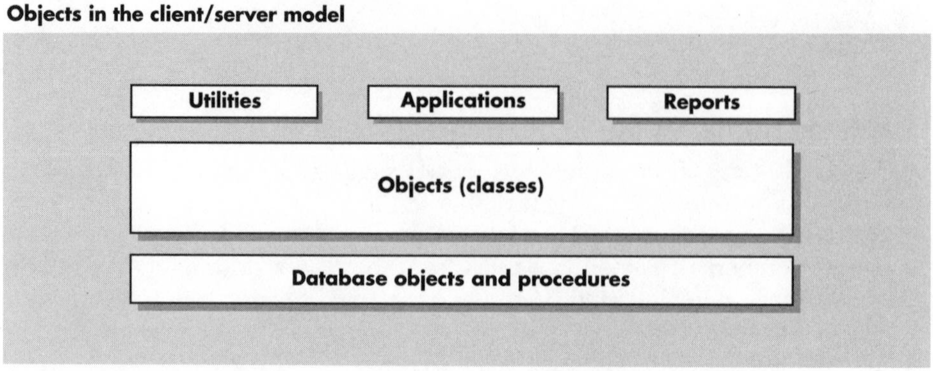

Objects in the client/server model

Utilities	Applications	Reports

Objects (classes)

Database objects and procedures

Figure 1-5. *This view of the object model shows the objects we create in tier 2 as a large part of the foundation of our system.*

The database objects and procedures in the bottom layer are truly the foundation of your entire client/server system. If your database is not designed well, your system is in big trouble from the start.

The long-term success of your system depends on your object model. If it is designed correctly, you can build most of your system by choosing from the objects in your collection and assembling them in your application. Correctly built object collections are well tested and small enough that you can use them in lots of different ways. For instance, let's say you build your application this year to help with running the customer service department. Next year, the department reorganizes and splits into two departments, requiring that the software be rewritten. Using the same objects, you can simply re-create the user interface and work flow and then turn on the system. Not much debugging is needed because all the components were previously tested. For an example of how easy it is to use this approach, see the different options in the section on splash screens beginning on page 156. This is an OLE automation version of the splash screen that can be reused without code changes or even loading the splash form into your project.

For more information on multitiered client/server applications, see "Building Three-Tiered Client/Server Business Solutions Whitepaper," by George J. Febish and David E. Y. Sarna (January 1995) in the Microsoft Solution Developers Kit.

Useful Features of Client/Server Systems

Client/server databases typically provide powerful features not found in desktop databases such as Access, FoxPro, Paradox, or dBASE. These features not only automate database management, but they also provide powerful application development capabilities.

Some features, such as cursors, are performance related, while others, such as MAPI, are designed for adding new functionality to applications. In addition, many features that have been designed for a particular activity can be used for other activities as well. For instance, MAPI can be used to add electronic mail capabilities to an application, but it is also useful in handling queries and results to and from remote systems.

In this section we introduce some of the features you are likely to use in a remote database. The correct use of features is actually critical to the success of your applications. For example, cursors are important for providing functionality and maximizing performance, but using them in previous versions of Visual Basic was difficult, at best. As Visual Basic 4 supports the implicit use of cursors, you might be using them and not even know it (which might not be optimal for your particular application). Of course, explicit use of cursors isn't as simple as utilizing them transparently (implicitly), but it is now far easier than it was before.

Stored Procedures and Triggers

The *stored procedures* technique is provided by most client/server databases (including Access and, therefore, Jet databases) to store executable SQL code directly in the database. Stored procedures are compiled as they are saved, resulting in significantly faster execution. You can use stored procedures to create a batch of tasks that execute as one task or to create a macro that looks for files in different paths depending on the parameters passed to it.

For instance, you can use the SQL Server *xp_sendmail* stored procedure to send the results of a query to a user. You could use this functionality to build an agent that monitors the database and then sends the results of a query to a particular user when a trigger occurs.

A *trigger* is typically used to kick off a stored procedure, which then does the real work of handling the triggering event. Triggers are just what they sound like: events that are triggered—in this case, when data is added, modified, or deleted from a table. Triggers can be written to fire under conditions programmable by you.

One of the primary uses of stored procedures and triggers in earlier versions of SQL Server was to maintain referential integrity. Referential integrity is just a fancy way of saying that SQL Server makes sure that information in one table is in sync with the information in another table when the two tables are related. An example will serve to illustrate the importance of maintaining referential integrity. Let's say we are teachers and we have created a database to track our students' grades in several subjects. The Students table, which contains the students' names, is related to the Grades table, which contains a list of classes and their associated grades by student numbers. Figure 1-6 on the next page shows this relationship.

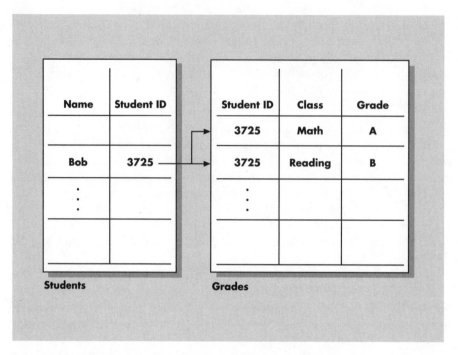

Figure 1-6. *The relationship between Students and Grades tables.*

It's necessary to maintain the relationship once it has been established. For example, if a StudentID is changed in the Students table but not in the Grades table, the records with the old StudentID in the Grades table are orphaned. Not only would the student whose StudentID was changed lose his or her grades, but if another student later assumed the StudentID of the orphaned records in the Grades table, that student might have two grades listed for each class or the application might not be able to deal with the inconsistency and might stop functioning.

In complex relational databases, there are often many such relationships across multiple tables and maintaining their integrity manually is all but impossible. This is where referential integrity comes in. In previous versions of SQL Server (prior to 6.0), it was necessary to place a trigger on each table containing a relationship so that a stored procedure could be executed to maintain it. However, using declarative referential integrity (DRI), these relationships can now be described when the DBA is setting up the tables. This eliminates the need for triggers and stored procedures in maintaining referential integrity. Using declarative referential integrity is faster, easier, and less error prone.

With the advent of multitiered designs, stored procedures might take a back seat to OLE servers for the implementation of business rules. But you shouldn't abandon stored procedures and triggers in a multitiered design. Both of these technologies are useful, and each can be used within multitiered designs to provide lots of power for your system. The trade-offs between using OLE servers or stored procedures for business rules can be frustrating. Simply put, OLE servers are convenient because they fit well with the multitier philosophy. However, they can be significantly slower than stored procedures.

You can execute stored procedures in the following ways:

- If you are using RDO, use the *OpenResultset* method to execute a stored procedure. You must first set any parameters, however, by using the rdoParameters collection of the rdoPreparedStatement object.

- Use the *Execute* method to execute stored procedures that do not return result sets.

- Use the ODBC API to execute stored procedures.

- Use the new OLE automation stored procedures in SQL Server 6.5 to execute Visual Basic stored procedures.

Result Sets

The term *result set* might be self-explanatory, but to ensure we're on the same wavelength, a simple example is in order. A result set is most often obtained by issuing a SQL query against a database table. For example, for the Biblio database that comes with Visual Basic, the following query instructs the database to return all rows from the Publishers table that have a Name field beginning with a letter less than *J*:

```
SELECT Name, Address, City, State, Zip FROM Publishers
WHERE Name < "J" ORDER BY Name
```

Figure 1-7 on the next page shows the results of this query. (The query also includes the specific columns to return and the order in which they'll be displayed.)

This particular result set contains 11 rows. Result sets can contain any number of rows, including none, depending on the form of your query and the number of records in the table(s) against which it is issued. Certain queries, such as one that returns a Cartesian product (the result of all possible combinations of all fields in each of two or more tables), can produce many more rows than exist in your tables. Restricting the number of rows, properly building your application to handle result sets, and designing the user interface to ensure that the user maintains control over the size of result sets are all important considerations when creating client/server applications.

Name	Company Name	Address	City	State	Zip
ACM	Association for Computing Machinery	11 W. 42nd St., 3rd flr.	New York	NY	10036
Addison-Wesley	Addison-Wesley Publishing Co., Inc.	Rte. 128	Reading	MA	01867
Bantam Books	Bantam Doubleday Dell Publishing Group, Inc.	666 Fifth Ave.	New York	NY	10103
Benjamin/Cummings	Benjamin-Cummings Publishing Company Subs. of Addison-Wesley Publishing Co.	390 Bridge Pkwy.	Redwood City	CA	94065
Beta V	Beta V Systems Software	16212 N.E. 113th Ct.	Redmond	WA	98052-2773
Blackwell	Blackwell Sci	3 Cambridge Ctr., Suite 208	Cambridge	MA	02142
Boyd	Boyd & Fraser	20 Park Place, Suite 1405	Boston	MA	02116
Brady Pub.	Brady Books Div. of Prentice Hall Pr., Simon & Schuster, Inc.	15 Columbus Circle	New York	NY	10023
Business	Business One Irwin	1818 Ridge Rd.	Homewood	IL	60430
Chapman	Chapman & Hall	29 W. 35th St.	New York	NY	10001-2291
Computer Science Press	Computer Science Press Inc Imprint of W H Freeman & Co.	41 Madison Ave	New York	NY	10010
ETN Corporation	ETN Corp.	RD 4, Box 659	Montoursville	PA	17754-9433
Future	Future Communications Systems	92 Summit Way	Syosset	NY	11791
Gale	Gale Research, Incorporated	835 Penobscot Bldg.	Detroit	MI	48226-4094
Glencoe	Glencoe	15319 Chatsworth St.	Mission Hills	CA	91345
Gupta	Gupta Technologies	1040 Marsh Rd.	Menlo Park	CA	94025
Hayden	Hayden Books (Imprint for Sams)	11711 N. College Ave., Ste. 140	Carmel	IN	46032
IEEE	IEEE Computer Society Press	10662 Los Vaqueros Circle	Los Alamitos	CA	90720
Intertext	Intertext Publications/Multiscience Press	2633 E. 17th Ave.	Anchorage	AK	99508
Irwin	Irwin Pr. (for Richard D. Irwin, Inc., see Business One Irwin)	4 Gentry St.	Baldwinsville	NY	13027

Figure 1-7. *A subset of the Biblio database.*

Result sets are normally returned from *Select* statements like the one in the previous example, but they might also result from stored procedures. When the database server receives a *Select* statement, it must determine how it will obtain the result set. This is called the query "plan." Huge differences in execution times can often exist between different plans that return the same result. For this reason, the database engine can justifiably spend a significant amount of time, often as much as 90 percent of the time it takes for a *Select* statement to execute, to determine the most efficient plan.

Wouldn't it be nice to formulate a plan ahead of time and use it only when the *Select* statement is issued? This is precisely what a stored procedure does. When you create a stored procedure, the database engine determines the best plan for that *Select* statement and stores it. When you actually issue the query, because the plan is already determined, the query can execute as much as 10 times faster. Using stored procedures probably provides the single greatest impact on performance in your client/server applications.

Of course, you can't anticipate every possible *Select* statement that might be issued, and even if you could, it probably wouldn't be reasonable to save them all as stored procedures. So what's the answer? Parameters. When you execute the stored procedure, you also pass it a parameter that it uses in determining the result set. This works because the plan doesn't change based on the parameter. For example, you could use the same plan to return all publishers in New York or to return all publishers in Los Angeles—you would change only the parameter.

Both complex SQL statements and stored procedures can return multiple result sets. In earlier versions of Visual Basic, it was difficult to handle multiple result sets because this required programming calls directly to the VBSQL API. Because VBSQL has no object model but is simply a collection of API calls, it requires more complex programming than using ODBC or DAO.

Visual Basic 4 handles multiple result sets using the new Remote Data Objects (RDO). RDO provides an object model, much like DAO, but one that is specific to remote databases such as SQL Server. To learn more about retrieving multiple result sets, refer to "Building Client/Server Applications with Visual Basic," which is included in the documentation that comes with Visual Basic 4 Enterprise Edition.

Cursors

A *database cursor* is a pointer into a result set that indicates the current row or record in the result set. Figure 1-8 on the next page shows a cursor in a data grid.

The highlighted row with the selection arrow in the far left column of Figure 1-8 indicates the row in the result set that is currently active (pointed to by the cursor). You can move the selection forward or backward in the result set by moving the cursor on screen.

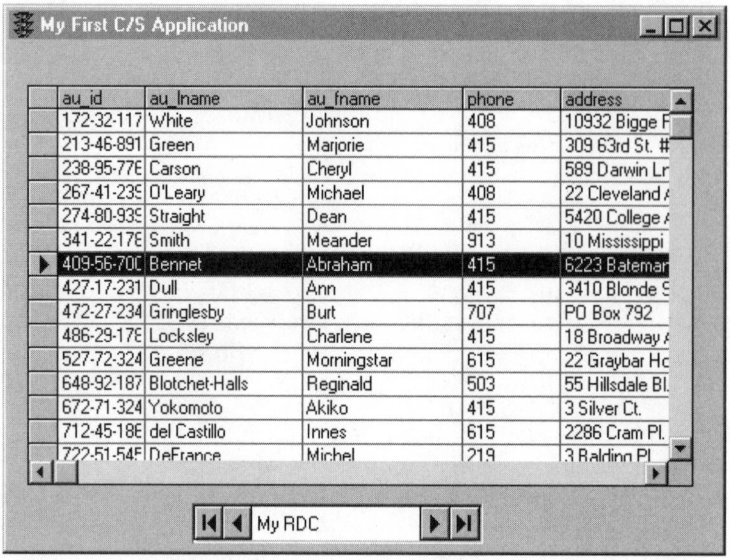

Figure 1-8. *The highlighted line in a grid behaves like a cursor and can be moved forward or backward.*

Visual Basic 4 and SQL Server 6 both support several types of cursors. Each type of cursor is useful for a specific task, and each places a different degree of overhead on the client, the server, or both. The more functional the cursor type, the more resources and/or execution time it requires.

The following table lists two broad categories of cursors and briefly describes their operation and the relative overhead they carry:

Cursor Type	Description	Relative Overhead
Server-side	Places the result set and cursor on the server. Offers improved performance.	High on server and low on client.
Client-side	Downloads the result set to the client and manages the cursor on the client. Used by Jet database engine's dynaset-type and snapshot-type Recordsets.	High on client and low on server.

As you can see from this table, both cursor types have advantages and disadvantages. In most situations, server-side cursors provide the greatest performance, reducing the demand on the client and network traffic and placing the cursor as close to the data source as possible. However, server-side cursors can be built using only RDO, ODBC, VBSQL, and the RemoteData control. The RDO and ODBC methods are recommended due to ease of development and performance, respectively.

Each server-side and client-side cursor can be set up as one of the types described in the following table:

Cursor Type	Description
Static	Rows updated in the result set are not visible to other users of the database unless the cursor is closed and then reopened. This type of cursor has the lowest overhead.
Forward-only	This type of cursor can move only in a forward direction through the result set. This cursor takes less overhead than a bidirectional cursor, but it cannot move backward through the result set. This is the default cursor for most activities.
Keyset	This is a bidirectional cursor. Rows updated are visible to other users. Rows added or deleted are not visible to others. Overhead falls between that of static and dynamic cursors.
Dynamic	This is also a bidirectional cursor. Rows updated, added, or deleted are visible to other users. This type of cursor has the highest overhead but is the most functional.

The various ways of accessing data using Visual Basic have implications for the kinds of cursors you use and the behavior of the entire system. For example, whenever a result set is created, the data in the result set must be stored somewhere. When a client-side cursor is used, the result set is stored on the client in RAM or as virtual memory in the Temp directory. A server-side cursor stores the result set on the server. In SQL Server 6, the cursor is stored in the tempdb database. Make sure both the client and the remote databases have adequate resources, including hard disk space, to handle the result sets generated by your system's actions.

You will find more information about cursors in the sections on Jet, RDO, and the RemoteData control in Chapter 5.

You might like to also know that you can choose which style of cursor to use with RDO and the RemoteData control. The following table lists the constants you can use with the CursorDriver property of either the rdoEnvironment object or the RemoteData control:

RemoteData Constant	Actual Value	Description
rdUseIfNeeded	0	Recommended. The ODBC driver chooses the appropriate style of cursor, using a server-side cursor when available.
rdUseOdbc	1	Uses the ODBC cursor library. Provides better performance for small result sets but degrades quickly as result sets get larger.
rdUseServer	2	Forces the use of a server-side cursor.

Recordset Objects

In Visual Basic 4, a *Recordset* object represents the records in a database table or the records that result from running a query. DAO provides three types of Recordset objects: table-type Recordsets, snapshot-type Recordsets, and dynaset-type Recordsets. Their differences are simple but fundamental and have wide-ranging implications.

Table-type Recordsets

A table-type Recordset object is a representation in code of a database table that you use to add, change, or delete records from the table. When you perform such an operation, only the current record is loaded into memory. The main advantage of table-type Recordsets is that they provide the fastest operations. Because of their speed, table-type Recordsets are handy when a local temporary table is required. Unfortunately, creating a table-type Recordset requires connecting directly to the table and is therefore supported only for Jet databases and ISAM databases such as FoxPro, dBASE, Paradox, and Btrieve. You cannot create a table-type Recordset for an ODBC data source or for an attached table.

Table-type Recordsets can be created from only a single underlying table—unlike snapshot-type and dynaset-type Recordsets.

Snapshot-type Recordsets

A snapshot-type Recordset object is a static set of records that you use to examine data in one or more underlying tables. The salient feature of a snapshot-type Recordset is that it is not updatable. No pointers to the data are kept, so the Jet database engine doesn't know where to return the data in the database.

The snapshot-type Recordset is efficient only for small Recordsets because the Jet database engine is forced to return all pertinent data to the client. One nice optimization that Jet performs is that OLE objects and memo fields are returned only when they are displayed. The snapshot-type Recordset has some performance advantages over the dynaset-type for Recordsets that have fewer than 500 rows.

The default cursor for a snapshot-type Recordset is bidirectional, but using a forward-only cursor is even faster. However, you need to remember that if you use the *Move* method on a Recordset created with a forward-only cursor, the rows argument can be a positive number only. (A negative number would cause the cursor to attempt to scroll backward.) Use the dbForwardOnly flag with the *OpenRecordset* method to create a Recordset with a forward-only cursor.

Snapshot-type Recordsets created with forward-only cursors are the most effective way to populate a list box from a list maintained in a database.

Dynaset-type Recordsets

Unlike snapshot-type Recordsets, dynaset-type Recordsets maintain a pointer to the information in the table (or tables) from which they are derived. This enables them to be updatable. Only a pointer to the data is transferred into memory, and when the data is required, the pointer is used to retrieve it.

Because a dynaset-type Recordset is dynamic, changes that other users make in the underlying tables are reflected, with the exception of adding a new record. New records are not visible until the *Requery* method is issued. If a user deletes a record, other users are notified when they try to access the deleted record.

The *Requery* method cannot be used on table-type Recordsets or on Recordsets for which the Restartable property returns *False*. Therefore, you should check that the Recordset supports the *Requery* method by checking its *Restartable* property prior to using the *Requery* method. If Restartable is *False*, use the *OpenRecordset* method on the QueryDef object currently in use to reopen the Recordset. This will show any changes made since the Recordset was originally created.

If you use an *Insert Into* statement to add new records to a dynaset-type Recordset, those new records don't become a part of your Recordset until you use the *Requery* method.

Both dynaset-type and snapshot-type Recordsets can be derived from heterogeneous (different) data sources. For example, you can create a dynaset-type Recordset by combining data from an Access database, a FoxPro database, and a SQL Server database and have it appear as a single Recordset. Any changes made to that Recordset will be reflected in the underlying tables.

Selecting a Recordset type

If you aren't sure which Recordset type to create, use the dynaset-type. It is the most functional type, and you are therefore least likely to experience difficulty. Of course, for maximum performance, spend the time to familiarize yourself with the benefits and uses of all the Recordset types.

Implications of ODBC data sources

Here are a few points to remember when working with ODBC data sources:

- When using DAO and creating a Recordset from an ODBC data source, you must fully populate the Recordset before attempting to create another Recordset. This is necessary in order to free the connection to the data source. Use the *MoveLast* method to fully populate the Recordset.

- You cannot create a table-type Recordset from an ODBC data source.

■ In order for an ODBC data source to be updatable, you must be able to create a dynaset-type Recordset for it. This requires that the data source have a unique index (an index with a unique key to identify each row).

■ Locking in an external database server (frequently accessed through ODBC) is under the exclusive control of that database server. Database locking is used to lock part of a database (typically a page or a row) to ensure data integrity. The Jet database engine cannot modify an external database server's locking mechanism.

Database Locking

Locking a database prevents a second user from modifying a record already in use and thus keeps data from being corrupted. Without locking, if two users were saving changes to the same row simultaneously, part of one user's information might be saved with part of the other user's information.

The simplest form of locking is *database locking*, which, for example, occurs when an Access database is opened for exclusive use. When the database is opened this way, no other users can modify it. While database locking is efficient in its use of resources and processing overhead, it precludes using the database in a multiuser environment. Locking an entire database is typically done only when administrative chores need to be performed, and the administrator must ensure that no one else is modifying the database at the same time.

The next most granular type of locking is *table locking*. If a table is locked, other users can't modify that table but they can modify other tables in the database. However, this form of locking also cannot be used for a database in a multiuser environment.

Page locking is commonly used because it affords a good trade-off among resource usage, performance, and data availability for modification. A *page* is a chunk of RAM of predefined size. When you request a row from a database, a chunk of data including that row is read into one or more pages. Access and SQL Server (which both support page locking) have 2-KB page sizes. As a result, if the row size is 500 bytes, for example, not only is the row that you are modifying locked, but the next three rows are also locked. So when constructing multiuser systems in Access and SQL Server, you need to be aware that when a user is modifying a row, other rows might be locked as well.

The next level of locking, *row locking,* ensures a high degree of availability of data for multiuser environments, but it can be costly with respect to the resources necessary to maintain the locks. (Locking can go even further, though. Some databases provide *field locking* in order to enable different users to modify different columns within the same row.)

Locks and deadlock

Whenever resources can be reserved for exclusive use and multiple users can request more than one resource, the potential for deadlock exists. Fortunately, SQL Server automatically detects and averts deadlock by rolling back the transactions of the user who would cause the deadlock. In other words, if two users are in contention for the same rows (or different rows on the same page, since SQL Server performs page locking), one user's transaction will be delayed. So far, so good. Unfortunately, the next step in the process is not so graceful. If deadlock occurs anyway, the second user's transaction, which is rolled back, is canceled and that user's application receives an error message (#1205) that must be handled by the application. Keep this issue in mind when you write error-handling code for multiuser applications.

Controlling locking

Although you cannot change the type of locking performed by either SQL Server or Jet—they both always lock 2-KB pages—you can fine-tune some of the parameters that affect locking (and other items). For Jet, you can find the parameter values in the Registry key HKEY_LOCAL_MACHINES/Software/Microsoft/Jet/3.0/Engines/xbase. (You can access the Registry by opening Regedit.exe or Regedt32.exe.)

The table below shows two parameters that effect locking. (For full information on all available parameters, see Visual Basic online help.)

Parameter	Description
PageTimeout (Integer)	The number of milliseconds that non-read-locked data can remain in an internal cache before being invalidated. The default is 5000 milliseconds (5 seconds).
LockRetry (Integer)	The number of times to attempt access to a locked page before returning a lock conflict message. The default is 20 times.

With SQL Server, locking can be modified in two ways: on a query-by-query basis using features of the *Select* statement or by the administrator for all users. If you're working on a query-by-query basis, you might find the Nolock, Holdlock, Updlock, Tablock, Paglock, and Tablockx options useful. (These keywords are actually optional parameters to the *Select* statement. For information on their syntax and usage, see the *Transact-SQL Reference* documentation or search SQL Books Online for the topic "SELECT Statement." The *Database Developers Companion* contains a description of what each of these keywords does. To locate this reference, search SQL Books Online for the topic "Customizing Locking With SELECT.")

The system administrator can control the Lock Escalation Level by utilizing the *sp_configure* System Stored Procedure. Escalation occurs when SQL Server determines that it would be more efficient to simply lock the entire table (or tables) for a query rather than maintain a large number of page locks. For SQL Server, locking information can be viewed by executing the *sp_lock* System Stored Procedure.

Replication

Replication is probably the most significant recent enhancement to client/server databases because replication is one of those paradigm shifters that has lasting implications for the industry. To show how replication works, we created a fictitious corporation with its master database on the server named "Master Database server." (See Figure 1-9.) In this simple example, the Master Database server distributes a subset of its corporate data to the other two servers in California and Tokyo. The two other servers also send data, such as daily transaction data, to the corporate Master Database server. Replication works great for this scenario, allowing both the master data to flow to the sites and the site data to "roll up" to the master system.

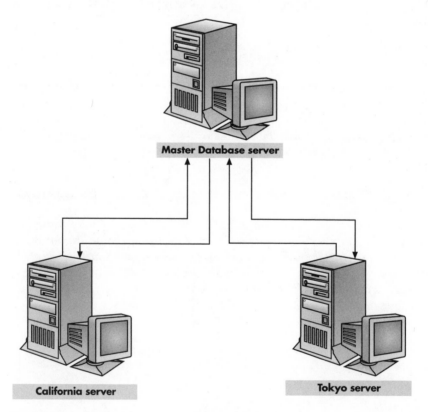

Figure 1-9. *A simple overview of how replication works.*

Using replication in SQL Server 6

The replication features in SQL Server 6 remove the need for the thousands of lines of code that were required to support replication in previous versions of database systems, such as SQL Server 4.21. In earlier versions of such servers, replication was implemented manually. Most of these techniques were problematic and prone to failure when the databases got out of sync. Problems were unfortunately the norm rather than the exception.

Replication, as well as virtually all other management activities of SQL Server 6, are performed from SQL Enterprise Manager—the graphical control center for SQL Server management. Replication is different from most SQL Server features in that it must be explicitly turned on before it can occur.

Be aware that a server that uses replication requires at least twice the minimum amount of memory of a server that does not replicate. If your server has minimal physical memory—say, 32 MB—you might need to manually adjust the amount of memory allocated to SQL Server before replication will work. To do so, choose Configurations from the Server Menu in SQL Enterprise Manager. Select the Configuration tab in the dialog box. From the spreadsheet-like display of values, locate the word *memory* in the left column. In the right column, change the value to 8192. This will allocate 8192 2-KB units of memory, or a total of 16 KB, to SQL Server the next time it is started. This process is necessary on some systems because when SQL Server is installed, it sets this value based on the amount of physical memory available in the system.

> **NOTE** The change in amount of memory allocated to SQL Server will not take effect until the next time SQL Server is started.

The publish and subscribe metaphor

SQL Server 6 uses a publish and subscribe metaphor for its replication services. This metaphor is modeled after the magazine industry: the server that provides the data is the "publisher," and the database that receives a copy of the data is known as the "subscriber." Just as you might subscribe to a particular magazine, a particular SQL Server can subscribe to the data published by another SQL Server. (Note that replication can be performed within SQL Server. That is, the same SQL Server that is publishing information can also subscribe to that information. Of course, the subscribing database must be a different database from the publishing database.)

The big picture

Replication, in the real world, can become quite complex. SQL Enterprise Manager presents a complete picture of the structure of the publishing and subscribing servers through the Topology option of the Replication Configuration item on the Server menu. You can even zoom in and out using the toolbar in the dialog box.

TIP This dialog box is also available from the SQL Enterprise Manager toolbar—it is the first button of the third group. This group on the toolbar also gives you quick access to the dialog boxes for managing publications and subscriptions by using the next two buttons on the toolbar.

Asynchronous Operations

There are several ways to implement asynchronous operations using Visual Basic 4 and SQL Server 6 or other databases:

- Asynchronous queries supported by RDO, ODBC, and VBSQL allow an application to request an operation and continue to function while the server processes the request. Once the request is processed, the server can hand data to the client piece by piece. Visual Basic 4 allows the application to pick up the data piece by piece and continue to service user requests. For more information, see "Background Processing" and "Options Property Remote Data" in Visual Basic online help.

- Remote Automation also supports asynchronous operations. This flexibility allows you to place different pieces of an application on several computers. By doing so, the improvement in efficiency is amazing. Remote Automation is another enabling technology that allows you to solve problems that were quite difficult to solve in the past. For a demonstration, see the sample in the samples\remauto\callback subdirectory of the directory in which you installed Visual Basic.

- MAPI and other messaging APIs provide a means of sending a query or a command to a remote system for execution. You can think of the messaging API as a "bus" on which you place a command for another system. The other system picks up the command, executes it, and then places its reply on the "bus" headed for you. For more information, review the MAPI sample applications available on the MSDN CD.

Figure 1-10 shows the three approaches you can use to implement asynchronous operations today.

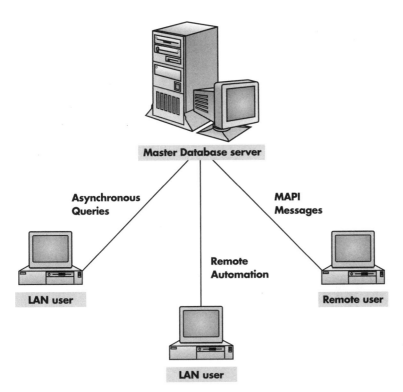

Figure 1-10. *The three approaches to implementing asynchronous operations.*

Asynchronous queries, Remote Automation, and MAPI all have an appropriate place in most progressive client/server systems being built today. The new concept of three-tiered client/server systems actually depends on features such as Remote Automation for building the middle tier.

2

The Planning, Design, and Management of Client/Server Systems

Microsoft has sold more than 3 million copies of Visual Basic in only a few years. This phenomenal record is primarily attributable to Visual Basic's Rapid Application Development (RAD) capability, but the latest release, Visual Basic 4, is also dexterous in the creation of client/server applications.

But don't be fooled. No RAD tool, including Visual Basic, eliminates the need for good planning. Before undertaking the development of your first project, review the following list. This list is far from being all-inclusive, but it serves to demonstrate that there is more to building a good client/server application than just writing the code.

- Define the business goals for the project.
- Determine the business rules for the organization.
- Develop an overall plan for the process.
- Carefully design the underlying data structure.

If you're unfamiliar with more than one of the tools you'll be using, the risk of failure increases dramatically. There are several ways to mitigate that risk. Control the projects you work on to reduce the number of unknowns, saving the more complex projects for later. If you don't have the luxury of time that this approach requires, consider hiring experienced talent. If the project is a one-shot deal, it might make sense to contract it out. Mentoring, or consulting, services provide another attractive alternative. The right consultant can help minimize project risk by both assisting in design decisions and providing on-the-job training with the tools you haven't yet mastered.

Most of the elements in this chapter relate not only to Visual Basic but to the development of client/server systems in general. We encourage you to read this material because most of these issues are at the heart of why systems either succeed or fail.

Customer, Management, and Development Roles

Corporate culture is a fact of life. Good, bad, or indifferent, it plays a part in everything we do. Instead of allowing it to drive your project, use it to your advantage as you define the roles and responsibilities of the various parties involved in planning and designing your client/server system, including end users, developers, and management.

Now for a real cliché: cultures can kill your client/server project. You must understand the culture in your organization.

Customer Partnership

One of the key factors to ensuring the success of your project is creating a partnership with your end users, or customers, to bring together complementary skills and attributes. The end user usually has the best understanding of the current process and can offer a necessary perspective, which can be of great benefit as you develop your application.

Partnership is equally applicable in those situations in which client/server expertise is brought in from outside the organization. In fact, partnership is even more vital with outside vendors because they rarely have the thorough understanding of the company's procedures, practices, objectives, and other factors that employees have absorbed over the years. Having an outsider involved in the process is also valuable because an outsider often questions assumptions that those familiar with the current process might tacitly assume to be correct. If you don't have a consultant working on the project, you can use someone from another department or another facility to fill the same role. Just be sure that he or she is not intimately familiar with the current process and is not afraid to ask questions.

Make sure you involve upper management in the process of creating partnerships. Support is fundamental at high levels in the organization because of the likelihood that a client/server project will cross departmental boundaries or even necessitate restructuring. Without such support, most client/server projects are never realized.

Management's Role

It is almost impossible to successfully implement a client/server project without top management support to back the project and drive the organization's adherence to project plans. Gaining management's support for the project at the outset is crucial because project plans are dynamic, changing over time as more information is gained about the project and the business environment.

Senior management must also support the organizational structure necessary to achieve the goals set for the organization. This not only includes the reengineering of business-related departments, but the creation of software teams for developing applications and for performing other tasks necessary for the project.

Any project of the magnitude of the typical first client/server project will at times require unpleasant decisions. Senior management must be willing to make these decisions and execute the plans to carry them out. It also must support the project teams in their efforts to discover problems and recommend solutions to management.

Cost/Benefit Analysis and Project Management

The main objective of any project is to provide a software solution that performs its tasks at reasonable cost (what the company can afford for the project). The cost effectiveness of additional work is questionable beyond a certain point. Remember the old 80/20 rule: 80 percent of the benefit can be obtained for 20 percent of the investment. This is true for almost any project. Obtaining the last 20 percent of the benefit is what drives the cost through the ceiling. Figure 2-1 on the following page shows the cost/benefit curve.

Low cost and high benefits are usually at opposite ends of the spectrum. To get more of one, you must sacrifice some of the other. Companies frequently undertake the development of low-cost projects that are never completed or are shelved after completion because they don't effectively solve the problem originally defined. For this reason and others, the rate of corporate software project failure is estimated to be greater than 90 percent.

Therefore, before anything else, you must determine whether you can achieve your goals with the resources available. If your objective is to create an order-entry system that can be integrated into an off-the-shelf accounting system, great care must be taken to ensure that the two systems work well together. Questions such as "How should users interact with customers to place an order?" can provide insight into the ease of use designed into the user interface. Other questions such as "Will the application interface directly with the general ledger or with the accounts receivable subsystem?" must be asked before the project proceeds too far.

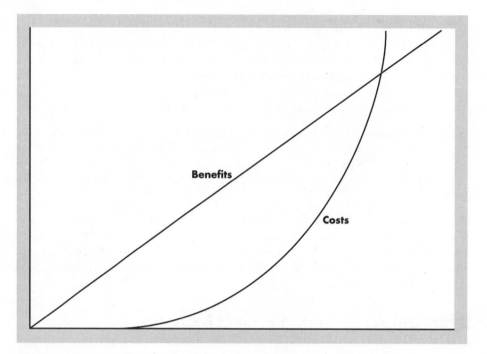

Figure 2-1. *The traditional cost/benefit curve.*

Sometimes goals are set that seem unattainable. If you can't achieve your goal with your available resources, you don't necessarily have to scrap the project. Often you can propose a useful solution that solves a significant portion of the problem. A partial solution that works is infinitely better than a complete solution that doesn't.

Project management plays a significant role in achieving the goals set for the project. Part of being a good project manager is the ability to recognize potential problems and deal with them before they arise. While this is the ideal, not all problems can be anticipated. When an unanticipated problem occurs, it should be dealt with expediently or you will pay the price in lost time. If your project runs up against an intractable problem, it is the responsibility of the project manager to modify or kill the project.

You might be surprised at the result of saying "No!" to an intractable problem. A truly good manager will reward someone who recognizes and addresses potential problems, rather than someone who simply plods along, deeper and deeper into the tar pit of failure. Use failures as learning opportunities. If you provide an environment that tolerates minor failures, you are providing an environment that encourages creative solutions.

Using On-Staff Specialists

You can take advantage of the skills your development team has to offer in a number of ways. One philosophy of employee utilization holds that specialization is the key to efficiency. This approach might lead to short-term efficiency, but it has some drawbacks. Namely, if the specialist leaves, so does the special skill. Also, the specialist might want additional responsibilities or experiences. If the person's specialty is in high demand within the company and no one is cross-trained to assist, he or she might not have the time to pursue other interests.

The specialist approach would be optimal if people were machines—the best for the task being used over and over until it was no longer usable and then being repaired or replaced—but people aren't like that, and specialists can be particularly difficult to replace.

A few years ago, one of us met an electrical engineer from a major auto manufacturer. It turned out that he was a specialist. Here's how the exchange went:

Author: So what kind of projects do you work on?

Engineer: The engine control module.

Author: That sounds interesting.

Engineer: Not really.

Author: Do you work on any interesting projects?

Engineer: No.

Author: How long have you been with the company?

Engineer: Three years.

Author: Have you worked on any other projects?

Engineer: No, just the ECM.

Author: Wow, I could never work on one control system for three years.

Engineer: I don't really work on the whole control system. I just work on R17.

Author: R17?

Engineer: Yeah, resistor 17.

Author: You've worked on just one resistor for three years?

Engineer: Yeah, no one else knows as much about R17 as I do.

Author: Do you like working on just R17?

Engineer: No, but that's how they want it. I'm looking for another job.

Granted, this is an extreme case, but look at the enormous potential for improving the situation for both the company and the employee. If this employee had been allowed to expand his role over time and learn more of the project, he would have been more valuable to the organization and to himself. Most likely, he would have stayed much longer, possibly making a huge impact on the organization.

Since you can afford neither high turnover nor employees who are ignorant of current technology, only a few alternatives remain. Provide a hospitable workplace for these valuable employees, and do your best to hire employees who fit reasonably well into the company culture. Grow a culture in which people are challenged and yet comfortable.

The Developer's Responsibility

Developers in a client/server environment must assume responsibilities over and above those they might have had in the past. Many development groups in traditional environments are accustomed to making unilateral decisions regarding systems. Users do not have much input, and planning is done at an operational or tactical level rather than at a strategic level.

Some organizations promote an approach that stipulates that each development group make its own decisions, which frequently leads to software systems that cannot communicate with one another. Often these systems are written in different languages or use different databases for storage. Strategic planning is a foreign language in many of these companies, while tactical thinking rules the day.

One common feature of organizations with high rates of successful client/server implementations is that they embrace change. They continuously evaluate technologies and determine how these technologies support the goals of the organization. The developer must contribute to and participate in all levels of planning and implementation—operational, tactical, and strategic.

An excellent book dealing with developers as they fit into the reengineering process is *Debugging the Development Process* by Steve Maguire (Microsoft Press, 1995). This book covers not only the developer's role but that of the entire team and the culture that should be cultivated for a successful development environment.

Where Do Consultants Fit?

Most organizations find that without knowledgeable assistance, their client/server projects are difficult or impossible to get up and running. Client/server programming is a new way of life and requires new tools and techniques, which can be overwhelming without outside assistance. This is a learning experience for the company, and a source of timely, reliable insight can make the difference between success and failure.

In-house staff who have been using the same tools for years cannot be expected to get up to speed on a powerful and complex tool such as Visual Basic from one or two training courses. The better developers will become truly productive only after they have their first major project under their belts. For others, it will take longer. Make sure that someone who understands the trade-offs is available to assist the staff in their efforts to learn the tools and to ensure that the project is completed successfully and on time.

Here are a few thoughts on choosing consultants:

- They must have demonstrable experience.

- They must fit in with the corporate culture.

- They must be able to provide references (and you must check them).

- In addition to having technical proficiency, they should be good mentors.

Many IS shops do not relish outsourcing development. Maybe they have been burned in the past, or maybe they prefer the control that comes with doing it all themselves. However, it is practically impossible for an internal staff to build a great client/server system the first time out. The staff must continue to maintain the in-house applications plus learn the new environment.

When we talk about outsourcing, we are *not* talking about using "contract programmers" who frequently only have a narrow range of skills and experience. A good consultant, on the other hand, usually has years of experience with a broader range of projects.

Concurrent Planning and Development

How do you plan and build concurrently? It's more natural than you might think. Natural learning is not a linear process. How did we learn to walk? It was trial and error, trial and error, trial and success. It wasn't until we entered high school that we were forced into a different learning model. Sure, iterative development can be a painful process with minor setbacks, but humans were meant to learn this way. The time between undertaking a project and its successful completion is minimized by allowing for a little stumbling along the way.

This isn't to say that you shouldn't plan. As you plan, just leave room for learning in the process, and don't punish failure. Everyone will make mistakes, and each person must have room for some failure in order to progress in his or her career.

Naturally, if you have developed a particular system, don't ignore the lessons you've learned along the way. The whole purpose of the exercise of iterative development is to learn throughout the process. Three-fourths of the trick is to develop a knack for recognizing processes of value and building on them. The other fourth is to recognize those that don't work for you and weed them out.

As in architectural planning, some things in planning a client/server system are almost intuitively obvious. For example, the concrete slab you intend to build a house on must be large enough to accommodate the entire house. The network, in today's "connected" world, is the equivalent of the concrete slab. If it won't support the full weight of its intended use, you are headed for trouble. If you provide network services of limited capacity, don't be surprised when your network support staff is working overtime and still is not able to solve all the problems popping up. You can beef up the servers, switch to 100-MB Ethernet, and partition the network. But it would have been far easier and, in the long run, less costly to do it right the first time. If you have the time and money, you can use an iterative approach even here. However, before doing so, consider whether your organization can afford the learning process. It might pay to hire an expert consultant or to hire an employee with demonstrated experience.

Training

Because the required software tools are often introduced into the organization for the very first time, training developers is often necessary and you might encounter a few obstacles. If the development team has been using the same tools for a number of years, you might lose some people from the team who are more comfortable using the old tools than learning the new ones.

An effective training technique is the use of mentors. A mentor can perform two roles. First, he or she can aid in the development effort because of background knowledge. Second, a mentor can transfer some of that knowledge to the development staff. The transfer of knowledge is a tricky business, however, as many excellent programmers are incapable of effectively conveying what they know to coworkers. Obviously, a mentor must be as much a teacher as a technician.

Why Traditional Design Methods Fail

The process of writing software has always been a hit-and-miss proposition. Some development efforts are successful while many more languish. It didn't take long for programmers and development managers to recognize that our understanding of the process of developing software is incomplete. As a result, software methodologies (step-by-step prescriptions to aid software development) were created to refine the understanding of the process.

Essential reading for developers and managers on the process of software development is *The Mythical Man-Month,* Anniversary Edition, by Frederick Brooks, Jr. (Addison-Wesley, 1995). Even though Brooks's observations are a result of his experiences managing the development of IBM's OS/360 project more than 20 years ago, much of what he has to say is still applicable. The fact that the industry continues to grapple with many of the same problems identified by Brooks indicates that software methodologies are a less-than-complete solution.

Most methodologies address only a portion of the increasingly complex development process, although some attempt to be all encompassing. One of the most useful has been the Systems Development Life Cycle (SDLC), which worked well for building traditional systems but is no longer sufficient. SDLC and other methodologies break down in today's business environment, where rapid development, frequent changes, and high functionality are expected on a regular basis. We can't wait years for an application or weeks for a simple report.

Since we are proposing that the process by which software is developed should change, you might wonder whether the traditional roles associated with software development, such as the systems analyst, are changing too.

In the past, the systems analyst would usually meet with the user to learn what the user needed and then produce a specification to which developers would code. The result of this process was an application that automated some task for the user. Today the opportunities to optimize organizational operations far exceed simple task automation; the available tools now allow for greater input from the users of the applications themselves. Accordingly, the role of systems analysts has changed: they now seek out opportunities to improve the organization, and their meetings with users are closer to interactive design sessions. These changes to traditional methodologies and roles are what the new design philosophies address.

Preferred Design and Implementation Philosophy

A software methodology is different from a design philosophy in the same way that a software algorithm is different from a heuristic: an algorithm is a specific set of steps; a heuristic is a more general description of the process by which an answer can be reached. A heuristic is used either when an algorithm cannot be developed that would address all cases of a particular problem or when an algorithm would be too complex if it covered all possible cases.

A methodology usually lays out inflexible rules and steps through which a design will evolve. Typical methodologies are also targeted at one part of the design process, such as a data model or a data flow diagram. Because of the high data content of corporate applications, most methodologies focus on the database, although several "business process" tools are also available.

In contrast, a good design philosophy provides a framework that guides the creation of software instead of micromanaging it. Design philosophies don't preclude the use of methodologies. In fact, certain methodologies are advocated (for example, the IDEF1X database methodology used by ERwin). Think of the design philosophy as a bag of tricks from which you and your organization can draw according to the requirements of the problem at hand. Your goal should be to adopt tools, methodologies, and guidelines that work to solve your organization's problems. Items such as checklists, specification documents, or even a database to track development projects or business rules can also play a significant role in a design philosophy.

A good design process is iterative, evolutionary, and traceable to the original business problem.

Iterative Design

An iterative design process is necessary when an organization moves to new technology. One of the most important steps in this process is the constant changing of a user's paradigm, or the window through which a person views the world.

Typical users in a traditional environment have a paradigm that matches the current system environment. This environment is often character based, requires many keystrokes, does not provide tips, might or might not have reports that can be viewed on screen or printed, and so forth. If you ask users what they want from a new system, guess what they answer? They want a system that works like the old one but with the problems fixed and a few new features added. In this scenario users are limited by their paradigm because they can only imagine the current solution with a few enhancements.

People naturally take small steps when changing paradigms. Small steps are safer and are frequently more successful than large leaps. The iterative design process accommodates this fundamental human characteristic, permitting users and developers to incrementally shift their paradigm. An efficient iterative design process has only recently become possible because of RAD tools. RAD, more than anything else, permits quick changes that enable "what if" design. For example, a good systems analyst tries to understand how the business environment can be improved and then quickly prototypes a system that can be demonstrated to the user. The user and analyst work together to improve the prototype incrementally. An opportunity for a little paradigm shift occurs each time the user sees a new implementation. Obviously, the shorter the turnaround time between implementations, the faster the paradigm shift. Traditional methodologies are too rigid to permit this type of feedback routinely, and today's RAD tools enable the process to occur in weeks rather than years.

Evolutionary Design

The design process must also be evolutionary as each iteration adds detail to the working specification. (For details about creating a specification document, see page 43.) As the process evolves, the application moves closer to solving the business problems that were targeted.

The specification document itself should evolve throughout this process, containing both the original information and the refinements made during development. Links to the application (storage path and project name) and database used by the application (database name, server name, and any other pertinent information) should also be in the document.

It is probably a good idea to also include in the specification document a hot link via OLE to the data model. Using a hot link will update the specification document automatically when the data model changes.

Design That Is Traceable to the Original Business Problem

One key element that is left out of most design specifications is the original business problem that the application is trying to solve. This element should be included first in your specification document. Clearly stating the business problem allows you to trace the application back to the original problem easily and documents the rationale for the application for future developers, managers, and users.

Design Phases

Before you crank up Visual Basic and start designing forms (screens), you must create a good design for the system. What does a good design consist of? For starters, define the problem you are trying to solve. The best applications result from answering this fundamental question before coding begins. As obvious as it might sound, quite a few development efforts are under way prior to this question being fully answered. Some related questions include the following: Who will use the application? Where will they use it? Who will want to see the results of their usage?

The goal is not to create a paralyzing design process, but rather a fluid and dynamic design process that guides development but does not constrain it. The design process is not a one-time phase; it must evolve and grow as the project continues. The stages of the design process should flow naturally to a conclusion that results in a good physical design for the application. Decisions made in the development stage should also be updated in the design document.

Conceptual Design

The purpose of the conceptual design is to get the ultimate user of the system involved in the design process. This step is critical to the design process because it is here that you try to understand the real vision for the application and begin to think of solutions to problems from the user's perspective. A typical solution might be included in one application, part of an application, or several applications. The key to effectively completing this step is understanding the user's view of the problem and the solution.

During conceptual design, you describe the problem in business terms and define usage scenarios:

- *Who* does *what*
- *How* they do it
- *Where* they do it
- *When* they do it
- *Why* they do it

The conceptual design might ask questions as well as answer them. For instance, you might determine that a series of graphs and grids is the most appropriate way to display particular information to the user. In the conceptual design stage, you can simply state what you know and ask, "How do we display this—using multiple forms or using tabs?" The question will be answered during the logical design stage.

Logical Design

The purpose of the logical design is to provide focus for the development team. The logical design addresses the requirements mandated by the various conceptual prescriptions. Logical designs do not concern themselves with exact procedures but concentrate on what needs to be done. For example, knowing that a list box needs to be displayed is more important than specifying at this stage what type of list box to display.

Physical Design

The physical design defines the implementation of the logical design. This is the specification that will guide coding. Here you define the components and interfaces necessary to address the requirements resulting from the analysis of the problem.

The physical design might also change during development as new information is acquired about how the application interacts with other applications and how the application works during user testing. Final changes to the application should be rolled into the specification to provide information for future development efforts.

Future Designs

In the specification document, be sure to include a section for the next version. In this section, you can collect features you've defined but decided not to implement in the current application. This section also attaches items for future versions directly to those in the current version in the specification document.

Microsoft, for example, included a Future Versions section in the Visual Basic 4 beta forum on CompuServe. As people were using the current version, they could post wish lists of features. Several major modifications in Visual Basic 4 resulted from the information posted in this section, and undoubtedly many of the ideas will find their way into Visual Basic 5. Imagine the wealth of information contained in that section for the development group! You can do the same for your developers, and you will always know where to find the information.

Using the Phases Together

Keep in mind that a great deal of overlap can occur among the stages. After all, conceiving a solution that is not possible to implement does no good. In fact, the best results occur when all three stages can be addressed simultaneously. Witness a product such as Mathematica, developed by the mathematical prodigy Jeffrey Wolfram.

Not only does Mathematica perform virtually any type of mathematical analysis, in both numeric and symbolic form, but it also runs on nearly every computer system of significance from a Cray down to a desktop PC. Mathematica works well on a wide array of equipment, and its interface is second nature to a mathematician (the intended user).

The key to Mathematica's technical success was not only Wolfram's ability to grasp the problem to be solved, its technical solution, and an appropriate implementation, but his ability to understand all three simultaneously. Minds like Wolfram's are one in a million. However, by using the array of tools in this book and following a sound design philosophy, you'll be able to achieve one-in-a-million results.

What Does a Specification Document Look Like?

Understanding the process of designing a client/server solution is only one part of the equation. You must have some type of specification document to track the process throughout the design.

Although specification documents can take many different forms, the form is not as important as the information the specification contains and how reusable the form is. Figure 2-2 on the following page shows the framework of a specification document in Microsoft Word for Windows 95. The document was generated using a Word template that we created in about 15 minutes for one of our projects. The bulleted text defines the standard requirements for the organization, so even outside developers can clearly understand the expectations and requirements for a project.

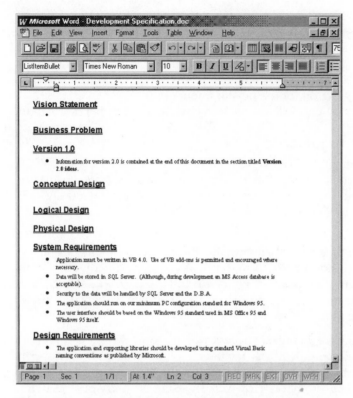

Figure 2-2. *An example of a specification document.*

Creating a new specification document is easy. If you own Word for Windows 95, first copy the ApplicationSpec.dot file from the Templates directory on the companion CD to your MSOffice\Templates directory (or the directory where you store you templates); then choose New from the File menu, select the ApplicationSpec template, select Document as the Create New option, and click OK. If you don't have Word for Windows 95, a version of this file in Rich Text Format (called ApplicationSpec.rtf) is also included on the CD. (You can use various editors, including WordPad, to open RTF files.)

We use the following section headers in our specification documents:

- Vision Statement

- Business Problem

- Version 1

- Conceptual Design

- Logical Design

- Physical Design

- System Requirements

- Design Requirements

- Database Requirements

- Version 2 Ideas

- Glossary

This format makes it easy to build a specification. The system and design requirements sections contain the standard boilerplate text that defines your organization's standards. This information can be typed in directly or linked to a file. (To create a hot link in your Word file, choose the Object command from Word's Insert menu.)

If you're using Word, make sure you set the document properties (choose Properties from the File menu) to include the appropriate information on each application or solution. This will allow you to use the advanced File Find features of Microsoft Office and Microsoft Windows 95 to sort and retrieve specifications.

You can also access the property fields of the Word document within Visual Basic. This is handy for those of you who have built a database to track development efforts. Just a little programming and you can hook Word and your specification documents right into your database!

Project Management

Good project management is critical to the success of any client/server project. Without it, the project reacts to outside forces and wanders from point to point. It might end up over budget and, worse yet, not achieve its goals. Goals become reality only when they are supported by at least a broad outline of how they will be reached. Sounds like a project plan to us! Project management is a balancing act: too many constraints and the final product is ineffective; too few and it is never finished.

One of the biggest advantages of a good plan is the structure it imposes on the project. When you develop a list of tasks and assign resources to them, it's easier for you to set deadlines and track progress for the tasks.

Several software solutions are available for tracking project management. One excellent package is Microsoft Project for Windows 95, which provides a software development template. (See Figure 2-3 on the following page.)

As you develop your project schedule, keep in mind the following:

- Schedule in identifiable and supportable blocks of time.

- Break down the task only to the level necessary.

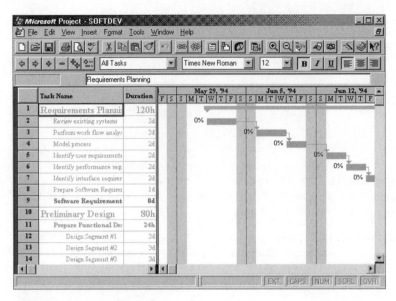

Figure 2-3. *The software development template included with Project is a good starting point for a project plan.*

Schedule major parts of the project down to at least the weekly task level to get a realistic idea of how long a particular task will take to complete. The schedule should be detailed enough to support a case for the length of time you've assigned to a specific task, but don't schedule task minutiae. Take the construction of a Windows help file as an example. If you have previously developed an application of similar complexity, you probably have a good idea of how long it will take to create the help file. Factor out the portion of the learning curve that won't have to be repeated. Factor in time for features that you haven't previously implemented—say, full-motion video. If you are considering features you haven't developed before, ask those with experience to estimate how much time the feature will need.

Scheduling

Once the project is scheduled, coordination between participants to meet the deadlines becomes necessary. Consider using Microsoft Schedule+ (shown in Figure 2-4) for both group and individual scheduling. Schedule+ integrates well with Project to both assign tasks and allow acceptance of tasks, simplifying project and time management for team members. Make sure you update the project plan as tasks are completed.

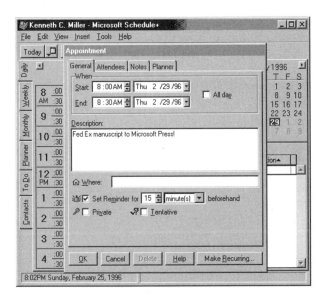

Figure 2-4. *Schedule+ simplifies project and time management, allowing you to view by weeks and months, as well as days.*

Version Control

Software version control is mentioned here in the planning section because it must be addressed at the outset of the project. Client/server systems tend to be large and complex because they often address multiple business problems. Planning for version control up front greatly reduces the support needed (and the potential for confusion) when the system goes on line. We can't emphasize enough that all software developed must include version information!

You should use major version numbers (1.0, 2.0, and so on) for significant product releases and minor version numbers for interim releases (for example, 1.5). The revision numbers are typically used for bug fixes to a minor release (for example, 1.51). A full description of each release should be kept in a project log or, better still, a project database.

Visual Basic 4 introduces several new wrinkles to the version control issue by allowing you to build several different types of OLE servers and components. You can develop a program easily that is both an OLE server and a fully functional application. Add the complexity of managing lots of different OLE components, and you can be overwhelmed in a hurry.

Microsoft Visual SourceSafe provides one form of version control. SourceSafe tracks source code and thus can help with version control for applications and their components. Take the time to master the version control capabilities of Visual Basic and understand how versions are maintained and generated. In addition, OLE versions must be carefully tracked. For example, what causes the OLE version of an OLE server to change? A simple modification such as changing an object's interface (adding a passed parameter to a method or a property, for instance) will change the OLE version and invalidate all references to that object used by all existing applications. Wow! For more information on version control in Visual Basic, refer to the Visual Basic documentation.

Visual Basic can also provide lots of version information for a project. After choosing Make EXE File from the File menu, click the Options button to open the EXE Options dialog box. Use of these options should be included in your organization's standards. Figure 2-5 shows the EXE Options dialog box. You can access version information for your program by checking the Version Number section of the EXE Options dialog box.

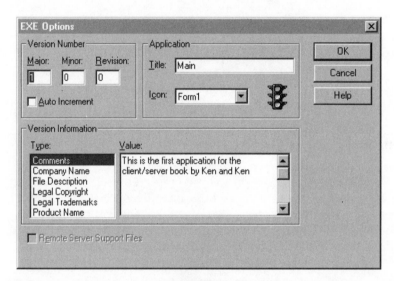

Figure 2-5. *Visual Basic 4 version information in the EXE Options dialog box.*

Text can be entered for each item that appears in the Type list box under Version Information. When the executable is built, this information is included near the beginning of the file. It is not readable with a text editor, however, because the EXE is a binary file. You can view the information from File Manager in Microsoft Windows NT or from Windows Explorer in Windows 95 by choosing Properties from the File menu.

Figure 2-6 shows the Properties dialog box from Windows Explorer. The Version tab displays information directly from the EXE file, including file version and other version information from the EXE Options dialog box. The Properties dialog box provides a handy way to retrieve this information when you need to quickly check the version of a file on a client's system or on the server.

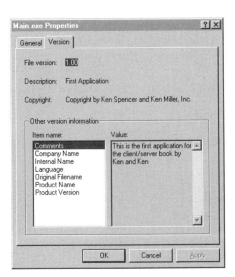

Figure 2-6. *Windows Explorer's Properties dialog box.*

A Few Practical Considerations

As you dig into the details of planning and building your client/server application, there are some basic issues you might need to consider. These include designing a user interface, converting data from an existing database, using a remote database, and finding appropriate and reliable development tools.

User Interface Design

How should users interact with the application? How do users perform the various tasks at hand? Do you use buttons or icons for actions? Do you use different forms in a complex application or simply use a tabbed dialog box? What about designing software to fit old and comfortable metaphors? Certainly an old metaphor would make users feel at ease with your new application. But it might limit you to warm and fuzzy things from the past, precluding you from really improving the interface in the future. These are but a few of the questions and considerations facing the interface designer.

Like so many aspects of programming, user-interface design has taken on a life of its own. Each operating system has its standards, which must be understood before a design for an application is undertaken. One of the advantages of such standards is that end users will intuitively understand how to use much of your application. So use these standards as your starting point. The role of the interface designer, however, is to make trade-offs between the published guidelines and the particular application's interface. The user interface is like an interpreter at the United Nations. It should facilitate, not impede or embellish.

In all likelihood, your client/server application will perform some task that the standard user-interface guidelines published by Microsoft and others do not cover. In this case, there are other volumes to guide you in selecting an implementation. One of the best recent works is Alan Cooper's *About Face: The Essentials of User Interface Design* (IDG, 1995).

How Do You Convert the Data?

What happens when it's time to move from the old system to the new one? You have several choices:

- Leave the old data and start over.

- Migrate the data from the old system to the new all at once.

- Set up a parallel migration path.

Most organizations cannot afford to skip the data conversion process, at least for major portions of their data. You might throw away some temporary data from various departments, but the VP of customer service will have your head if you suggest throwing away his or her customer database.

So, what happens when you start the transfer? One problem that is almost never mentioned is the need to convert the old data to the new format before moving it to the new system.

Data conversion is not a trivial task for most organizations. There are several issues to keep in mind as you consider moving data from one system to another:

- Determine where the data will go. There is seldom a one-to-one match between the old data files and the new database tables.

- Match up the new data structures with the old. The new database must be built without a complete dependence on the old file structure. This necessitates matching fields in one system to the other.

- Match data storage formats. Moving from a non-normalized system to a fully normalized relational database usually requires a vast restructuring of various parts of the data. For instance, a text field might contain several codes that must be stripped out and placed in individual fields. Numeric formats might require translation from one format to another for the new system.

Many other issues might arise and require some work to resolve. Fortunately, Visual Basic is adept at data conversion tasks and its file I/O has always been among the fastest.

Design Implications of Remote Databases

Client/server development implies the use of a high-performance database for back-end data services. Many applications grow from single-use or minimal count multiuse to client/server. For instance, let's take that cool Access-based application that has outgrown its intended user base of three and now is demanded by 100 people across the corporation. Just use the Upsizing Wizard, and, presto, it's a client/server, right? Well, maybe.

There are lots of differences between using a local database such as Access and using a remote database such as SQL Server. The latter is more powerful and robust but also more complex. Moving an application from a local database to a remote database without examination might lead to some surprises. For example, a lengthy query that ran fine on a local Access database might return a "Query too long" error when issued against SQL Server. There are differences in data types, how queries are issued, what can and cannot be done with the data, referential integrity, and so on.

Remote database features, such as stored procedures, triggers, and replication, present additional opportunities with which the developer might not be familiar. Tackling a large client/server project requires that you rethink how you build solutions, not just that you learn how to connect to the database.

Expected response time: local vs. remote

Response time is usually good from local databases (such as Access) but can be slow from a client/server database for several reasons. A local database doesn't have to contend with network traffic; an application connecting to a remote data source does. A local database doesn't have to service a large number of users; its remote counterpart might. In other words, don't expect that because a remote database is executing on a dedicated server and because it cost more to purchase than its local counterpart, it will necessarily be more responsive. Response time of a client/server system is much more dependent on outside factors than is a desktop database such as Access.

Here's a simple example to demonstrate this point. You build a company phone book application that contains a list box of names and numbers populated from a remote data source. Your testing during development shows snappy response so you deploy the application. At 8 A.M., 1000 users turn on the application. Since the list box is populated with all phone numbers at startup, 1000 queries are issued against your single remote data source. You receive a call from a rather perturbed help desk employee who wants to know why the help desk got calls from 100 users. This problem has a simple solution: don't populate the list box automatically on startup; populate it with the first query instead. Other potential problems might not be solved so easily.

Another example illustrating the differences in response time is the use of the asterisk (*) as a wildcard character. Many developers simply code the following SQL statement when they want to return data from a table:

```
Select * from MyTable
```

Perhaps they should instead consider using an explicit reference to a particular column:

```
Select MyColumn from MyTable
```

For certain types of data sets, the overhead to return all the columns from a table is much higher than returning only the column of interest. As a simple example, consider a table in which there are ten columns of the same type. For snapshot-type data sets, using an asterisk when you need only the contents of a single column creates 10 times the load on the network, the server, and the client. Each must handle 10 times the data of your one column. Multiply this by 100 or 1000 users, and you have a serious performance problem.

There are many other opportunities for enhancing the performance of remote databases. The section starting on page 68 has more general tips for building client/server applications.

System reliability

Client/server applications depend on a much larger number of interoperating components than do stand-alone solutions. The failure of a single component in your network or server can render your application unusable. Does your system have a good backup strategy? Do you have a support contract with a guaranteed response time? Have you tested the response time to gauge its accuracy?

Don't forget to stress test your applications. Even if every piece of hardware works flawlessly (and it won't), you must build applications that can support the unanticipated demands of production. If your application will support an estimated 50 users, test it with 60. Set up an automated process that bangs away at it, placing more demands on the system than normal production will.

Make sure you have looked at the environment that will support your applications. For instance, is your remote database going to run on a dedicated server or on a system that is also a file server? The former typically provides far better performance. Does the intended network segment that your server will use have the required bandwidth, or is it already hitting performance limits with existing applications? Regardless of the effort you put into preventing them, problems will occur. You need to have a system in place to deal with your plan when it goes astray.

Uptime requirements

How long must your system be up each day? If the answer is 24 hours a day, how do you perform backups when users are still working in the database? How do you perform updates to system software and application programs in such an environment? Widely deployed client/server solutions can touch far-reaching parts of the organization, bringing about vast changes in uptime requirements and system support for the solutions. Considerations such as these should be included in your plan.

Eliminating duplicate data

Normalization is the process of defining a database schema (architecture) that by virtue of its design eliminates redundant data. Eliminating redundancy is important because you don't want to have to update multiple instances of a piece of data when an update is required. Because it is virtually impossible to inform every new person who works on the database about every new redundant location, it is inevitable that your database will end up with corrupt data.

Normalization has long been used to create schemas that were fine-tuned to eliminate redundancy at the expense of efficiency. The trade-off of normalization vs. performance has been around for a long time and will remain with us for the foreseeable future. Why the performance penalty? A truly normalized database will include a large number of tables. For instance, if your database includes a customer master table, you must include a place in which contact names are stored for each company. One scenario is to define your customer master with the following structure. (Many details are missing to keep it brief.)

```
CustomerName
Address1
Address2
City
State
Zip
ContactName1
ContactPhoneNumber1
ContactName2
ContactPhoneNumber2
```

This structure is *not* normalized. Let's say that for the customer named MyCompany, our contact is Ken Smith. What happens if Ken Smith also works part-time for YourCompany? It just so happens that YourCompany is also a customer of yours. Now Ken Smith is listed in both companies' records—redundancy happens.

Now let's look at the same type of table with a normalized schema.

```
CustomerMaster
  CustomerKey
  CustomerName
  Address1
  Address2
  City
  State
  Zip
ContactMaster
  ContactKey
  ContactName
  ContactPhoneNumber
ContactCustomerLink
  CustomerKey
  ContactKey
```

In this normalized structure, Ken Smith would be listed only once—in the ContactMaster table. The ContactCustomerLink table would contain two records, one linking Ken Smith to MyCompany and the second linking Ken Smith to YourCompany. With a correctly defined set of triggers or referential integrity rules, this database can contain no redundant data.

Looking up a customer contact in the first table structure requires access to only one table. Performing the lookup in the second example, with our normalized tables, requires searching three tables. You can easily see the performance penalty that a normalized structure can create as the number of tables in your design proliferates.

With this structure in mind, we can begin to understand the trade-off of a truly normalized database vs. ease of use. Users could quickly understand how to find a contact name in our first example but would be hard-pressed to work their way through the normalized example and return the correct data. Fortunately, using SQL Server, we can define views to create a "virtual" table that looks the same as a table in the database. Users have the same ease of use they would encounter from the first table in our example.

Data warehousing

A data warehouse usually is designed to contain all types of data from an organization. For instance, multiple online databases will roll up the information to the warehouse, which becomes a source for all data inquiries for the organization. What a cool concept!

The data warehouse is also useful for improving the performance of online databases. We suggest setting up a warehouse from the start. Move all data that is not for the current period into the warehouse on a regular basis. The frequency with which you move data can be monthly, weekly, daily, or even hourly depending on your application. All user queries can be made against the data warehouse and not the online database. Done properly, this approach improves performance because reporting and ad hoc queries don't interfere with live transactions. Using this scenario, you have built some performance-tuning into your system. Even when a user goes after everything in the database, it won't cause a major impact on the online databases. The ease of replication using SQL Server makes this approach very convenient.

A Few Good Tools

In our consulting work, we use many of the same tools over and over. To save you the trial and error we endured, we suggest you consider using the utilities and applications described in this section.

Data modelers

In this book, we use a modeling technique known as IDEF1X, primarily because of its effectiveness. A secondary consideration is that it can be used with ERwin, a product from Logic Works that permits the interactive construction of Entity Relation diagrams and then directly implements the data structures in SQL Server. One version of the product can even create your Visual Basic forms as the starting point for a particular design.

Upsizing Wizard for Access

No book that discusses Visual Basic and SQL Server would be complete without at least mentioning the Microsoft Upsizing Wizard for Access. This free tool is a boon to developers because of its ability to quickly migrate an Access database to SQL Server and because of the management tools it provides. In fact, this is probably the quickest, least expensive route to a good SQL Server database: design the database, including data validation rules, in Access and then use the Upsizing Wizard. Your SQL Server database will be created for you, and a report will be generated describing its structure and any problems encountered in the conversion.

sp_Assist

One tool that we were fortunate enough to find and that we use in examples in this book is sp_Assist from Sheridan Software. This tool assists the developer and system manager in building and managing client/server systems. You can use it to build and manage stored procedures, triggers, queries, Visual Basic code, and all kinds of other neat stuff. You can interactively build and test a query and then paste it into your Visual Basic program.

3

Implementation Techniques for Visual Basic

Microsoft Visual Basic has grown into a powerful tool that supports many different ways of developing client/server applications. Because Visual Basic 4 introduces so many new features, it can be difficult to decide what the best method is for solving a particular problem. In this chapter, we'll discuss the variety of database access techniques available, as well as one option you can use to create the forms that make up your user interface.

Database Access Techniques in Visual Basic 4

Prior to Visual Basic 4, your choices were far simpler. If the application would use a large amount of data, you selected DAO, ODBC, or VBSQL, depending on the amount of performance you required and the amount of development time you could afford. Visual Basic offers several alternatives for storing and retrieving data, from sequential file access at the lowest level, followed by random file access. Using the Microsoft Windows API, it is a simple matter to store and retrieve information to and from INI files and the Registry.

Visual Basic 4 changes the landscape for constructing any type of database application, particularly client/server applications. The new bound controls ("data-aware" controls that are linked to the database) are more flexible than their predecessors, and their performance is much closer to programming DAO directly. In addition, DAO and Remote Data Objects (RDO) in Visual Basic 4 are incredibly robust. The additional features of DAO, as implemented in Visual Basic 4, finally make available to Visual Basic programmers all of the power of the Jet database engine.

The Jet database engine provides several ways of accessing data in a variety of formats, including native support for Microsoft Access databases and ISAM support for dBASE, Paradox, and Btrieve. Jet, an acronym for Joint Engine

Technology, arises in part from the fact that both Access and Visual Basic use it. Earlier implementations reserved some of Jet's most useful functions only for Access. As implemented for Visual Basic 4, Jet provides the same functionality provided for Access. Jet also supports ODBC, which really opens up the choice of database back ends as manufacturers and third-party vendors provide ODBC drivers for more than 100 different databases. Visual Basic 4 has a new DAO object model that has been expanded to include the features of Access. This new model, shown as part of Figure 3-1, makes both stand-alone and client/server development a more reasonable undertaking.

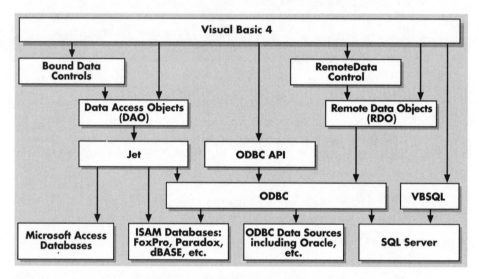

Figure 3-1. *Options for accessing data using Visual Basic 4.*

Although the Jet database engine provides extensive functionality, the Jet DLLs consume a lot of memory and disk space as a result. RDO and the RemoteData control are new to Visual Basic 4. Both use ODBC to connect directly with the remote database engine, bypassing Jet and eliminating the overhead the Jet database engine incurs when talking to a remote database. They can be used to access any ODBC-compliant database, including flat files (using an ODBC driver), Access, Microsoft SQL Server, and Oracle. If you are building an application that talks only to a remote database such as SQL Server, using RDO and the RemoteData control is your best bet. Using them does not preclude you from using Jet in order to access a local data source within the same application. However, RDO can be used only on Microsoft Win32 clients, such as Windows 95 or Windows NT. The small footprint data solution, such as CodeBasic by Sequiter Software or Rocket from SuccessWare, is yet another option to use and avoids Jet's high overhead.

RDO is covered extensively in the Visual Basic manual *Building Client/Server Applications with Visual Basic* and in the Entprise.hlp Windows help file (included with Visual Basic Enterprise Edition), so we don't go into it in depth in this book. Instead we concentrate on using the features and functionality of RDO and the RemoteData control in several examples.

One major difference from previous versions of Visual Basic is the use of object libraries in Visual Basic 4. Object libraries are created using class modules to build both internal objects for a project and OLE automation objects. Methods and properties for a class are created by building procedures and variables, respectively. Using object libraries overcomes source-code maintenance problems while still providing full functionality. We cover this subject in more detail in Chapter 8.

Both DAO and the original Data control have undergone significant changes in Visual Basic 4, so existing applications will need to be modified to take full advantage of the new features and performance enhancements.

The Jet Database Engines

Two versions of the Jet database engine are supplied with Visual Basic: version 2.5 (for creating 16-bit applications) and version 3.0 (for creating 32-bit applications). You must select only one version for each Visual Basic project that will use Jet. Use the References command on the Tools menu to display the References dialog box, in which you can select the appropriate library. If you are building a new application that will use only the Access 95 database format, Visual Basic 4, and applications that use the latest version of Jet, select Microsoft DAO 3.0 Object Library in the dialog box. If your application must coexist with another application that uses only an Access 2.0, 1.1, or 1.0 database, select Microsoft DAO 2.5 Object Library.

The Microsoft Developer Network CD-ROM (MSDN) includes a good reference article on DAO, "Guide to Data Access Objects." This article contains lots of information, plus a table that lists the changes in DAO for Visual Basic 4. The definitive reference on the Jet database engine is a book by Jim Ferguson and Dan Haught, *Microsoft Jet Database Engine Programmer's Guide* (Microsoft Press, 1995).

ODBC

A major component in virtually all client/server development today is ODBC, which was created to resolve long-standing incompatibilities between database back ends. In the past, an application written for a specific back end was difficult to migrate to a different database server because each database manufacturer had a proprietary API to which the front-end applications were written. ODBC provides an answer to this problem by defining a client-side API that is independent of the database on the other side. You can access the database transparently through its ODBC driver.

Today is an especially exciting time for developers using ODBC because the ODBC drivers have improved from barely usable to the most robust and fastest way of accessing high-performance databases. As evidence of the prominence of ODBC, it has become a native API on Microsoft SQL Server 6 and provides the fastest means of executing Transact-SQL on SQL Server.

Another standard, albeit one that has been around a little longer, is vitally important in the development of client/server applications. Structured Query Language (SQL) was developed as a standard for programming databases and returning result sets from them. The American National Standards Institute (ANSI) publishes a SQL standard with which virtually all vendors' SQL implementations comply.

Using ANSI standard SQL has its drawbacks, however. The standard is updated only every five years, and if vendors offered only the functionality described in the standard, developers would miss out on a lot of useful functionality. Many vendors enhance the language to include capabilities not included in the standard, which offer significant performance improvements over their equivalent ANSI implementations.

The net result is that although ODBC sounds like the panacea of database independence, developers of high-performance applications still tie their applications to a particular database back end. ODBC does, however, significantly reduce the effort required should a developer need to port an application to a different back end, because at least 80 percent of the code in the application is probably database independent. ODBC is a great API that allows a wide variety of vendors to create all types of tools that can access almost any database. If your database back end supports ODBC, you can use almost any package that is ODBC compliant—which is practically anything these days.

Keep in mind that ODBC plays a vital role in the life of RDO and the RemoteData control, permitting them to bypass Jet. RDO provides an easy-to-use layer that is also fast and powerful. An application that relies on RDO will typically be much easier to implement and maintain than one that uses ODBC directly.

VBSQL

VBSQL is a Microsoft implementation of the SQL Server DB-Library for Visual Basic. DB-Library for Visual Basic is an API to the Transact-SQL features of SQL Server. In past versions of Visual Basic, VBSQL was arguably the fastest way to get to a SQL Server database. It was also the most difficult way.

Microsoft continues to maintain and enhance VBSQL, and it is still available to Visual Basic 4 programmers. VBSQL still offers a few convenient features such as its asynchronous error handling. But the real action is with ODBC. VBSQL is not needed very much these days due to the power and flexibility of ODBC, RDO, and the RemoteData control. For more information on VBSQL, see *Hitchhiker's Guide to Visual Basic and SQL Server* by William Vaughn (Microsoft Press, 1996).

ODBC Data Source

A *data source* is an ODBC database or database server. You use the ODBC application in Control Panel to specify unique names for all connections to a data source. The data source is used by ODBC, RDO, and the RemoteData control.

Configuring ODBC

Before you can use a database, it must be registered as an ODBC data source. This registration usually occurs from the ODBC application in Control Panel.

Figure 3-2 shows the ODBC application for Windows 95 with the registration definition for the sample Publishers database from Chapter 5.

Figure 3-2. *The required text box items in the ODBC SQL Server Setup dialog box are Data Source Name, Description, and Server. It is usually beneficial to also enter the name of the database the data source will use.*

You follow these general steps to create a data source definition:

1. Start the ODBC application in Control Panel.

2. Select the driver you want to use from the list of User Data Sources, and click Setup to open the ODBC Setup dialog box. (If the driver you need is not in the list, click the Add button to display the Add Data Source dialog box. Select the ODBC driver you want to use, and click OK.)

3. Enter the data source name. This is the name you will use to refer to the data source in Visual Basic and other applications. Make sure you use a descriptive name for easy reference later.

4. Enter the description for the data source.

5. Enter the name of the server on which the database is located. The server name should not contain double backslashes (\\).

6. Click the Options button to display the advanced options.

7. If you want the data source to point to a particular database, enter the database name. (This is highly recommended. Otherwise, the data source points to the "Master" database in SQL Server as it is the default.)

8. Make sure the Generate Stored Procedure For Prepared Statement option is checked. This is a SQL Server–specific option that causes SQL server to generate stored procedures for all prepared statements.

Sample Program: Using One Command to Create or Update an ODBC Data Source on Multiple Clients

The RegisterODBC application, which you can find in the Utilities directory on the companion CD included with this book, uses a simple command to create or update an ODBC data source on all of your clients. Just open the application to see the Register Datasource form, shown in Figure 3-3. Enter information in the form, and click the Create Data Source button.

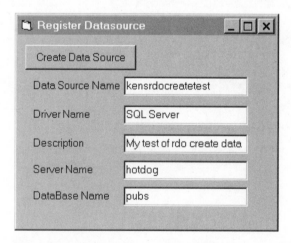

Figure 3-3. *The Register Datasource form of the RegisterODBC application.*

frmRegisterDataSource Form

This form contains all the code in the application.

cmdCreateDatasource_Click **event procedure**

This event procedure uses the *rdoRegisterDataSource* method to create a new data source. The implementation of this method is fairly straightforward, except that the documentation on *rdoRegisterDataSource* is a little vague as to how it works. The Attributes parameter must contain a list of items, with each item separated from the next by a carriage return. The most frequently used attributes are shown in the following table:

Attribute Name	Description
Description	A description of the data source.
Server	The name of the SQL Server.
Database	The name of the database.
FastConnectOption	Set to *True* or *False*. If *True*, uses the fast connection method to shorten connection time when the client connects.
UseProcForPrepare	Set to *True* or *False*. If *True*, automatically creates stored procedures for prepared statements.
OEMTOANSI	Set to *True* or *False*. If *True*, SQL Server automatically translates character sets when necessary. If *False*, a character set translator must be used if the client and server are using different character sets.
Language	Specifies the national language used by SQL Server.

In our sample, the *strAttributes* variable is used to build the description of the ODBC attributes for a data source to be created. The complete attributes list is built by copying an item from the appropriate text box on the form and appending it to the *strAttributes* string. You add the necessary carriage return to separate it from the next item in the list by concatenating a *Chr(13)* to each individual attribute.

```
Private Sub cmdCreateDatasource_Click()

  Dim strAttributes As String

  strAttributes = "Description=" & txtDescription & Chr(13)
  strAttributes = strAttributes & "Server=" & txtServerName & _
    Chr(13)
  strAttributes = strAttributes & "Database=" & txtDatabaseName & _
    Chr(13)
  strAttributes = strAttributes & "FastConnectOption=Yes" & Chr(13)
  strAttributes = strAttributes & "UseProcForPrepare=Yes" & Chr(13)
  strAttributes = strAttributes & "OEMTOANSI=No" & Chr(13)
  strAttributes = strAttributes & "Language=" & Chr(13)
```

(continued)

```
rdoEngine.rdoRegisterDataSource DSN:=txtdsName, _
    Driver:=txtDriverName, Silent:=True, Attributes:=strAttributes

End Sub
```

The last statement in our subroutine actually executes the *rdoRegisterData-Source* method. Notice that we got most of the information from the two text boxes on the form and then set the Attributes parameter from our local variable (*strAttributes*).

The RegisterODBC application doesn't include any error handling. Although the *rdoRegisterDataSource* method is pretty foolproof, you must provide a valid driver name or runtime error number 40000 ("An error occurred configuring the DSN") will occur. (DSN stands for Data Source Name.) The results of our actions on the Registry are shown in Figure 3-4.

Notice that all data source information is located under the HKEY_CURRENT_USER\Software\Microsoft\ODBC.INI key. Look here when you need to modify the information manually or simply check out its validity.

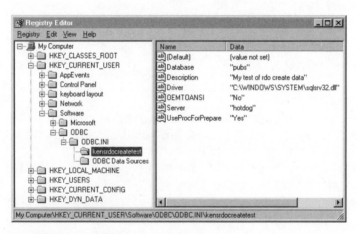

Figure 3-4. *The Registry after running RegisterODBC.*

Automating Form Design and Generation

Generating a user interface is typically done at the start of constructing a new client/server application. It is a useful step in the iterative design process because it provides accessible and visual feedback to the prospective user.

Using an automatic form design tool can take a big chunk of design time out of a data-centric form. This is especially true for database maintenance forms that contain all the fields in a table. A simple form, such as a table maintenance form, can be generated automatically with a form designer.

Visual Basic 4 includes the Data Form Designer sample add-in program (Dfd.vbp) to give you a jump start on form generation. Figure 3-5 shows the form designer as it is preparing to build a new form from the Biblio database.

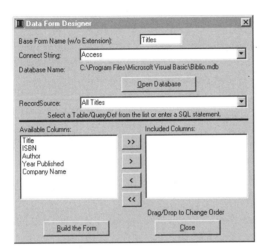

Figure 3-5. *The Data Form Designer included with Visual Basic 4.*

Although you can generate more complex forms with grids, drop-down lists, and other complex controls using the form designer, these forms will require additional manual work to get them up and running. One problem with automatic form design tools is that most of them generate undescriptive names for controls, such as Text1 and Text2 for text boxes. Why use a form generator if you must go back and rename each control? Instead, we use the syntax *pfxFieldname* for all our control names, where *pfx* is a standard prefix and *Fieldname* is a unique name that we assign the control. Using this scheme, a text box might be named *txtMyField*.

Because Visual Basic 4 includes the source code for the Data Form Designer, you can quickly modify it to generate field names properly. In its default format, the Data Form Designer generates all the data fields in control arrays. This could be useful for some purposes, but on many occasions you might want controls that are not part of an array. For example, you might want individual field names to match exactly the name of the column they reference in the database (except for the prefix, of course).

To use the Data Form Designer, you simply follow these steps:

1. Choose the Add-In Manager from the Add-Ins menu.

2. Check Data Form Designer, and then click OK.

3. Activate the Data Form Designer by choosing it from the Add-Ins menu.

Having available the source code for this little program is very useful. You can include your own code standards for generated forms, build in automatic error handling, create default splash screens, and add any other goodies specific to your style of application development.

Other Tools for Generating Forms

You can use other tools to generate Visual Basic 4 forms, including Logic Work's ERwin (versions 2.1 and later) and VBAssist from Sheridan Software. After you have installed ERwin, the forms wizard is located on the Add-Ins menu. ERwin's claim to fame is its ability to define, create, and maintain relational databases. ERwin provides for graphical definition of the structure of the database and then implements that structure in an Access or a SQL Server database. Another nice feature of ERwin is its ability to keep its model synchronized with the database. You can change the database directly, and those changes will be reflected in ERwin. After using ERwin once, you can't imagine being without it.

VBAssist can also generate Visual Basic forms. If you are running VBAssist, its toolbar will be located under the Visual Basic toolbar.

Form Generators in the New World of Multitiered Development

There is a big caveat to using most form generators in the multitiered environment we find ourselves in today: most generators will build the form using a link to a Data control or will generate code to manage the form using DAO or possibly RDO. These are not necessarily bad, as long as you remember to migrate the form to use the correct data-service layer. For more information on building multitiered solutions, see the section "Multitiered Solutions Based on a Services Model" in Chapter 1. You can also read Chapter 6, "OLE Automation and Remote Automation," for more information on building OLE Automation servers.

Another issue we briefly mentioned earlier is common to all forms generators: almost all of these packages expect you to conform to their standards, including coding style, error handling, naming conventions, module designs, and so on. While this might not seem like a big deal at first, it might become inconvenient at some point in your project. Developing your own forms generator is relatively easy and gives you a flexibility not provided by any commercially available forms designer.

4

General Client/Server Development Tips

Let's start delving into the code generation for our client/server systems. Lots of people, particularly managers, think that you don't start making progress on a development project until you begin generating code. We'll jump into coding in Chapter 5, but we need to go over a few tips and techniques first.

Dos and Don'ts for Client/Server Programming

Unless you've previously created production applications using Microsoft Visual Basic and a true remote database, you probably don't know which way to turn when it comes to writing the code for your client/server project. The following sections offer lots of tips for client/server development using Visual Basic. Some of these tips seem to apply to simple Visual Basic applications, but even simple actions become very important when implemented in the more complex client/server world. Some of these tips are Visual Basic 4–specific. Other tips are valid for any software development effort and are so important that we repeat them here even though you've undoubtedly heard them before.

Also remember that there is no clear-cut formula for success in a project as big as the typical client/server development effort. Good programming techniques and a thorough analysis of the problem are absolute necessities for success. Only by applying the right analysis and tuning the steps will you create the type of system that meets your users' demands and performs reliably over time.

General Tips

Place procedures and functions in modules and class libraries instead of placing them in forms Localizing your code in modules has always been a good programming practice. Because class libraries and modules are not loaded until they are used, placing code in modules and in-process DLLs saves resources but ensures that the code will be available when needed. Furthermore, placing code in class libraries builds reusable components that can shorten all of your project life cycles.

Start your application with a Sub Main procedure instead of a startup form Create a Sub Main procedure in a standard module, and explicitly load the forms you want. This avoids the potential problem of your startup form not unloading from memory because the code to unload it exists in that form. This is important, for example, when creating a startup splash screen. To set up your application in this manner, follow these steps:

1. Write a Sub procedure called Main, and save it in a standard module.

2. Choose Options from the Tools menu to display the Options dialog box.

3. Click the Project tab.

4. Select Sub Main from the Startup Form drop-down list box.

5. Click OK.

Use error handlers frequently You cannot have too many error handlers, and you will never have enough. Unfortunately, Visual Basic does not support global error handling, so you need to manually place an error handler in every significant routine. To add global error handling to Visual Basic, we recommend a super product from Avanti Software, VB/Rig.

Database Tips

Use the new Remote Data Objects (RDO) and RemoteData control when dealing with a remote database The new remote features of Visual Basic 4 remove the overhead (execution time and memory requirements) of the Jet database engine when using a remote database, dramatically improving performance.

Use attached tables instead of direct Jet connections to ODBC database tables For attached tables, Jet caches much database information, making subsequent access faster.

Reattach tables when a structure (schema) change occurs To update the information Jet stores in an attached table, the table must be reattached when a change in its structure occurs.

Use snapshot-type Recordsets for small tables (fewer than 500 records) As snapshot-type Recordsets return actual data to the client system, using that type of Recordset is faster than using table-type or dynaset-type Recordsets. Don't return too many rows, or you lose this advantage because virtual memory will be required to store the data. Also remember that snapshot-type Recordsets cannot be updated.

Use transactions to improve performance Transactions can dramatically improve performance and increase the reliability of a database. Transactions allow Jet to buffer its operations—collecting a sequence of commands and then sending them off for execution. Jet typically does not allow nested transactions on ODBC databases, however.

Use the *ExecuteSQL* and *Execute* methods on selected SQL statements These methods pass a SQL statement directly to the database for execution. The SQL statement must use the syntax of your database server rather than Access SQL.

Use SQL *Where* clauses instead of loops for retrieving results and updating records Both Jet and remote database servers are optimized to return Recordsets. Even if the back-end database supports cursors, creating a cursor and stepping through all the data will be slower than the equivalent SQL command.

Use a *Where* clause on ODBC databases instead of the *Seek* method, one of the *Find* methods, or the Filter property in Visual Basic *Where* is faster because it can be optimized by the database server.

Don't use the *Refresh* method on a database object unless necessary *Refresh* rebuilds a dynaset-type Recordset in its entirety. If it took 60 seconds to create it the first time, it will take another 60 to *Refresh*.

Use SQL *Join* statements when joining tables *Inner Join*, *Left Join*, and *Right Join* are more efficient at building joined Recordsets than other approaches.

Use stored procedures and triggers instead of placing SQL statements in your source code Stored procedures and triggers are compiled by the database engine the first time they run. Subsequent executions are faster because they do not need to be recompiled and are already optimized.

On Microsoft SQL Server 6, use Declarative Referential Integrity (DRI) rather than stored procedures and triggers DRI stores the integrity rules for a table in the database when the schema is defined. DRI executes faster and is easier to set up and maintain than defining stored procedures and triggers to support referential integrity. For more information, see the section on Constraints in the Database Developer's Companion of the SQL Server 6 documentation.

Use bookmarks to flag a record and then return to the record Bookmarks point to a specific record using its unique key and provide the quickest way to return to the record.

Don't use *Select* * except for tables with few columns and records, unless you need to return all columns Using the asterisk when you don't need all the columns reduces performance because accessing every row and every column requires resources. Explicitly specifying column names lowers overhead to the minimum, thereby maximizing performance.

Be wary of using single or double quotation marks (' or ") in strings If your database engine uses quotation marks to delimit SQL strings, you can create big problems by allowing them to creep into the database. For instance, the user might enter the word *"Jone's"* in a text box, which could end up in the SQL string and result in an extra apostrophe: *Select Name From Customers Where Name = 'Jone's'.* See the *FixSQLString* method in the CSUtilities class on page 23 for an example of how to handle single-quoted or double-quoted strings.

Make sure your client workstations have plenty of free disk space If memory is exhausted, Jet and all client-side cursor Recordsets will overflow to the Temp directory (which acts as virtual memory space) on a client workstation. This can reduce performance, and it can even cause the client to run out of disk space. Both snapshot-type and dynaset-type Recordsets are susceptible to this problem.

Development Standards

You should create a *standards document* that specifies coding conventions for your organization. For instance, do you want all label controls to be as wide as the text they contain? If so, specify in your document that the AutoSize property for label controls be set to *True*. Here are a few other questions to answer:

- Should all labels on a form be part of a control array?
- Will all forms have menus and toolbars?
- How big are bitmaps on toolbars?
- What types of images do the toolbar bitmaps contain?
- Where should functions be placed?

There is a seemingly limitless number of things to consider. As a result, collect your standards in a living document that can change as the organization gains experience. Make your standards clear, concise, and short and your document easy to read and search.

This standards document will be handy for your internal staff, such as quality assurance personnel. It will also be helpful when you use consultants or contract programmers—just hand them the document and they will know what standards the code they test or produce should meet.

Creating a useful standard is more art than science. You don't want to be too loose, but, on the other hand, a 5000-page document that no one can possibly utilize effectively is just as useless. Instead, try to provide some latitude for individual programmers. For example, "All variable names shall begin with a 3-letter descriptor as outlined in the chart below and shall have a minimum character length of 8 and a maximum length of 24" is more useful and not as restrictive as "All variable names shall have a length of between 8 and 10 characters."

Coding Conventions

As consultants, when we examine code for a project we can often identify the number of programmers working on the project and each individual's level of experience—just by looking at the source code. You don't want this to happen because what it really means is that some portions of your code are well written and others aren't. (We presume that you want all of your code to be well written.) Coding conventions ensure a uniform level of quality.

There are many possibilities for confusion during development unless you address them up front. For instance, how big should a single method be? Good coding standards usually define a procedure as a single block of code that is roughly 50 or fewer lines in length. Many developers write procedures that are 100 to 200 lines long—some go into thousands of lines of code. Their argument is that longer procedures run faster than a procedure that calls numerous smaller ones. The actual savings in speed is trivial and is usually less important than the code readability and ease of maintenance. The first objective should be to turn out programs that work reliably. If your programs are fast but give incorrect results, all they do is generate incorrect results faster. Without a standard, the novice developer has no idea of how to proceed.

The following list describes some things to place in your coding standards document:

- Global flags: These can be useful in an application but present their own brand of trouble. Scoping of variables exists specifically to reduce the number of things the developer needs to keep track of. Before using global flags, make sure they are really necessary. If they are, it is especially important that you document them. Your coding standards should address these items.

- Objects (class modules): Will object libraries be in DLLs, EXEs, project source code, or (more likely) all three? What part of your code base will be in an object library vs. a form or source module?

- Methods: What should the procedure length be? What about coding style—the number of spaces to indent, for example? What type of documentation (description of parameters, author's name, creation and revision dates, and so on) do you require at the beginning of each procedure?

- Projects: You should create a standard for the options in the Make EXE File dialog box (which you access from the File menu). You might also want to standardize project names.

Naming Conventions

Naming conventions are one thing that definitely must go into your standards document. They determine to a large extent how easy your application is to debug and how easy it is to maintain in the future. The following list includes several items you should consider creating conventions for:

- Control names

- Databases

- Database columns

- Stored procedures

- Triggers

- Forms

- Code modules

- Objects (class module names)

- Methods (subprocedures and functions)

- Properties (variables and property procedures)

You can obtain the latest naming convention recommendations from the Microsoft Developer Network (MSDN) CD-ROM. Microsoft Consulting Services publishes them periodically, and virtually everyone in the Visual Basic community uses them.

Striving for Optimization

One activity that often preoccupies programmers is optimization. Possibly because of some academic residue or maybe because programmers like solving puzzles, some seem to take every opportunity to squeeze the very last CPU cycle of speed out of their code. This behavior borders on programming insanity. The purpose of corporate programming is to provide adequate solutions that are maintainable, not to create the smallest or fastest executing piece of code in 99 percent of instances.

You can find many articles on optimizing. Few of them warn the developer of the danger involved in relentlessly chasing optimization or indicate when it is appropriate to target optimization. These hazards have been well known for many years. In 1974, Donald Knuth addressed the issue of optimization. For those unfamiliar with Knuth, he is quite possibly the single most influential individual in the history of computer science. His "The Art of Computer Programming" trilogy addresses virtually every significant aspect of programming in detail and provides the most thorough analysis of computer science to date. So what did Knuth have to say about optimization?

> There is no doubt that the "grail" of efficiency leads to abuse. Programmers waste enormous amounts of time thinking about, or worrying about, the speed of noncritical parts of their programs, and such attempts at efficiency actually have a strong negative impact when debugging and maintenance are considered. We should forget about small efficiencies about 97 percent of the time. Premature optimization is the root of all evil.

> —originally published in *Computing Surveys*, Volume 6, December 1974. Reprinted in 1992 in *Literate Programming* by Donald E. Knuth, p. 28.

Keep in mind the following points as you consider code optimization:

- Don't optimize unless necessary. If a program serves its purpose, calculates adequate results, and does so in a timely fashion, "improving" its performance can only negatively impact the organization.

- Only optimize the offending code. If performance necessitates optimization, positively identify the portion of code that needs to be optimized. This might sound obvious, but a surprisingly large number of programmers will begin optimizing the first piece of code they encounter that can be optimized. If a program has been properly designed, less than 10 to 20 percent of code should require optimization.

- Document optimizations. Almost without fail, optimization will obscure the original purpose of the code. The secrets of optimization are easy to learn, but until then their purpose might escape less experienced programmers. This is doubly important because a less experienced programmer is more likely to perform code maintenance than is the programmer who wrote the code.

■ Don't overdo it. The number of hours spent on optimization should be no more than the time saved as a result of optimizing. For example, if one person uses a program once every working day of the year and if each time the user does so he or she incurs a 10-second delay, at the end of the year he or she will have wasted less than an hour. Therefore, spend no more than one hour optimizing this application, which basically means you shouldn't waste your time optimizing it at all. However, if the application is used by 500 people twice a day and if they each have to wait 10 seconds every time, the wasted time is almost 1000 hours per year. This delay is worth optimizing.

Software maintenance

Visual Basic brings an easy-to-use object model to the development arena that you can use to create easy-to-maintain multitiered solutions built around reusable parts or components. Applications, even those written by the best programmers with the greatest foresight, inevitably will require maintenance, at the least because needs for the system will change. How many times have you heard a programmer maintaining code say something like "Whoever wrote this stuff wasn't a programmer; he was a pasta chef!" (A pasta chef creates "spaghetti code.") Since maintenance is inevitable, plan for it in advance, by focusing your early development efforts on creating a component foundation that your applications can build from.

Variable and Property Definitions in Procedures

While the standard convention for where you declare variables is at the beginning of the module, this is not a requirement of the language. On those occasions when the length of a module exceeds the height of a single screen, you might want to use a different technique. For easier overall comprehension, move the declaration of a variable closer to the location where it is first used.

Take the following code snippet:

```
Dim iLoopCounter, iCharacterCount, iItemsFound, _
   iTotalCharacterCount as Integer
Dim sWorkString, sSeekString, sSearchedString As String
Dim vTextField As Variant
Dim bFound As Boolean

' Database field extraction code here.
⋮

' Does this field contain the string we seek?
iTotalCharacterCount = Len(sSearchedString)
For iLoopCounter = 1 to iTotalCharacterCount
  If InStr(sSearchedString, sSeekString) <> 0 Then
    bFound = True
```

```
   Else
      bFound = False
   End If
Next iLoopCounter

' More code here.
⋮
```

Why clog the beginning of the routine with *Dim* statements when it is perfectly acceptable to move some of them closer to where their declared variables are actually used?

```
' Database field extraction code here.
⋮


' Does this field contain the string we seek?
Dim iLoopCounter, iTotalCharacterCount As Integer
Dim sSeekString, sSearchedString As String
Dim bFound As Boolean

iTotalCharacterCount = Len(sSearchedString)
For iLoopCounter = 1 to iTotalCharacterCount
   If InStr(sSearchedString, sSeekString) <> 0 Then
      bFound = True
   Else
      bFound = False
   End If
Next iLoopCounter

' More code here.
⋮
```

An even better approach would be to break the above routine into several routines of smaller scope. In fact, a good location for the break is immediately before any *Dim* statements that appear in the body of the code. Structuring methods carefully along these lines will fit within the object model philosophy discussed earlier in Chapter 1 and will make your code much easier to debug and maintain.

Tracking Your MDB File

You should never hard code a reference to a local database in your application. Instead, use either the Registry, an INI file, or some other approach that will provide flexibility in where you locate your database. It is no longer necessary to use the Microsoft Windows API for writing to either the Registry or INI files because that functionality is now inherent in the Visual Basic 4 *SaveSetting* statement and *GetSetting* function. Because *SaveSetting* and *GetSetting* work on Registry entries that are specific to a particular user, they use the HKEY_CURRENT_USER key.

Error Proofing with "Kevlar Code"

Kevlar is a lightweight material used extensively by the U.S. military to "bullet-proof" both its soldiers and vehicles. Kevlar code is similarly bulletproof. The key to writing Kevlar code is to minimize the complexity of any one portion of the program. Einstein paraphrased Occam's razor as "Everything should be made as simple as possible, but no simpler." When writing applications, 100 simple modules are infinitely easier to comprehend than 5 large ones. (Of course, having well-designed small modules doesn't eliminate the need for a good overall system design.)

Part of ensuring an effective conglomeration of these smaller modules is to ensure that each interface (that is, the parameters that are passed to and from a module) is both well designed and appropriate. Interfaces take on a new importance with the introduction of the class module in Visual Basic 4. If the interface to an OLE object changes, any existing reference to the object is no longer valid. This can get messy when you have a large client/server solution with hundreds or thousands of OLE client applications and OLE servers sitting on your network. The moral: use care in creating the interface to all objects.

5

Building Your First Client/Server Applications

Now we can start building your first client/server applications. For this chapter, we created a couple of sample applications to show you how to connect to a remote database using bound controls and using Data Access Objects (DAO) and Remote Data Objects (RDO).

Sample Program: A Simple First Application

The first thing you need to know to create a client/server application is how to connect to the remote database. While this isn't difficult, it is different from connecting to a local database. As a demonstration, we have created a simple application called Main, which you can find in the FirstApplication directory on the companion CD. It uses the pubs sample database shipped with Microsoft SQL Server and accesses it via Microsoft Visual Basic bound controls. A bound or "data aware" control can be linked to a Data control to provide an automatic interface between the database and the control. This application uses only the RemoteData control and the DBGrid control. (The DBGrid control is data aware and requires no coding for its normal functions. You can, of course, control the grid manually, but that's left for a later project.)

Figure 5-1 on the next page shows our sample's main form in design mode. Note that the RemoteData control looks just like a normal Data control.

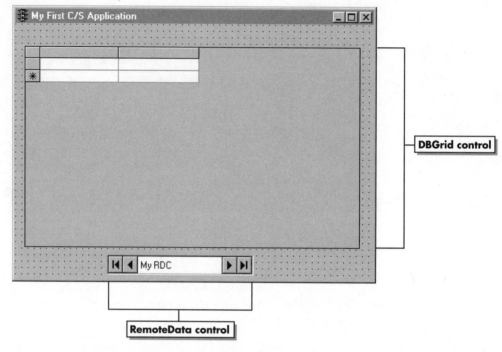

Figure 5-1. *The main form in design mode.*

In order to be able to run this application, you must first create a data source for the pubs database. To do this, open the ODBC application in Control Panel to display the Data Sources dialog box. Click Add to display the Add Data Source dialog box, select SQL Server from the Installed ODBC Drivers list box, and click OK to display the ODBC SQL Server Setup dialog box. Enter *Publishers* for the Data Source Name, enter your server name for the Server, and click the Options button. Enter *pubs* for the Database Name in the Login panel that appears, and click OK to return to the Data Sources dialog box. After verifying that Publishers (SQL Server) is listed in the User Data Sources list box, click Close and exit Control Panel.

Now we will tell you how to create this application from scratch. Open Visual Basic 4, and choose New Project from the File menu. Using the toolbox, place a DBGrid control and an MSRDC control on your form.

NOTE	If the DBGrid and MSRDC controls are not in your toolbox, choose Custom Controls from the Tools menu to display the Custom Controls dialog box. Check Apex Data Bound Grid for the DBGrid control and Microsoft RemoteData Control for the MSRDC control. Click OK to see the controls in your toolbox.

ActiveX Controls

ActiveX controls (formerly called OLE controls) extend the functionality of Visual Basic and many other languages and applications. The ActiveX specification from Microsoft is a standard for creating extensions to perform a wide variety of tasks. Visual Basic ships with a number of ActiveX controls, depending on which edition you have (Standard, Professional, or Enterprise). Examples of standard Visual Basic controls include the Microsoft Gauge Control (Gauge32.ocx) and the Microsoft Key State Control (Keysta32.ocx).

Before you can use an ActiveX control in a Visual Basic application, you must load the control in your project using the following steps:

1. Choose Custom Controls from the Tools menu.

2. If the control that you want is not listed, use the Browse button to add it to the list.

3. Check the control that you want to use.

The control is displayed in the Visual Basic toolbox, and you can use it just like any other Visual Basic control in the toolbox.

Using the Properties toolbar button, set the controls' properties according to the following table. Leave any unlisted property at its default setting.

Control	Property	Setting
DBGrid	DataSource	rdcAuthor
MSRDC	Caption	My RDC
	DataSourceName	Publishers
	Name	rdcAuthor
	SQL	select * from authors

NOTE To simplify the sample application, we used a *Select* * statement. However, to reduce overhead in your applications, always specify the exact column names that you wish to retrieve.

If you have not already done so, create a data source called Publishers that points to the pubs database on your server. You can use the ODBC application in Control Panel to do so. (See the section "ODBC Data Source" on page 61 for more information on setting up your data source.)

Now press F5 to execute your application. The first thing you should see when the application runs is the Login dialog box shown in Figure 5-2, which you use to log in to the SQL Server database. For more information, see "Logging in to a Remote Database" on page 81.

Figure 5-2. *The SQL Server Login dialog box.*

After you successfully log in to SQL Server, data will be returned to your form as shown in Figure 5-3.

au_id	au_lname	au_fname	phone	address
172-32-117	White	Johnson	408	10932 Bigge F
213-46-891	Green	Marjorie	415	309 63rd St. #
238-95-77E	Carson	Cheryl	415	589 Darwin Lr
267-41-23S	O'Leary	Michael	408	22 Cleveland /
274-80-93S	Straight	Dean	415	5420 College /
341-22-17E	Smith	Meander	913	10 Mississippi
409-56-70C	Bennet	Abraham	415	6223 Batemar
427-17-231	Dull	Ann	415	3410 Blonde S
472-27-234	Gringlesby	Burt	707	PO Box 792
486-29-17E	Locksley	Charlene	415	18 Broadway /
527-72-324	Greene	Morningstar	615	22 Graybar Hc
648-92-187	Blotchet-Halls	Reginald	503	55 Hillsdale Bl.
672-71-324	Yokomoto	Akiko	415	3 Silver Ct.
712-45-18E	del Castillo	Innes	615	2286 Cram Pl.
722-51-54E	DeFrance	Michel	219	3 Balding Pl

My First C/S Application

My RDC

Figure 5-3. *The results of a fully functional application that required no programming.*

One interesting aspect of this first sample application is that it contains no code—it drives everything using bound control features. In this example, the DBGrid control is bound to the RemoteData control. To see details of this binding, look at the RemoteData Control Properties dialog box shown in Figure 5-4.

This dialog box is opened by right-clicking the control while in design mode and choosing Properties from the pop-up menu.

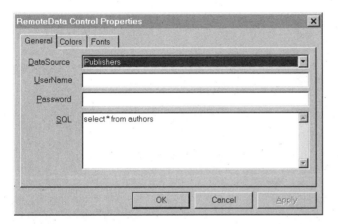

Figure 5-4. *Always check the information in the properties dialog box for new controls and for old ones you have not used for a while.*

Although bound controls are easy to use, they don't always offer optimal performance for heavy-duty, real-world applications. Instead, you can augment Data controls by using DAO and RDO to retrieve the data and then use the *Set* statement to set the RecordSource property of the RemoteData control to the Recordset generated by DAO and RDO.

> **TIP** To interactively build and test long Select statements, use a tool such as sp_Assist from Sheridan Software. Then copy the statement to the clipboard, and paste it into your application. You can also create an sp_Assist project to maintain Select statements and objects in SQL Server, such as stored procedures and triggers. Give the sp_Assist project the same name as your Visual Basic project to make tracking much easier.

Logging in to a Remote Database

Logging in to a remote database can be an exasperating experience for your users. The SQL Server Login dialog box (expanded to display the Options frame) shown in Figure 5-5 on the next page is the default. This dialog box appears to the user for every data control and connection accessed by your application if you do not explicitly set the Login ID and Password for the application before the connection is made.

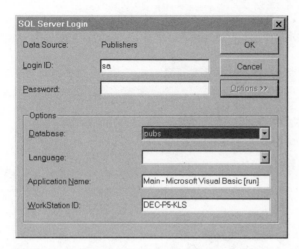

Figure 5-5. *The expanded SQL Server Login dialog box.*

If you are switching to another database of the same structure or if your application allows you to choose different tables from a database, you can select your database from the drop-down Database list. (Remember that this list points to your defined ODBC data sources.) This dialog box is often useful to developers but should be hidden from most users.

You can enter the user name and password in the dialog box shown in Figure 5-4 to disable the display of the Login dialog box. You will need to supply the user name and the password to each RemoteData control in your application. You can also enter *UID=sa;PWD=;* in the Connect property of each Remote-Data control to hard-code the user name and password.

NOTE	Our examples use the *sa* User ID. This is the SQL Server default system administrator user ID and should not be used in your production applications.

Security Modes in SQL Server

SQL Server supplies three different security modes for connecting users. The mode you choose will depend on your network environment, your organization's security needs, and how much hassle you want your users to go through when they log in to the database.

■ **Standard**
 This is the default security mode. Standard security mode uses SQL Server's own security model for every connection to a database. The only exception is when a client explicitly requests a trusted connection using Integrated mode.

■ **Integrated**

Integrated mode uses the Microsoft Windows NT security system for all connections to any database. Any user name and password sent from a client at connection time is ignored by the database. Instead, the network user name from the client workstation is used. Only clients using named pipes and multiprotocol connections are supported under this mode.

■ **Mixed**

This mode is a combination of Standard and Integrated modes. When a client tries to make a connection using Mixed mode, SQL Server first checks the login name supplied with the connection. If the login name is blank or is the same as the network user name, the Integrated mode is used. If the login fails at this point, SQL Server tries the login name and password using Standard mode. SQL Server also attempts Standard mode if the login name isn't blank but does not match the network user name.

Integrated and Mixed modes are by far the easiest to manage if your network is composed of Microsoft Windows, Windows for Workgroups, Windows 95, or Windows NT clients. Integrated and Mixed security modes allow you to use the standard NT user accounts for SQL Server. These clients can use named pipes and multiprotocol connections to enable them to use either of the preferred modes. How should you choose between Integrated security mode and Mixed security mode?

■ You can safely use only the Integrated mode if every user of your database has an NT account and everyone always accesses the database from a system running named pipes and multiple protocols.

■ You must use the Mixed mode if you have users without NT accounts who need to access the database or if there are client workstations that do not run named pipes or multiple protocols.

On the other hand, if you want your users to use Standard mode only, you can obtain the user name via an API call as demonstrated in the *"UT_NetUserID* Method" section starting on page 146. Use Standard mode only when you can't use either Integrated or Mixed mode or when you don't want users accessing the database with their normal user account for the network.

You can also bury the user name and password in the application as discussed in *Building Client/Server Applications with Visual Basic* (pages 155–157), included with Visual Basic Enterprise Edition.

Building Your Database Schema in SQL Server

You must build your database schema in SQL Server before you can run many client/server applications. The following procedure demonstrates how to do this by creating a database containing the tables necessary for all of the remaining samples in this book.

If a server is not already connected, use SQL Security Manager to connect one. For system administrator privileges, use *sa* as the login ID and leave the password blank. Then, if you haven't already registered your server, choose Register Server from the Server menu of SQL Enterprise Manager.

Once you have a registered server, you create a device on which your database will reside. A *database device* is just a file—not one that necessarily consumes an entire physical disk. To create a database device on SQL Server, choose Devices from the Manage menu of SQL Enterprise Manager. The window shown in Figure 5-6 appears. Click the first toolbar button (New Device) to display the New Database Device window, and enter the name of the new device, the drive it will reside on, the path to the file, and its size. (A good default is 10 MB.)

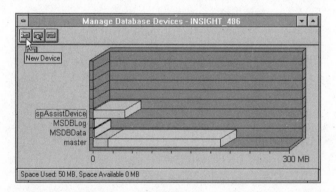

Figure 5-6. *SQL Enterprise Manager enables you to create new database devices in this window.*

Next you create a database by choosing Databases from the Manage menu of SQL Enterprise Manager. First click the toolbar button (New Database) to display the New Database window, and then enter the name of the database (our samples use ClientServerBook for the database name), the data device where you want it to reside (use the database device you just created), and its size. (See Figure 5-7.)

Now you are ready to export the tables from the client to SQL Server. To do this, you must first add your data source on the client. Go to the ODBC application in Control Panel to display the Data Sources dialog box. Click Add to display the Add Data Source dialog box, select SQL Server from the Installed

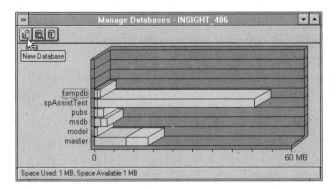

Figure 5-7. *This is the window you use in SQL Enterprise Manager to create a new database.*

ODBC Drivers list box, and click OK. In the ODBC SQL Server Setup dialog box that appears, enter ClientServerBook for the Data Source Name; enter your server name for the Server; and then click the Options button. In the Login panel that appears, enter ClientServerBook for the Database Name and click OK to return to the Data Sources dialog box. After verifying that ClientServer-Book (SQL Server) is in the User Data Sources list box, click Close.

Next open ClientServerBook.mdb, which you will find in the root directory on the companion CD. Select the Client table and choose Save As/Export from the File menu to display the Save As dialog box. Select the To An External File Or Database option and click OK to display the Save Table In dialog box. In the Save As Type drop-down list box, select ODBC Databases ( ) to display the Export dialog box. Simply click OK (without changing the table name) to display the SQL Data Sources dialog box. Select ClientServerBook and click OK to display the SQL Server Login dialog box. Enter a valid login ID and password (if you are a system administrator, use *sa* for the login ID and leave the password blank), click OK, and voilà!—you have just successfully exported the Client table to SQL Server.

Repeat the process described above for each of the remaining eight tables in ClientServerBook.mdb.

Now you are ready to complete the configuration of the database in SQL Server. First copy BuildIndexProcedure.sql, which you will find in the root directory on the companion CD, to the server. Then open ISQL/w (shown in Figure 5-8 on the next page) in SQL Server, and connect to the server using the Connect Server dialog box that appears. In the Query window, choose ClientServerBook from the drop-down list box labeled DB. Then click the Load SQL Script toolbar button to display the Open File window. Open BuildIndex-Procedure.sql to display the script in the Query tab of the Query window. Click the Execute Query toolbar button, and you are done.

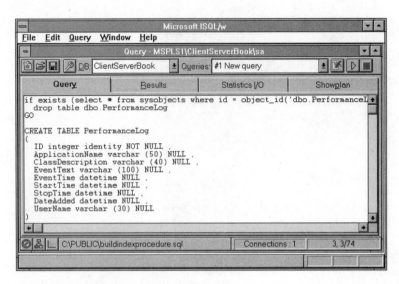

Figure 5-8. *The ISQL/w application.*

Generating SQL Scripts

SQL script files usually have a SQL extension (as in Kens.sql). You can, of course, generate scripts manually, or you can use an automated tool such as Microsoft SQL Enterprise Manager (which comes with SQL Server 6). SQL Enterprise Manager can generate scripts for rebuilding an entire database or just part of a database, which is extremely useful when you want to transfer the database structure to another database. How do we generate these scripts?

1. Start SQL Enterprise Manager.

2. In the Server Manager window, select the database you want to create a script for.

3. Choose Generate SQL Scripts from the Object menu.

4. Select the options for your script, and check the All Objects check box. (Selecting All Objects will generate a script to build the entire database.)

5. Click the Script or Preview button to generate the script.

6. If you clicked Preview, click Save As to save the script.

7. In the Save As dialog box, select the directory and filename to use.

After you have generated the script, you can use it anywhere you can execute a set of SQL commands against the desired database. For instance, you could use ISQL/w or the ISQL command at the MS-DOS prompt.

Sample Program:
Batch Loading a Country and State Database

Now to add some zip to our application by switching from the RemoteData control to RDO. How do we use RDO to perform the same functions as in our first sample? Let's see how we connect to a default database using the Remote Data Objects.

The next sample application, which is named Batch and is in the BatchLoad-Country directory on the companion CD, demonstrates the power of DAO and RDO in Visual Basic and SQL Server. We use DAO to read two tables (one a list of countries and the other a list of states) from a local Microsoft Access database, and we then use RDO to load the data into corresponding tables in a remote SQL Server database.

This is a good starter application for demonstrating how both DAO and RDO work. As it reads through the Country or State table from the Access database (using DAO), it appends the data to the corresponding table in the remote database. Running the application named Batch displays the form shown in Figure 5-9.

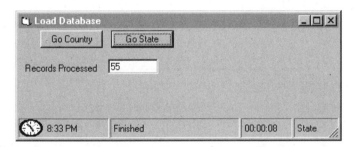

Figure 5-9. *The form used by the Batch sample application.*

Click either the Go Country or Go State button (which work in the same manner) to load the local data to the server. The status bar displays statistics on the progress of the application, showing the current time, the current operation, the time to perform the action, and the name of the table that was loaded. (The operation of the status bar is explained in the section "Using the StatusBar Control" on page 91.) The total number of records processed is shown in the Records Processed text box.

frmLoadDatabase Form

This form contains all of the code in the application.

cmdGoCountry_Click **event procedure**

The *cmdGoCountry_Click* event procedure is triggered when you click the Go Country button.

The first part of the procedure creates lots of variables. The most interesting are the variables used for the database connection, which are shown below:

```
Private Sub cmdGoCountry_Click()

    Dim CountryDb As Database, CountryInTable As Recordset
    Dim ConnectString As String
    Dim cnCountryConnection As rdoConnection, _
      enCountry As rdoEnvironment
    Dim rsCountryIn As rdoResultset
    Dim i As Integer, StartTime As Date, _
      StopTime As Date, TotalTime As Date
```

CountryDb is created as an instance of the Database object to provide access to our database through DAO. The CountryInTable object is created as an instance of a Recordset object. These two objects are all that's required to communicate to an Access database through DAO. *ConnectString* is a string variable that will be used to hold our SQL statement for both tables.

The three properties in the table below are used to create instances of RDO objects:

Property	RDO Object	Description
cnCountryConnection	rdoConnection	This property provides a reference for connecting to the ODBC database. Once the connection is created, you don't need the object until you're ready to close the connection.
enCountry	rdoEnvironment	This property is the reference to the RDO environment. You can create multiple, named environments, each with multiple connections. Each environment can support multiple transactions and lots of other features.
RsCountryIn	rdoResultset	This property will be used the most because it points to the Resultset from our RDO connection.

The next part of the *cmdGoCountry_Click* event procedure is shown here:

```
pnlTableToProcess.Text = "Country"
StartTime = Time()
frmLoadDatabase.MousePointer = vbArrowHourglass
txtRecordsProcessed = 0
pnlStatus.Text = "Connecting"
DoEvents
```

The second line captures the current time in the StartTime property to be used when the routine completes. For the user's convenience, we set the mouse pointer to an arrow with an hourglass to indicate that other tasks can be performed while this procedure runs. We also initialize the txtRecordsProcessed control to *0* and execute the DoEvents function to update the panel text.

The two statements below open the Access database and create a new Recordset based on the SQL statement in the second line.

```
Set CountryDb = Workspaces(0).OpenDatabase _
  ("..\ListAndGridDemo\CountryIn.mdb")
Set CountryInTable = CountryDb.OpenRecordset _
  ("Select CountryCode, CountryCode, RegionCode, " _
  & "Country from Country", dbOpenDynaset)
```

Once the *OpenRecordset* method is used to create the CountryInTable object, we can use the Recordset in our application. Notice that we create a dynaset-type Recordset in this sample by using the dbOpenDynaset constant with the *OpenRecordset* method.

Now that we have our Recordset from the Access database, we can build a Recordset for the ODBC database. First we create the ODBC connection string and store it in the ConnectString property.

```
ConnectString = "DSN=ClientServerBook;UID=sa;PWD=;"
```

Does part of this look familiar? The data source name (ClientServerBook), the login name (sa), and the password ( ) are the same as the ones we used in our first application earlier in this chapter.

After building the connection string, we need to create our connection. The next statement creates a numerical reference to the RDO environment we are going to use, in this case *0*. We actually open the connection to the database using the *OpenConnection* method against the environment reference created in the previous statement.

```
Set enCountry = rdoEnvironments(0)
Set cnCountryConnection = enCountry.OpenConnection _
  ("", rdDriverNoPrompt, False, ConnectString)
```

Now that we have our connection established, we can begin to perform some useful tasks. The following statement deletes all the rows from the Country table to prepare it for our update. Notice how simple the *Execute* method is.

```
cnCountryConnection.Execute "Delete from Country"
```

We create our result set by using the *OpenResultset* method against the open connection. The rdConcurRowver parameter tells the method which type of locking we want to use on the database. This example uses *Optimistic locking,* which makes the page containing the row available to other users, except at the moment an update is being performed. Notice the refresh after we change the Text property of the status panel.

```
Set rsCountryIn = cnCountryConnection.OpenResultset _
  ("Select * from Country", , rdConcurRowver)
pnlStatus.Text = "Processing"
DoEvents
```

Now we start the fun stuff. This next section of our procedure is where most of the work is accomplished.

We begin by setting a counter (i) to track the number of records processed. Next we use *DoWhile* to start looping through our Access table. Once in the loop, we use the *AddNew* method to create a new record on the rsCountryIn result set. Then we simply set the values of this result set to the corresponding values in the Access database.

When the values are set, we use the *Update* method to actually update the remote database. A *MoveNext* method takes us to the next record in our Access database.

Once again, notice that after we set a control on the form, we use the *Refresh* method to update the form's display. We update our counter for total records as the last action in the loop.

```
i = 1
Do While Not CountryInTable.EOF
  rsCountryIn.AddNew
  rsCountryIn("UniqueCountryCode") = i
  rsCountryIn("CountryCode") = CountryInTable("CountryCode")
  If CountryInTable("RegionCode") = "" Then
    rsCountryIn("RegionCode") = 0
  Else
    rsCountryIn("RegionCode") = CountryInTable("RegionCode")
  End If
  rsCountryIn!Country = CountryInTable("Country")
  rsCountryIn.Update
  CountryInTable.MoveNext
```

```
   txtRecordsProcessed = i
   txtRecordsProcessed.Refresh
   i = i + 1
Loop
```

Once our loop terminates, the databases can be closed. We use the *Close* method on the CountryDb object (for the Access database) and on the cnCountry-Connection object (for the remote database). We update our times, reset the mouse pointer, and are done.

```
   pnlStatus.Text = "Closing Databases"
   DoEvents
   CountryDb.Close
   cnCountryConnection.Close
   StopTime = Time()
   TotalTime = StartTime - StopTime
   pnlStatus.Text = "Finished"
   pnlTimeProcessed.Text = Format$(TotalTime, "hh:mm:ss")
   frmLoadDatabase.MousePointer = vbDefault

End Sub
```

cmdGoState_Click event procedure

We will not go through the details of this event procedure here because it is identical to the *cmdGoCountry* event procedure except that it uses the State tables.

Using the StatusBar Control

The StatusBar control is a new addition to Visual Basic 4 and is handy for displaying status messages to the user. There are several things you should know about using it.

The first thing to do after placing a StatusBar control on your form is to set up the status bar's individual panels, using the Panels tab in the StatusBar Control Properties dialog box shown in Figure 5-10 on the next page. To display this dialog box, right-click the StatusBar control and choose Properties from the pop-up menu.

The Index property in the Panels tab contains the number of each status panel. When a new status bar is first placed on a form, it contains one panel and the Index property is *1*. The Key property contains the name that is used to access the individual panel. Our sample in the figure is named *CurrentTime*.

We placed a clock on the panel using the Picture frame in the lower right corner of the Panels page. Click the Browse button to find a picture on your system and load it into the panel. We set this panel to display the current time by choosing *5-Time* from the Style property's drop-down list. We will leave you to discover the other properties and their uses in your application.

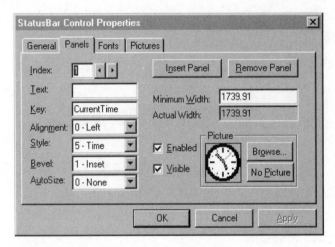

Figure 5-10. *The Panels tab in the StatusBar Control Properties dialog box.*

How do we access the StatusBar control in our program? The easiest way is to create an object reference to each panel that allows you to directly access that panel. Our sample uses the declaration section to declare four form-level properties, one for each panel.

Declarations

Notice that we always use the *Option Explicit* statement to turn on explicit variable declaration in our applications. Use of *Option Explicit* significantly reduces the time you'll spend tracking down spelling errors during the debugging process.

```
Option Explicit
Dim pnlCurrentTime As Panel
Dim pnlTimeProcessed As Panel
Dim pnlTableToProcess As Panel
Dim pnlStatus As Panel
```

Form_Load event procedure

After creating the properties, use the *Form_Load* event procedure to preset four object references, one for each panel in the status bar:

```
Private Sub Form_Load()

    Set pnlStatus = StatusBar1.Panels("Status")
    Set pnlCurrentTime = StatusBar1.Panels("CurrentTime")
    Set pnlTimeProcessed = StatusBar1.Panels("TimeProcessed")
    Set pnlTableToProcess = StatusBar1.Panels("TableToProcess")

End Sub
```

Now we can simply access each panel directly—for example, using this syntax:

```
pnlStatus.Text = "Processing"
```

This sets the status panel's Text property to *Processing*. Using the object reference shortens your code, makes it easier to read, and executes faster than directly using the full syntax to access a panel.

TIP   We learned another thing from using the StatusBar control: don't display items in the status bar while in a tight loop. This causes the status bar to flash during each loop pass. Instead, use a normal text box to display the number of records processed during the loop.

6

OLE Automation and Remote Automation

How many times do you have to make a change in your application, rebuild the executable file, and distribute that file to your users over the network? Every user of the executable needs a new copy, right? What if you could update only one file on the network and have everyone's executable use it without rebuilding? Wow!

Welcome to OLE automation. To begin to understand how we can use this technology to our advantage in a client/server project, refer back to Figure 1-3 on page 11, which shows the object model used as the foundation of our project. A typical project makes use of lots of different objects. Some objects, such as a splash screen, serve utilitarian purposes. Others can contain business rules, mathematical functions, and other functions that you had no idea of at the inception of your project. The first step is to begin defining what objects are required for a project. You should also look at what objects reside in your corporate database that you can reuse with minor changes.

Introduction to OLE Automation

OLE automation works by allowing an application to expose methods (subroutines and functions) and properties (variables) contained in the application to other applications. An application that exposes methods and properties is referred to as an *OLE server*. Any application that can access an OLE server can use a method from the server as if it were a normal procedure or function within the application. When it does so, it is called an *OLE client*. (Note that the terms *OLE client* and *OLE server* do not refer to the client and server in a client/server database system.) All of the applications in Microsoft Office are OLE servers. Let's try an example with Microsoft Excel.

To find out what Excel offers in the way of OLE automation methods and properties, refer to the Microsoft Excel 5.0 Object Library. To see what the library makes available, open Excel and create or go to a module sheet. (To create a module sheet, choose Module from the Macro option on the Insert menu.) Now you can choose Object Browser from the View menu to display the Object Browser dialog box, shown in Figure 6-1. Selecting Excel from the Libraries/ Workbooks drop-down list box displays all the methods and properties that Excel exposes to all OLE clients, including your Microsoft Visual Basic program.

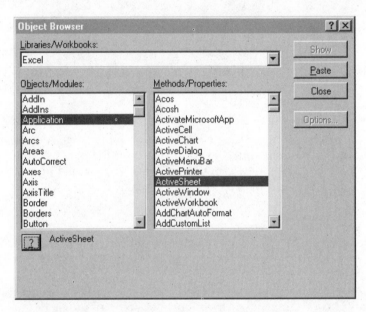

Figure 6-1. *Excel's Object Browser shows you all the methods and properties exposed by the Microsoft Excel 5.0 Object Library.*

For instance, let's say you need to find out the name of the currently active worksheet. The following code snippet will retrieve it for you:

```
activeSheetName = Application.ActiveSheet.Name
```

This line of code assumes that your application already has a connection to the OLE automation object. The Name property of the active sheet in the currently running Excel application is retrieved and stored in the local variable *active-SheetName.*

Applications such as Excel, Microsoft Word, Microsoft Access, Microsoft Project, Visio, and many others provide rich libraries of time-proven functionality.

Tapping into these libraries is easy and provides a wide array of tools that can dramatically shorten the development time for the project and provide a more robust solution.

The GeoFacts sample application included with Visual Basic 4 further demonstrates OLE automation. You can find GeoFacts in the samples\oleauto subdirectory under the directory in which you installed Visual Basic. Figure 6-2 illustrates the interface of this application.

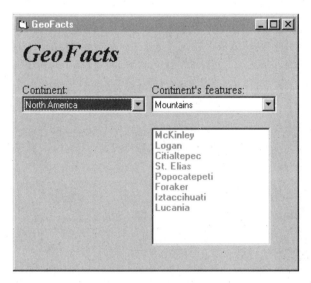

Figure 6-2. *The GeoFacts application ships with Visual Basic.*

This seems to be a simple application at first glance—a database program that reads information about the features of a continent and displays it, right? The data for this program is actually included in an Excel spreadsheet named World.xls in the same directory as the GeoFacts sample application. OLE automation is used to retrieve the data from Excel and hand it to the Visual Basic program.

This technology is much more powerful than most realize. One of our clients recently needed a new application that did lots of calculations and then printed a pretty report with graphs. The estimate of time it would take to create the application using traditional methods was 10 months for four people. We worked with one of their developers, who produced the application in 6 weeks using Visual Basic, Excel, MS Query, and, of course, OLE automation. Excel was used for the calculations, graphics, and printing tasks. Imagine, all of the power of Excel at your fingertips, and all you need to do is call on it!

How does the GeoFacts application work? Most of the code is straightforward, so we leave it for you to discover, but let's look at the basics of using OLE automation in this application. There are two things you must always do to use an OLE automation method or property:

1. Create an object reference to the OLE automation object you will use.

2. Destroy the reference to the OLE automation object when you are finished with it.

The *Setup* and *CleanUp* methods in Module1 of GeoFacts take care of these chores for the application. When the application loads, *Setup* creates the object references by creating an object (shtWorld) that points to the spreadsheet file and another object (wbWorld) that points to the workbooks in the spreadsheet file:

```
Sub Setup()
    ChDir App.Path
    ChDrive App.Path
    ' Get the first sheet in WORLD.XLS.
    Set shtWorld = GetObject("world.xls")
    ' Get the workbook.
    Set wbWorld = shtWorld.Application.Workbooks("world.xls")
End Sub
```

The *CleanUp* method sets both of these objects to *Nothing* to destroy the reference to the Excel spreadsheet and free the resources used by the object references:

```
Sub CleanUp()
    ' This should force an unload of Microsoft Excel,
    ' providing no other applications or users have it loaded.
    Set shtWorld = Nothing
    Set wbWorld = Nothing
End Sub
```

The *FillContinentsList* method, shown below, loads the Continents combo box with a list of the valid continents.

```
Sub FillContinentsList()
    Dim shtContinent As Object

    ' Iterate through the collection of sheets and add
    ' the name of each sheet to the combo box.
    For Each shtContinent In wbWorld.Sheets
        Form1.listContinents.AddItem shtContinent.Name
    Next
```

```
        ' Select the first item and display it in the combo box.
        Form1.listContinents.Text = Form1.listContinents.List(0)

        Set shtContinent = Nothing
End Sub
```

Each sheet in the World.xls file is named after a particular continent. The *Fill-ContinentsList* method creates a new object (shtContinent) that is used to reference the name of each sheet and load the name in the listContinents ComboBox control. The object reference is destroyed just before the procedure ends.

OLE automation is the primary way we are moving to a component model for building applications. Wouldn't it be great if all applications provided OLE automation support in this way?

Introduction to Visual Basic OLE Servers

Visual Basic 4 is the first version of Visual Basic that allows us to create OLE servers. With this new capability we can build component applications that can be mixed and matched, object libraries, multitasking applications, and lots more. Let's look at how to create a simple OLE server and then see how it can be turned into a Remote Automation Server.

A *class module* is roughly equivalent to an object in most object-based languages, including Visual Basic. Methods and properties in a class module are accessed just like normal Visual Basic methods and properties, using the dot separator (.) syntax. Class modules can be used in three different ways:

- Within the local application. (The Public property in the class library must be set to *False*.)

- As an in-process server, implemented in a DLL. (The class library's Public property must be set to *True*.)

- As an out-of-process server, implemented in an EXE. (The class library's Public property must be set to *True*.)

An *in-process server* is a DLL created with Visual Basic that runs in the same address space as the application making calls to it, making it faster than an out-of-process server. An *out-of-process server* runs in its own address space and incurs the additional overhead of passing data back and forth between the OLE client and the OLE server. The more data you pass from client to server or vice versa, the greater the incremental overhead.

Out-of-process servers offer advantages of their own. An out-of-process server can multitask with its client application, effectively simulating multithreading in your Visual Basic application. (Multithreading is the means by which Windows NT operating systems can take advantage of more than one CPU in the computer. There are also advantages to multithreading on single CPU systems. Although Visual Basic doesn't inherently support multithreading, you can simulate it by using out-of-process servers.) Out-of-process servers are also the only OLE servers you can use with Remote Automation.

Creating an OLE Server

The first step in building an OLE server in Visual Basic is to create your server application. This process is so simple that you might think you have missed something after you read this list. There has been a lot written on creating OLE servers in Visual Basic 4, so we will cover the basics here and move quickly on to using the functionality in our client/server projects.

1. Create a class module in your server. (Choose Class Module from the Insert menu.)

2. Click the Properties toolbar button to display the Properties dialog box for the class module.

3. Change the Name property of the class module.

4. Change the Public property to *True*.

5. Change the Instancing property to *Creatable SingleUse* or *Creatable MultiUse* to allow the class to be used by another application. (For more information, see the sidebar titled "The Instancing Property.")

6. Create properties for the class.

7. Create methods for the class.

8. Compile the program into an EXE or DLL.

Using an OLE server is also simple:

1. In your project, create a reference to the OLE server you will use by choosing References from the Tools menu and clicking the check box to the left of the server description.

2. Create an object to reference the OLE server.

3. Use the OLE server's methods and properties in your application.

The Instancing Property

Class modules in Visual Basic have an Instancing property, which is used to determine the behavior of the class module as an OLE server. The Instancing property is only useful in applications that are out-of-process servers (EXEs). This property has three possible values:

- **0 = NotCreatable** Does not allow the class to be used as an OLE server.

- **1 = Creatable SingleUse** Causes every instance created from this object to run as a separate process, simulating multithreading.

- **2 = Creatable MultiUse** Causes all instances created from this class to share a single process.

The Creatable MultiUse option is useful for many OLE servers, depending on the loading of the file server. Applications that access a multiuse server are susceptible to queuing and deadlock problems. As the number of users increases, the performance of a multiuse server will also degrade if the task the OLE server performs is complex and time-consuming.

Single-use OLE servers are usually preferred when many users require concurrent access to the OLE server because each instance of the OLE server runs as a separate process. However, single-use servers are memory intensive—each instance of the server takes a minimum of 500 KB of RAM. A single-use server will also load the processor on your system. (While Windows NT is good at multitasking, there is a limit to the magic it can perform.) For instance, on a dual processor system, a few highly compute-intensive servers could easily max out the system.

In most situations, using a pool manager to manage the number of OLE servers you use has a lot of merit. The pool manager could load two of these intensive servers, for example, and parcel out the references to them to requesting client applications. The pool manager could also track how many users were using each server and alert you when the load began increasing drastically. For more information about pool managers, see the PassPoolManager sample application in Chapter 9 (page 234).

Setting Options for an OLE Server

OLE servers require a little housekeeping. One of the first things you should do is to set a few options for your OLE server, which is a two-step process.

First, set the Project Name and Application Description before you build the application. To do this, choose Options from the Tools menu to display the Options dialog box and then click the Project tab. (See Figure 6-3.) For Project Name, enter a descriptive name for the application. The Application Description should be meaningful and well thought out, as both it and the Project Name will be used in many places to refer to the OLE server.

Second, after you have generated either a DLL or EXE file, open the Options dialog box again and select a Compatible OLE Server. Click the ... button next to the open field, and select an EXE or DLL file in the Compatible OLE Server dialog box that appears. This tells Visual Basic to use that file to compare against future versions of the OLE server. Each time you build the application, Visual Basic will check the current project against the compatible file. When you change any existing properties or the parameters of a method, Visual Basic will warn you that your new version may be incompatible with any applications that use it. Setting the Compatible OLE server should be done for all OLE server applications. If you don't do this, each time you build a new EXE or DLL file, another entry will be made in the Registry on your system. By selecting this option you effectively tell the system to recycle the existing Registry entry.

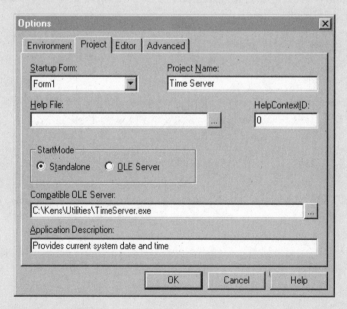

Figure 6-3. *The Project tab on the Visual Basic Options dialog box.*

Introduction to Remote Automation

The functionality of Remote Automation allows you to perform lots of tasks that were previously available only to the hard-core C programmer. Remote Automation is founded on OLE automation, allowing you to take an OLE server and run it on a separate computer from the client. This is Remote Procedure Call (RPC) functionality using Visual Basic.

RPC handles the distributed network part of Remote Automation when a call from a local system is made to a method or property on another system. The beauty of Remote Automation comes from its simplicity: you do not need to understand the underpinnings or details of Remote Automation to make effective use of it. Remote Automation servers can run only on Win32 systems (currently Microsoft Windows 95 or Microsoft Windows NT 3.51 or higher); they cannot run on Win32S. Client applications, however, can run on both Win32 and Win16 systems.

The concept of Remote Automation takes a little while to fully understand. The capabilities are so incredible that they open up entirely new opportunities for corporations that are reengineering or developing new applications.

Creating a Remote Automation Program

Remote Automation in Visual Basic 4 comprises several support utilities for managing different aspects of an OLE server's operations. An OLE server does not need a single change to any existing code or the addition of any code to become a Remote Automation server. Only an out-of-process server can be used as a Remote Automation server. You can, however, use the concept of a pass-through server to run an in-process server remotely. A pass-through application simply starts an OLE server and then passes a reference to that OLE server to another application. An application does not even need recompiling to work as a Remote Automation server as long as the correct options were set when you created the EXE.

What do we do differently in the creation of an OLE server to make it a Remote Automation server? Choose Make EXE File from the File menu, and then click the Options button. The EXE Options dialog box is shown in Figure 6-4 on the following page.

Check the Remote Server Support Files option in the lower left corner of the dialog box. This causes Visual Basic to generate the optional Remote Automation files when it builds the application. These files are the VBR and TLB files found in the same directory as the EXE file and contain information used by the various Remote Automation support utilities and the Setup Wizard.

After setting the Remote Server Support Files option, click the OK button and then click OK in the Make EXE File dialog box. This is all you need to do to turn that cool OLE server into a Remote Automation server.

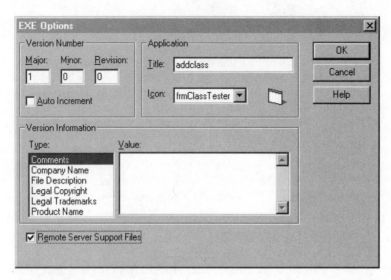

Figure 6-4. *Use the EXE Options dialog box to enable the Remote Automation Support Files option for your OLE server.*

When you create this Remote Automation server, it is still a standard OLE server. If it has an interface, it is also a standard application. Let's say this one more time: *your application can be a standard application, an OLE server, and a Remote Automation server at the same time.* No changes to the EXE or source code are necessary!

Executing a Remote Automation Server on Another System

Now that you have rebuilt your executable, you should test the application and make sure it still runs correctly. Be sure to run both the client and server applications on the local system to thoroughly test their functionality.

Part of the support structure for Remote Automation is the Automation Manager that ships with Visual Basic (located in the Visual Basic 4.0 program group). The Automation Manager must be running on each system that will run Remote Automation servers; you need to run the Automation Manager only once and leave it running. If you look at its form, you will see something similar to Figure 6-5.

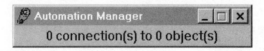

Figure 6-5. *The Automation Manager shows how many connections it is currently handling and how many objects are currently active with those connections.*

Figure 6-5 shows the Automation Manager running with no connections. The information displayed by the Automation Manager is dynamic and changes as clients connect and disconnect to Remote Automation servers. It is a good idea to place the Automation Manager in the Windows\Start Menu\Programs\-StartUp directory (or in the Startup group for Windows NT) to make sure it is restarted automatically should the server go down.

Once you have the Automation Manager running on the system that will run your OLE server, you are ready for the next step. Copy the OLE server executable to your server system where the Automation Manager is running. Run the executable once on this system to register it. Alternatively, you can add the /REGSERVER option to the command line to cause the executable to automatically register itself in the Registry and then terminate.

Next you need to change your application into a Remote Automation application. You use the Remote Automation Connection Manager, located in the Visual Basic 4.0 group, to manage connections and security settings for your Remote Automation applications. Run the Remote Automation Connection Manager (shown in Figure 6-6 on the following page) on the computer that will run the OLE client application, and perform the following steps:

1. Select the application in the list of OLE Classes.

2. In the Network Address text box, enter the name of the server the application will run on. (You can optionally enter the network address, but we do not recommend that approach.)

3. Enter the network protocol to use for Remote Automation. Both the client and the server must be running the same protocol.

4. If you want to use an authentication level, select it from the list.

5. Switch the application to Remote Automation by doing one of the following:

   - Right-click the class name in the list, and choose Remote.
   - Choose Remote from the Register menu.
   - Press Ctl-R.

Run the OLE client application again, and try the operations supplied by the remote OLE server. This time the OLE server should start on the remote system and perform the requested actions. Data passed to or from either application will be handled transparently by your application. If your two systems are close to each other, you should be able to see the disk drive access light go on or hear the disk drive rattle on the system running the OLE server.

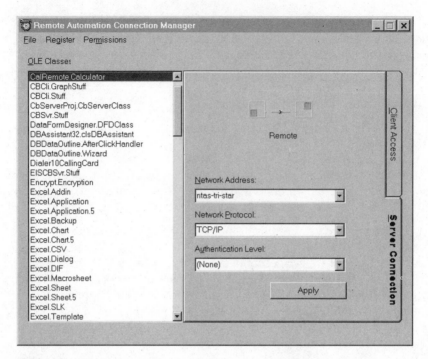

Figure 6-6. *The Remote Automation Connection Manager.*

The Remote label on the upper portion of the Server Connection tab indicates that the selected application is currently configured to run remotely. The Client Access tab lets you set the security options for your Remote Automation servers.

Sample Program: Teaming Up OLE Automation and Visio

To completely illustrate the capabilities of OLE automation, we used our favorite drawing package, Visio Technical Version 4, to create the sample application named SetTable, which you can find in the TableSetting directory on the companion CD. (This sample won't work with the standard edition of Visio version 4, because of a bug in that edition of Visio.) Before you can build or run this application, you must make sure that project's Splash Screen reference has the correct path for your system. Choose References from the Tools menu, and make sure that the Splash Screen reference points to Splash.exe in the Splash directory for this book. You must also create the ClientServerBook data source as described in "Building Your Database Schema in SQL Server" on page 84 in Chapter 5.

Visio contains a number of shapes (objects) called SmartShapes. A SmartShape has intelligence, as it can size itself, handle text, and more. You can easily create your own shapes and modify existing shapes to create both templates and "shape sheets." Figure 6-7 shows Visio running on Windows 95 with a completed drawing for this sample application. The shape sheet is on the left, and the drawing is on the right.

You create a drawing in Visio by dragging a shape from a shape sheet to the drawing. Once in the drawing, you can resize the shape, add text, glue the shape to other shapes, and lots of other stuff. The drawing in this picture was created completely via OLE automation from Visual Basic.

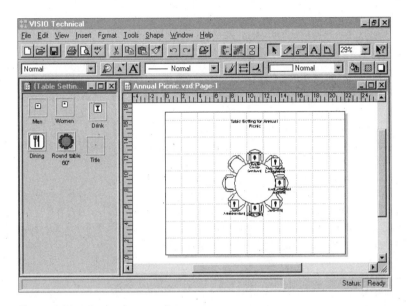

Figure 6-7. *The Visio interface.*

There are several reasons why Visio appeals to us:

■ Each SmartShape in Visio is really an object with its own properties. You can actually modify the master for a shape in a shape sheet and change the operation of your application without touching your Visual Basic code! Cool.

■ We can use a Visio template to build our initial drawing. Like the SmartShapes, the template can be modified without changing any code in your application.

■ Using an application such as Visio allows you to leverage the power of the tools at your disposal. For instance, it took only part of two evenings during Comdex to create this sample. This was the first time we had created an application with Visio, so it took longer than normal. It's impossible to know how long it would have taken if we had started this application from scratch and had had to create the graphic objects, the drawing tools, and so on.

In this example, we are partially solving a problem for one of our clients. Our sample is somewhat simplified, but it provides the basic functionality required. This client delivers weeklong seminar programs that include dinners that require custom seating plans. The plans are determined by the following criteria (and are cumbersome to create, to say the least):

■ Build the layout for a specific event (picnic, meeting, class, and so on).

■ If possible, the seating layout must be: female, male, female….

■ The description for each person must include name and department.

■ If the person wants to drink wine, the word *Wine* must appear in parentheses after the department.

A couple of limitations in this sample program are that we set only one table and allow no more than eight people per table. Some fairly simple logic must be added to make this a fully functioning application.

Figure 6-8 shows a close-up of the definition for one person. Notice how the shape indicates the individual's gender.

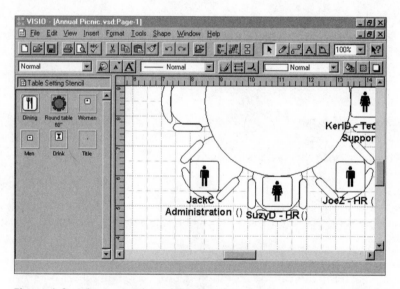

Figure 6-8. *The SmartShape illustrated in this figure was modified from a sample that was included with Visio.*

Before we go on, take a look at Figure 6-7 to understand how the drawing is set up. The table contains spaces for eight people in the configuration shown.

We designed the program to place a shape in the appropriate location at the table. The application also places a simple title on the drawing.

This application provides a simple interface that allows the user to perform the following tasks:

- Select an event from the combo list

- Automatically create the table layout drawing by clicking a button

- Save the drawing

- Print the drawing

- Exit the application

The application is built using the new RemoteData control and OLE automation. The RemoteData control allows Visual Basic to talk to our ODBC database.

Overview of the Application's Operation

As this application starts, all three of the command buttons used to manage the drawing are disabled, as shown in Figure 6-9. This is good programming practice because you should always visually clue users for actions they can take. In this case, the buttons are disabled until a visit description is selected from the drop-down list box. It also simplifies your error checking because a user can't click the wrong button if the button is disabled. In our sample, the only action the user can take is to select a visit from the drop-down list box or to close the application by clicking the Close button.

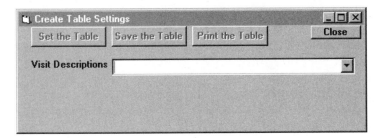

Figure 6-9. *The interface of the SetTable application when it is started.*

Figure 6-10 on the following page shows the application after the user has selected an item from the Visit Descriptions drop-down list box. Notice that only the Set The Table button is enabled. It makes no sense at this point to enable the other buttons, as there is no drawing open in Visio to save or print.

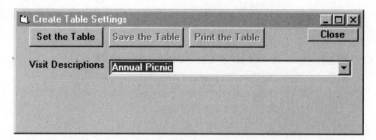

Figure 6-10. *The application interface after a visit description is selected.*

Another item we included in this sample is a status display that updates as each major step is completed during the processing cycle. Figure 6-11 shows how our example uses a simple Label control as an alternative to the StatusBar control for displaying messages. The updates to the Label control are in the *SetThe-Table* method.

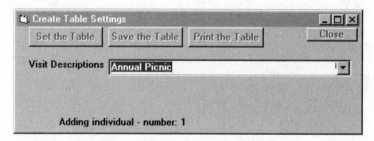

Figure 6-11. *Use of a Label control to show status messages.*

frmSetTable Form

The frmSetTable form includes the user interface for the application and miscellaneous procedures.

cmdClose_Click event procedure

The *cmdClose_Click* event procedure checks to determine if a table has been set using the bTableSet property. If the property is *True*, the *ClearObjects* procedure is called to clear all the objects. The *End* statement shuts down the application.

```
Private Sub cmdClose_Click()

   If bTableSet Then
     ClearObjects
   End If
   End

End Sub
```

Providing Feedback

Providing up-to-date and detailed feedback is absolutely necessary when using OLE automation because of the variability of a particular system. There is no way to know how many applications a user will be running or what the applications will be doing.

Most networks also have lots of different workstation configurations. Memory, processor type and speed, disk type and speed, network bandwidth, and many other factors come into play with client/server applications. Providing feedback to users in these situations can stop them from getting into lots of trouble (like repeatedly killing the application when it seems too slow) and can reduce support calls.

Figure 6-12 shows the application after processing is complete. Notice that all the buttons are now enabled and the status label shows the user that the process is finished.

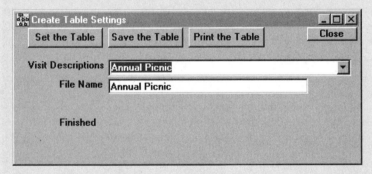

Figure 6-12. *The SetTable application after processing is complete.*

ClearObjects method

ClearObjects is a simple but important method that does exactly what its name implies, clearing all the objects in the application. If an object is not cleared, it can take up valuable resources on the user's system. It is good programming practice to set all objects equal to *Nothing* when they are no longer required.

You should use care when creating a method such as this one. The potential problem in a production application arises from the fact that you might not create instances of all the objects in an application. Depending on the flow of an application during execution, the program might create all, some, or none of the objects. You can create some way of tracking which objects are in use and which are not before clearing all of them in one procedure, as in this sample:

```
Sub ClearObjects()

    Set Visio = Nothing
    Set objTableDiagram = Nothing
    Set objTableSettingStencil = Nothing
    Set shMaster = Nothing
    Set Shape = Nothing
    Set objTextShape = Nothing
    Set objTableRound60 = Nothing
    Set objTitle = Nothing
    Set objControlCell = Nothing
    Set objConnectCell = Nothing
    Set objChars = Nothing

End Sub
```

cmdSetTable_Click event procedure

The *cmdSetTable_Click* event procedure fires when a user clicks one of the three buttons: Set The Table, Save The Table, or Print The Table. These controls are in a control array, which is more efficient in terms of resource usage than having three separate controls. The result of using a control array is that you have one event procedure for all the controls in the array. See page 129 for more information on using control arrays.

This procedure is similar to other examples in this book. It sets the mouse pointer and uses a *Select Case* statement to determine which action to take.

Our *Select Case* statement uses *cmdSetTable(Index).Caption* instead of *Index* to determine the button's position in the control array. Most developers just use the Index property to determine the action to take, but that makes the code very unreadable. Using only *Index*, you must look at the button's ordinal position in the control array each time you want to modify this code. Using the *Caption* property, you can instantly see which button relates to which action.

NOTE Be careful using any control array. If you change the ordinal position of a button or its caption, you can trash every procedure based on the control array. One handy trick is to put some error checking code in the *Select Case* statement using a *Case Else* clause as shown at the end of this procedure.

The Close button is also disabled at the beginning of this method. This prevents the user from clicking the Close button before the method completes, which would queue up a command to close the application.

The *Select Case* statement handles three different cases:

- Set the Table: The main action in this section of code is executing the *SetTheTable* method, which actually does all the work of executing Visio and so forth. The code must also take care of several housekeeping functions. Setting bTableSet to *True* indicates that you have created a table drawing. The Set The Table button is disabled to prevent an impatient user from getting click happy and trying to start the method again.

  The *SetTheTable* method is executed to create the drawing in Visio. The name of the visit selected and the description for the visit are passed to the procedure from the dbcboVisitorListDBCombo control. Once the method completes, the *EnableCmdButtons* method is executed to enable all three buttons in the control array.

- Save the Table: This section of code temporarily disables all the buttons on the form and saves the document. Notice that we have hard-coded the document name. In a normal application this might or might not be the case. The *objDocument.SaveAs* statement performs the save action. (This action is the same as choosing the Save As menu command in Visio.)

- Print the Table: This section of code also temporarily disables all the buttons on the form, and it prints the document.

The mouse pointer is reset to the default, and the Close button is reenabled.

```
Private Sub cmdSetTable_Click(Index As Integer)

  Dim sFileName As String
  Dim objPage As Object, junk As Variant

  Me.MousePointer = vbArrowHourglass
  cmdClose.Enabled = False

  Select Case cmdSetTable(Index).Caption
    Case "Set the Table":
      bTableSet = True
      cmdSetTable(0).Enabled = False
      SetTheTable dbcboVisitorList.BoundText, dbcboVisitorList.Text
      txtFileName.Visible = True
      Label1(1).Visible = True
      EnableCmdButtons True
```

(continued)

```
    Case "Save the Table":
      DisableCmdButtons True
      If Len(txtFileName) = 0 Then
        txtFileName = "tablefile.vsd"
      End If
      sFileName = App.Path & "\" & txtFileName
      objDocument.SaveAs sFileName
      EnableCmdButtons True
      If Not UpdateVisitMasterFileName(sFileName, _
        dbcboVisitorList.BoundText) Then
        MsgBox "VisitMaster could not be updated with File Name"
      End If
    Case "Print the Table":
      DisableCmdButtons True
      Set objPage = objDocument.Pages(1)
      junk = objPage.Print
      EnableCmdButtons True
    Case Else
      MsgBox "A Control error has occurred." & vbCr _
        & "Please call support - Error" & _
        "               ControlArray SetTheTable"
  End Select

  Me.MousePointer = vbDefault
  cmdClose.Enabled = True

End Sub
```

dbcboVisitorList_Click event procedure

This event procedure simply executes the *EnableCmdButtons* method with a
parameter of *0* to turn on the first command button. See the definition of this
method on page 115 for an explanation of its parameters.

```
Private Sub dbcboVisitorList_Click(Area As Integer)

  If Area = 2 Then
    EnableCmdButtons 0
    txtFileName = dbcboVisitorList.Text
  End If

End Sub
```

Form_Load event procedure

This event procedure sets the bTableSet property to *False* and disables the
three command buttons using the *DisableCmdButtons* method.

```
Private Sub Form_Load()

   OpenVisitMaster
   bTableSet = False
   DisableCmdButtons True
   Me.Show
   DoEvents
   SplashComplete

End Sub
```

DisableCmdButtons method

This method is almost exactly like the *EnableCmdButtons* method, except that the current procedure sets the Enabled property of the buttons to *False* while the *EnableCmdButtons* method sets the Enabled property of the buttons to *True*. The trick to these two methods in their current implementation is that passing *True* to either method will set all the buttons, whereas passing the Index property of a button will set only that button.

```
Sub DisableCmdButtons(ButtonIndex As Integer)

If ButtonIndex < 0 Then
   cmdSetTable(0).Enabled = False
   cmdSetTable(1).Enabled = False
   cmdSetTable(2).Enabled = False
 Else
   cmdSetTable(ButtonIndex).Enabled = False
 End If

End Sub
```

EnableCmdButtons method

As mentioned earlier, this method sets either all or one of the buttons in the control array to *True*. In a production application, you could simply add one more parameter to set all the buttons with one method.

```
Sub EnableCmdButtons(ButtonIndex As Integer)

  If ButtonIndex < 0 Then
    cmdSetTable(0).Enabled = True
    cmdSetTable(1).Enabled = True
    cmdSetTable(2).Enabled = True
  Else
    cmdSetTable(ButtonIndex).Enabled = True
  End If

End Sub
```

modTableSetting Module

This module contains the methods that do most of the work in this application.

Declarations

This is where we put all the properties defined as objects in this application. Locating them in one place makes them easy to find during the maintenance phase of the application.

We'll skip most of the gory details of all the definitions here, but there are a few things you need to know.

The VisitorType is a user-defined type that holds the information required for one user record. The MaleVisitors and FemaleVisitors arrays use this type to establish the tracking structure for each group. By using these arrays, we split up the males and females when each record is loaded from the database. This removes the need to do any fancy sorting and matching as we process the records during the drawing process in the *SetTheTable* method.

```
Option Explicit

Dim XPos As Double, YPos As Double
Dim YCounter As Double, XCounter As Double
Dim YCenter As Double, XCenter As Double
Dim stDrinks As String, stSex As String, stLabel As String
Dim IndexCounter As Integer, SQL As String, stTemp As String

Public bTableSet As Boolean
Public ConnectString As String
Public enVisitMaster As rdoEnvironment
Public cnVisitMaster As rdoConnection
Public rsVisitMaster As rdoResultset
Public rsVisitorDemographics As rdoResultset

' Visio application object, objTableDiagram drawing
Public Visio As Object, objTableDiagram As Object

' Stencil
Public objTableSettingStencil As Object

' objDocument
Public objDocument As Object

' shMaster shape, Shape as object
Public shMaster As Object, Shape As Object

' objTextShape for label, objTableRound60 shape
Public objTextShape As Object, objTableRound60 As Object
```

```
' objTitle
Public objTitle As Object

' Shapesheet cell, connection point
Public objControlCell As Object, objConnectCell As Object

' Characters
Public objChars As Object

Dim iTableCount As Integer

Public Type VisitorType
  Name As String
  Department As String
  Wine As String
End Type

Dim MaleVisitors(1 To 9) As VisitorType
Dim FemaleVisitors(1 To 9) As VisitorType

Dim objSplash As New clsSplash
Dim CounterMale As Integer, CounterFemale As Integer
```

SetTheTable method

All of the major action takes place in this method or is driven from here. The main elements of the procedure are the following:

- Execute the *LoadVisitorTables* method to load the FemaleVisitors and MaleVisitors arrays. The VisitName property is passed to the procedure to provide the lookup criteria for retrieving records from the database.

- Use the *StartVisio* method to create an instance of the Visio object.

The balance of the procedure is concerned with creating the new drawing in Visio and placing the other objects on the drawing. As you will see, there is lots of housekeeping for this process.

The first thing you might notice is that this method uses lots of properties and constants. Many of these are used as counters or temporary variables to hold information for the current visitor.

This method also uses the frmSetTable.labStatus control, which is the status label on the form where we track the actions of the OLE server as this method executes. To process the updates to the Label control, we followed each statement that sets the Label control with a call to the *DoEvents* function. Otherwise, the status label won't be updated until after the process for which we're providing feedback is completed.

There is not a lot of database processing in this method, so we won't spend a lot of time discussing that here. The database processing is encapsulated in the *LoadVisitorTables* method, which is called early in this method.

The other items of interest here are related to driving Visio. The actual functions are reviewed in the sidebar below.

Be aware that using OLE automation might not be included in a vendor's standard support options and contracts. Visio is a good case in point. Neither the registration card nor the manual indicate that developer support is excluded from the standard technical support, but instead is fee-based and has different hours of operation.

Using OLE Automation with Visio

The code used in our application to drive Visio from Visual Basic is fairly simple.

The *StartVisio* method creates the instance of our Visio object:

```
On Error Resume Next

' If Visio is already running, create an object reference.
  Set Visio = GetObject(, "Visio.Application")

' Otherwise, start Visio and create an object reference.
  If Err Then
    Set Visio = CreateObject("Visio.Application")
  End If
```

The first *Set* statement uses *GetObject* to obtain a reference to a running copy of Visio. If Visio is not running, an error will occur. The *On Error* statement causes Visual Basic to simply execute the next statement after the error. The *If* statement checks the Number property (the default property) of the Err object for a nonzero value. When an error occurs, the *CreateObject* function is used to start Visio. Obtaining the object handle to Visio in this manner is the most user friendly. If the user has Visio running, the application simply uses that instance; if Visio is not running, it will be started. If the application is running on a server, you can opt to leave Visio running at all times.

The statements shown below are located in the *SetTheTable* method and add a new drawing, based on the template TableSetting.vst, to Visio using the *Add* method.

```
Set objTableDiagram = Visio.Documents.Add _
  ("TableSetting.vst").Pages(1)
```

After the drawing is created, we set objDocument to point to our new drawing.

```
Set objDocument = Visio.ActiveDocument
```

The following statement is commented out in our sample. In a production application, you would enable this statement to turn off the Visio interface while placing objects. This will drastically improve the performance of the system as Visio will not do any visible drawing until the routine is finished.

```
' Visio.ScreenUpdating = False
```

Next we begin placing objects on our drawing. First we place a table in the center of the drawing. The stTemp property is used to hold the definition of the name of the master shape for our table. The next statement creates an object reference to the master shape (in the Masters collection) using our property. The *Drop* method places the object in the drawing.

```
stTemp = "Round Table 60"""
Set shMaster = objTableSettingStencil.Masters(stTemp)
Set objTableRound60 = objTableDiagram.Drop _
  (shMaster, XCenter, YCenter)
```

Next we will add the title for the drawing using the same process we used for the table. Notice that we add 7 feet to the Ycenter value to place the title at the top of the drawing. The (7 * 12) formula calculates the number of inches by multiplying 7 by 12. The Text property is set in the last statement to change the text of the title shape.

```
stTemp = "Title"
Set shMaster = objTableSettingStencil.Masters(stTemp)
Set objTitle = objTableDiagram.Drop _
  (shMaster, XCenter, YCenter + (7 * 12))
objTitle.Text = "Table Setting for " & VisitDescription
```

In the code below, we create a reference to the appropriate icon for each visitor based on his or her sex. The stSex property has been previously set to either *Men* or *Women*. (As you might expect, the two shapes are named *Men* and *Women*.) The Drop and Text properties are used as in previous statements to place the shape and set its title.

(continued)

Using OLE Automation with Visio *continued*

```
Set shMaster = objTableSettingStencil.Masters(stSex)
Set Shape = objTableDiagram.Drop(shMaster, XPos, YPos)
stLabel = sCurrentName & " - " & sCurrentDepartment
stLabel = stLabel & " (" & sWine & ")"
Shape.Text = stLabel
```

The next group of statements sets the text of our SmartShapes label to boldface. We get the count of our current shape, set an object reference to the current shape, and then select all of the characters in the label up to the first "(" and make those characters bold. This effectively makes the entire label bold, except for the word (Wine).

```
IndexCounter = Shape.Shapes.Count
Set objTextShape = Shape.Shapes(IndexCounter)
Set objChars = objTextShape.Characters
objChars.End = InStr(objTextShape.Text, "(") - 1
objChars.CharProps(visCharacterStyle) = visBold
```

The following statement turns the ScreenUpdating property back on to allow Visio to paint the screen:

```
Visio.ScreenUpdating = True
```

You can see from the sidebar how Visio is controlled using OLE automation. The balance of this procedure controls the sequencing of events around the operation of Visio and how the SmartShapes are placed.

```
Sub SetTheTable(VisitName As String, VisitDescription As String)

    Dim bCurrentSex As String
    Dim sCurrentName As String, sCurrentDepartment As String
    Dim sWine As String

' Used to calculate SmartShapes locations at 0 and 45 degrees.
' Multiplying by the number 12 converts the value to inches.
    Const Degree0 = 3 * 12
    Const Degree45 = 2.5 * 12

' Establish the center of the table in the X and Y directions.
    XCenter = 11 * 12
    YCenter = 8.5 * 12
```

```
' Set two variables to point to the next
' SmartShapes location in the drawing.
  XPos = XCenter
  YPos = YCenter + Degree45

' Update the status label.
  frmSetTable.labStatus = "Loading table from database"
  DoEvents

' Load the names of the visitors, and related information, from
' the database. LoadVisitorTables loads each visitor record from
' the database, checks if the individual will drink wine or not,
' and then loads the individual into the appropriate array:
' MaleVisitors or FemaleVisitors. (The advantage of loading the
' visitors into arrays is that later, the logic used to process
' the individuals is very simple--requiring no database
' manipulation. All of the database access is localized in the
' LoadVisitorTables method.) Notice that we pass the method the
' name of the visit we want to retrieve.
  LoadVisitorTables VisitName

' Update the status label and start Visio.
  frmSetTable.labStatus = "Starting Visio"
  DoEvents
  StartVisio

' Reset to no error handler.
  On Error GoTo 0

' Control Visio using OLE automation: create a new drawing,
' drop a table on the drawing, and set the table's title.

' Create a new drawing.
  frmSetTable.labStatus = "Creating new document in Visio"
  DoEvents
  Set objTableDiagram = Visio.Documents.Add _
    ("TableSetting.vst").Pages(1)
  Set objTableSettingStencil = Visio.Documents _
    ("Table Setting Stencil.vss")
  Set objDocument = Visio.ActiveDocument

' Drop a table on the drawing.
  frmSetTable.labStatus = "Adding table to new document"
  DoEvents
  ' Visio.ScreenUpdating = False
```

(continued)

```
   stTemp = "Round Table 60"""
   Set shMaster = objTableSettingStencil.Masters(stTemp)
   Set objTableRound60 = objTableDiagram.Drop _
     (shMaster, XCenter, YCenter)

' Set the table's title.
   frmSetTable.labStatus = "Adding title to new document"
   DoEvents
   stTemp = "Title"
   Set shMaster = objTableSettingStencil.Masters(stTemp)
   Set objTitle = objTableDiagram.Drop _
     (shMaster, XCenter, YCenter + (7 * 12))
   objTitle.Text = "Table Setting for " & VisitDescription

' Prepare to place the SmartShapes for each person around the table.

' Initialize variables. Force the system to
' place a female guest in position one.
   iTableCount = 1
   bCurrentSex = "F"
   CounterMale = 1
   CounterFemale = 1

' Loop through our two arrays to retrieve the visitors.
   While iTableCount <= 8
     sCurrentName = ""

' Determine the position of the visitor SmartShape around the table.
' (Using variables to hold the X and Y positions for the shape, and
' the Degree0 and Degree45 constants, allows for easily adding an
' outer loop to handle multiple tables.)
     Select Case iTableCount
       Case 1:
         XPos = XCenter
         YPos = YCenter + Degree0
       Case 2:
         XPos = XCenter + Degree45
         YPos = YCenter + Degree45
       Case 3:
         XPos = XCenter + Degree0
         YPos = YCenter
       Case 4:
         XPos = XCenter + Degree45
         YPos = YCenter - Degree45
       Case 5:
         XPos = XCenter
         YPos = YCenter - Degree0
```

```
      Case 6:
        XPos = XCenter - Degree45
        YPos = YCenter - Degree45
      Case 7:
        XPos = XCenter - Degree0
        YPos = YCenter
      Case 8:
        XPos = XCenter - Degree45
        YPos = YCenter + Degree45
    End Select

    frmSetTable.labStatus = "Adding individual - number: " _
      & iTableCount
    DoEvents

' Check whether we have a male or female visitor and make sure that
' the counter for that gender is less than 9, which is the size of
' each array. Set variables to hold the visitor's name, department,
' wine preference, and sex. Increment the counter for the gender and
' toggle the bCurrentSex variable to the opposite gender.
    If bCurrentSex = "M" And CounterMale <= 9 Then
      sCurrentName = MaleVisitors(CounterMale).Name
      sCurrentDepartment = MaleVisitors(CounterMale).Department
      sWine = MaleVisitors(CounterMale).Wine
      stSex = "Men"
      CounterMale = CounterMale + 1
      bCurrentSex = "F"
    Else
      If CounterFemale <= 9 Then
        sCurrentName = FemaleVisitors(CounterFemale).Name
        sCurrentDepartment = FemaleVisitors(CounterFemale).Department
        sWine = FemaleVisitors(CounterFemale).Wine
        stSex = "Women"
        CounterFemale = CounterFemale + 1
        bCurrentSex = "M"
      End If
    End If

' Create a reference to the appropriate icon for each visitor
' based upon his or her sex. Place the shape and set its title.
' Set the text of the SmartShapes label, up to the word (Wine),
' to boldface.
    If Len(sCurrentName) > 0 Then
      Set shMaster = objTableSettingStencil.Masters(stSex)
      Set Shape = objTableDiagram.Drop(shMaster, XPos, YPos)
```

(continued)

123

```
            stLabel = sCurrentName & " - " & sCurrentDepartment
            stLabel = stLabel & " (" & sWine & ")"
            Shape.Text = stLabel
            IndexCounter = Shape.Shapes.Count
            Set objTextShape = Shape.Shapes(IndexCounter)
            Set objChars = objTextShape.Characters
            objChars.End = InStr(objTextShape.Text, "(") - 1
            objChars.CharProps(visCharacterStyle) = visBold
            iTableCount = iTableCount + 1
        Else
            iTableCount = 10        ' drop out of loop
        End If
    Wend

' Update the status label and allow Visio to paint the screen.
    frmSetTable.labStatus = "Finished"
    DoEvents
    Visio.ScreenUpdating = True

End Sub
```

LoadVisitorTables method

The *LoadVisitorTables* method takes the visit name to retrieve as its only parameter. Then it looks up the visit and loads the visitors for that visit in the two arrays.

```
Sub LoadVisitorTables(VisitName As String)

' Build our Select statement.
    SQL = "SELECT DISTINCT * FROM VisitorDemographics " & _
        "WHERE VisitName = '" & VisitName & "'"

' Open a Recordset. (If the visit name is invalid, the
' OpenResultset method will generate a SQL error or return
' no rows from the database. In the real world, you should
' perform error checking for both syntax and validity on
' parameters.)
    Set rsVisitorDemographics = cnVisitMaster.OpenResultset(SQL, _
        rdOpenKeyset)

' Set up the counters for this method.
    iTableCount = 1
    CounterMale = 1
    CounterFemale = 1

' Begin marching through our Recordset.
    rsVisitorDemographics.MoveFirst
```

```
' Loop through the entire Recordset.
  While Not rsVisitorDemographics.EOF

' The variable stDrinks stores the current value of the
' Wine column; then the If statement sets the same variable
' to "Wine" or "" depending on whether the column is True.
    stDrinks = rsVisitorDemographics("Wine")
    If stDrinks = "True" Then
      stDrinks = "Wine"
    Else
      stDrinks = ""
    End If

' If the visitor is male, load the current record
' into the MaleVisitors array. Otherwise, load the
' current record into the FemaleVisitors array.
    If rsVisitorDemographics("Sex") = "M" Then
      MaleVisitors(CounterMale).Name = _
        rsVisitorDemographics("Name")
      MaleVisitors(CounterMale).Department = _
        rsVisitorDemographics("Department")
      MaleVisitors(CounterMale).Wine = _
        stDrinks
      CounterMale = CounterMale + 1
    Else
      FemaleVisitors(CounterFemale).Name = _
        rsVisitorDemographics("Name")
      FemaleVisitors(CounterFemale).Department = _
        rsVisitorDemographics("Department")
      FemaleVisitors(CounterFemale).Wine = _
        stDrinks
      CounterFemale = CounterFemale + 1
    End If

' Move to the next record.
    rsVisitorDemographics.MoveNext
    iTableCount = iTableCount + 1
  Wend

' Close the database.
  rsVisitorDemographics.Close

End Sub
```

StartVisio method

This method is used to start Visio. Encapsulating a function, such as starting an OLE server, in a separate method is good programming practice. We can perform whatever error checking is required and never have to worry about cluttering up another method with code specific to our task.

```
Sub StartVisio()

  On Error Resume Next

' If Visio is already running, create an object reference.
  Set Visio = GetObject(, "Visio.Application")

' Otherwise, start Visio and create an object reference.
  If Err Then
    Set Visio = CreateObject("Visio.Application")
  End If

End Sub
```

The technique above should work for all OLE servers. Using the *GetObject* function is called *late binding* because the OLE object is not "bound" to the application until the application executes. It always takes longer to create the reference using late binding, but it is more flexible.

modVisioConstants module
This module contains the constants for Visio that ship with the application. These constants are typically used by any application that uses Visio via OLE automation.

Declarations
The Declarations section comprises the entire module. A few of the constants are shown below:

```
' Class name to be used with Create/GetObject.
Global Const visApi$ = "visio.application"

' Unit codes to be used with cell.result and similar methods.
Global Const visNumber% = 32
Global Const visDate% = 40
Global Const visTypeUnits% = 48
```

7

Choosing and Using Components Wisely

Now it's time to pull together one of these client/server applications. Microsoft Visual Basic has always been the number one tool for taking lots of different components and incorporating them into an application. The VBX format for custom controls that we learned to love and hate was a big benefit to developers as the number of tools using VBX technology increased dramatically. Visual Basic 4's ActiveX format for custom controls takes the component idea to a new level. Not only can Visual Basic use this format, but so can almost any Microsoft Windows–based application, as long as the developer builds in the ability to extend the application with ActiveX Controls (formerly called OLE controls).

The major question facing a developer these days is: "What components do you use in your client/server application?" Another side of this discussion concerns how to use components wisely, including how to use an individual control and choosing the maximum number of controls to use on one form. For instance, in Visual Basic 3 you used fewer controls on a form to improve load time and overall performance. But what happens when you use a TabStrip control with 10 Tab objects instead of using 10 separate forms? Every control is on the same form, which can slow your load time to a crawl.

This chapter introduces Visual Basic 4's bound controls and discusses resource limitations on client workstations, including a number of approaches to minimize a program's resource usage. Control arrays are discussed in depth, and a sample program demonstrates how to use them effectively. Another sample application provides a number of general-purpose utilities for client/server systems. This CSUtilities sample offers a good overview of how to build small, functional class libraries. The application also demonstrates how to use SQL Server to log application performance information and any problems that occur during your application's operation.

Bound Controls

Bound controls are shipped with Visual Basic and are also available from a number of vendors. When bound controls were introduced in earlier versions of Visual Basic, developers were ecstatic! Finally there was an easy way to build an interface to a database. Unfortunately, an application that used bound controls was painfully slow—so slow, in fact, that very few successful production applications were developed using bound controls because they ran out of power as users and complexity were added to a system.

The implementation of bound controls has been greatly improved in Visual Basic 4. For instance, one of the enhancements to the Data control, to which bound controls are bound, is the ability to create a result set programmatically using Data Access Objects (DAO) or Remote Data Objects (RDO). You can then assign that result set to the Data control. You can also use bound controls with the new RemoteData control, which has much better performance with a client/server database than DAO. RDO also offers improved performance when working with a remote database such as Oracle or Microsoft SQL Server. Managing the database interface using RDO and a little source code will provide much better performance than bound controls. The following table describes the bound controls that are included with Visual Basic:

Control Name	Description
DBList	List box that contains items based on a database query.
DBCombo	Same as DBList but also contains a text box.
DBGrid	Displays and enables manipulation of multiple columns of data based on a Recordset object.
Label	Displays text that a user can't change directly. Set the text by using the Caption property or by binding the control to a Data control.
TextBox	Displays information entered at design time, input by the user, or assigned by code during runtime.
CheckBox	Displays an X when selected; the X disappears when the check box is cleared.
PictureBox	Displays a graphic from a bitmap, icon, or metafile.
Image	Lightweight control that displays a graphic from a bitmap, icon, or metafile. Uses fewer system resources and repaints faster than a PictureBox control but supports only a subset of the PictureBox properties, events, and methods.
OLE Container	Enables you to insert an OLE object into your application.
Rich TextBox	Text box with advanced formatting features.
Masked Edit	Text box that allows restricted (masked) data input and formatted output.

Control Name	Description
3D Check Box	Emulates the standard check box but also allows you to align 3-D text to the side of the check box.
3D Panel	Use to group controls. The Caption property can be bound.

A number of other vendors also provide bound controls. It is almost impossible to build an industrial-strength application without using third-party controls, but choose which ones to use carefully. Be sure to test and test and test your application with all of the controls that will be in the final version.

Resource Limitations on Clients

Windows resources are the areas in memory where Windows puts icons, window handles, controls, data, code, and so forth. The operating system makes a finite number of resources available to all applications, and when your application runs out of resources, weird things can happen. For example, users can't start the application, or part of the application doesn't display.

To solve the problem of resource limitations, you can play tricks with Visual Basic and spend lots of time debugging. A better solution, however, is to adopt some nice programming techniques and use an operating system that alleviates most of the problems.

The best operating system in terms of resources is Microsoft Windows NT, which effectively has no resource limitations. It will always return the same number of available resources.

Windows 95 is your second-best option. When resources do become scarce, Windows 95 degrades cleanly—slowing down rather than quitting. You can minimize the use of resources in your applications by optimizing your control usage. You can also monitor the resource status of your users' systems. Brian Livingston covers resources in detail in his book, *Windows 95 Secrets* (IDG Books, 1995).

Using Control Arrays

There are many reasons to optimize the usage of controls, in addition to conserving Windows resources. For example, how fast your form loads depends not only on what happens in your *Form_Load* event procedure but also on the number of controls on a form and how the controls are used.

Control arrays optimize usage of controls by treating a group of controls as one. Each control in a control array shares the same Name property, type, and event procedures. Having 10 text boxes in a control array is a much more efficient use of resources than having 10 separate text boxes, because only one resource is required instead of 10.

You can create a control array by placing a control on a form and setting its Index property to *0*. This will create a control array with one element. To add more controls to the array at design time, add the same type of control and give it the same name. (The Index property will change automatically.) The easiest way to build control arrays during design, however, is to add the first control to a form, set its properties (location, size, and so on) to the values you want, and then copy the control to the clipboard and paste it into the form. Visual Basic will ask if you want to create a control array. If you want more than two elements in the array, simply continue to paste the elements into the form. Visual Basic will automatically increment the Index property for each.

> **NOTE** Controls that are copied and pasted into a container appear in the upper left corner of the container—even if that container is another control. However, controls that are pasted as part of a control array appear on top of the first control in the array.

Another nice feature of a control array is the ability to add members to the array at runtime. This is useful whenever you want to allow a user to add elements to a form. Controls are added to a control array by using a statement such as *Load cmdButtons(3)*, where *cmdButtons* is a valid control array. In this case, *3* would be the next highest index after the current upper bound of the control array.

A control can be unloaded using a statement such as *Unload cmdButtons(3)*.

You can use the *Unload* command to remove any control that was added at runtime. This includes removing controls out of order. For instance, you might add five controls and then use *Unload* to remove the control with an index of *3*. Keep in mind, though, that you can't easily use a *For...Next* or other type of loop to increment through your control array if it is not contiguous. *Unload* cannot remove controls from an array that were added at design time.

A new control added to a control array at runtime will have its Visible property set to *False*. The location of the control (Left and Top properties) will also be set to the location of the first element of the control array.

Sample Program: Adding to a Control Array at Runtime

Our Control1 sample program, which you can find in the ControlArrays directory on the companion CD, uses a single control array to provide the command buttons on a form. The user can add a new button simply by clicking the New Button command button.

Figure 7-1 shows the form when the application starts with just two buttons displayed, in addition to the New Button command button.

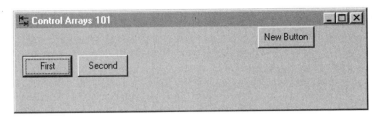

Figure 7-1. *Control1 application at startup.*

Figure 7-2 shows the same form after the New Button button has been clicked four times. Notice that all of the buttons are correctly spaced and have the proper titles.

Figure 7-2. *The form after the New Button command button has been clicked four times.*

How does this work? Read on.

Form1 Form

The Form1 form contains all of the code in the application.

cmdButtons_Click event procedure

The *cmdButtons_Click* event procedure occurs when a user clicks any command button in the control array. The value of the Index property is passed to the event procedure, identifying which button was clicked. Most developers check the value of the Index property in the event procedure itself to determine the button that was clicked and what action to take. We prefer to check the Caption property of the clicked button, as this makes the code much more readable. In this sample procedure, you can see how *Case "First":* is much more understandable than *Case 0:*, which means the same thing.

```
Private Sub cmdButtons_Click(Index As Integer)

    Select Case cmdButtons(Index).Caption
      Case "First":
      Case "Second":
      Case "Third":
      Case "Fourth":
      Case "Fifth":
      Case "Sixth":
      Case "Seventh":
      Case Else
    End Select

End Sub
```

cmdNewButton_Click event procedure

The *cmdNewButton_Click* event procedure is the heart of this sample application. This procedure is where we actually create the command buttons and set their properties.

```
Private Sub cmdNewButton_Click()

' The last array index and the next array index.
    Dim iLast As Integer, iNext As Integer

' The caption to use for the new button.
    Dim strCaption As String

' Determine the current upper bound of the control array.
    iLast = cmdButtons.ubound

' Set the next array index.
    iNext = iLast + 1

' Set the new caption based on the new index.
    Select Case iNext
      Case 2: strCaption = "Third"
      Case 3: strCaption = "Fourth"
      Case 4: strCaption = "Fifth"
      Case 5: strCaption = "Sixth"
      Case 6: strCaption = "Seventh"
      Case Else
    End Select

' Create the new button.
    Load cmdButtons(iNext)
```

```
' Set the new button's properties--Caption, Left, Top, and Visible.
  cmdButtons(iNext).Caption = strCaption

' Locate the new control to the right of the last one.
' Add 100 to (Left + Width) to include a uniform amount
' of space between all the controls.

  cmdButtons(iNext).Left = cmdButtons(iLast).Left + _
    cmdButtons(iLast).Width + 100

' Ensure that the new control is positioned the same as the last one,
' even if that control has been moved.
  cmdButtons(iNext).Top = cmdButtons(iLast).Top

' Make the new control visible. (When a new control is added
' to a control array, the Visible property defaults to False.)
  cmdButtons(iNext).Visible = True

End Sub
```

Miscellaneous Issues with Control Arrays

When you use the *Load* command to add a new control to a control array, you must set the tab order for the control, which is stored in its TabIndex property. The default TabIndex value for a new control in a control array is one higher than the last TabIndex value in use for the form. Our sample program demonstrates this after you have added at least one control. Notice the tab order: First, Second, New Button, Third.

Control arrays are very useful for letting users add fields to a form on the fly. For instance, you could easily write a query front end that lets users pick a table and then pick which fields to display. You can then use a control array to add the fields to the form as the user picks them.

Changing the Parent of a Control

Using the Container property and the *SetParent* Win32 API function is one way to add some zip to an application, by moving a control to another container. A container can be a form, picture box, or frame and might contain other controls. When you move a control from one container to another, not only does the control move, but all of its data and code moves too. Contrast changing the parent of a control with placing a duplicate of the control in another container. Adding the duplicate control doubles the amount of resources used by those controls. Changing the parent essentially uses no additional resources and requires only a minimal amount of additional code to manage multiple parents.

Sample Program:
Moving a Control to a New Parent Container

The MoveList sample program, which you can find in the MoveList1 directory on the companion CD, demonstrates how to use the Container property and the *SetParent* Win32 API function to move a control to a new parent container. Figure 7-3 shows the main form when the application starts.

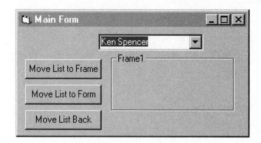

Figure 7-3. *The main form of the MoveList sample application at startup.*

Figure 7-4 shows the form after the Move List To Frame button is clicked. This apparently simple operation actually changes the container for the list box from the form to Frame1.

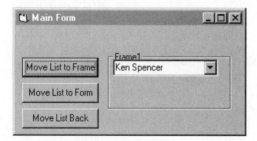

Figure 7-4. *The main form of the MoveList sample application after the list box has been moved to a new parent container.*

Figure 7-5 shows the same list box on a new form. The list box was moved to the secondary form by clicking the Move List To Form button on the main form. The name in the list box stays the same on each form.

By reusing a control on different forms, you benefit from the lack of overhead. In the following code for the frmMain form, you'll note that there are a few tricks to this approach, such as using explicit references to forms in the code behind the control that you plan to move.

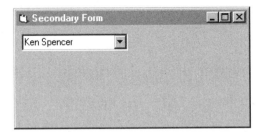

Figure 7-5. *The secondary form after the list box has been moved from the main form.*

frmMain Form

This form contains the interface and code for the main form.

Declarations

The declarations section contains the declaration of our *SetParent* Win32 API function and three variables to hold location information and a return value.

```
Option Explicit

Private Declare Function SetParent Lib "user32" _
  (ByVal hWndChild As Long, ByVal hWndNewParent As Long) As Long
Private iOrigListLeft
Private iOrigTop
Private RetValue As Long
```

cmdMoveList_Click event procedure

This event procedure uses the Container property to change the parent of a control. In this procedure, we change the Container property of the ListBox control (named cboMyList) from *frmMain* to *frame1*. Only a Frame or PictureBox control can be used to contain other controls using the Container property. Notice that we set the Left and Top properties of the control after it is moved.

```
Private Sub cmdMoveList_Click()

  Set cboMyList.Container = frame1
  cboMyList.Left = 100
  cboMyList.Top = 150

End Sub
```

cmdMoveListToForm_Click event procedure

This event procedure uses the *SetParent* Win32 API function to move the control. Using this function, you can move a control to any object that has an hWnd property and can serve as a container. This example moves the ListBox control to the frmSecondary form. Notice how quickly the list box moves to the second form.

135

```
Private Sub cmdMoveListToForm_Click()
  RetValue = SetParent(cboMyList.hWnd, frmSecondary.hWnd)
End Sub
```

cmdMoveListBack_Click event procedure

This event procedure uses *SetParent* to move the cboMyList control back to the main form. Notice that the Left and Top properties are reset to their original values. The original values of these two properties were captured in the *Form_Load* event procedure.

```
Private Sub cmdMoveListBack_Click()

  RetValue = SetParent(cboMyList.hWnd, frmMain.hWnd)
  cboMyList.Left = iOrigListLeft
  cboMyList.Top = iOrigTop

End Sub
```

Form_Load event procedure

The *Form_Load* event procedure performs several housekeeping chores, such as displaying the secondary form (frmSecondary), saving the Left and Top properties of the ListBox control, and loading the list items.

```
Private Sub Form_Load()

  frmSecondary.Show
  iOrigListLeft = cboMyList.Left
  iOrigTop = cboMyList.Top
  cboMyList.AddItem "Ken Spencer"
  cboMyList.AddItem "Ken Miller"
  cboMyList.AddItem "Jane Jones"
  cboMyList.AddItem "John Smith"
  cboMyList.AddItem "Jill Mason"

End Sub
```

Miscellaneous Issues with Changing a Control's Parent

In the *cmdMoveList_Click* event procedure, we used the Container property of cboMyList. By setting the Container property to another container (*PictureBox* or *Frame*), you can move a control to another container on the same form. This is useful when you have multiple frames or tab controls that are shown one at a time and you want to move the current list between them. The Container property can be set only to other controls on the same form or to the form itself, but *SetParent* can move a control to almost any form in the application.

The *SetParent* function is best used when you need the same control with the current data contents in another location in the application, such as on another form. But you cannot use the control in its original location after the move, at least while the control is used in the new location. When the application is through with the control in the new location, you can move it back to the original location.

SetParent can greatly enhance your application. Imagine that you have a list with 5000 customer names. The user selects a customer from the list, which causes another form to display and the first form to disappear. However, the user needs to be able to select another customer from the new form. How do you handle this?

SetParent makes this fairly simple. We have modified the code from our last example to perform this task in the next example.

Sample Program:
Moving a Control in a Real-World Application

The second MoveList sample application, which you can find in the MoveList2 directory on the companion CD, demonstrates a more complex version of moving controls. The major change to the interface was to add a text box to the secondary form as shown in Figure 7-6.

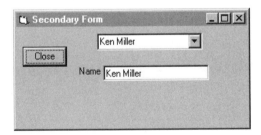

Figure 7-6. *The new and improved secondary form.*

MoveListSupport Module

We have moved the declarations section from the frmMain form to the Move-ListSupport module.

Declarations

We have added a property, *sCurrentListForm*. This property will be used to determine which form currently contains the ListBox control cboMyList.

```
Option Explicit
Public Declare Function SetParent Lib "user32" _
  (ByVal hWndChild As Long, ByVal hWndNewParent As Long) As Long
Public iOrigListLeft
Public iOrigRight
Public RetValue As Long
Public sCurrentListForm As String
```

frmMain Form

The code behind frmMain has changed the most. To determine which form (frmMain or frmSecondary) contains the cboMyList control, we use the variable *sCurrentListForm*. (Even though the parent of the ListBox control has been changed to the new form, checking the Me object inside of a list procedure will still show frmMain as Me. This means you can't check the form's Caption property.)

cboMyList_Click event procedure

The code for the *cboMyList_Click* event procedure is shown below:

```
Private Sub cboMyList_Click()

  Select Case sCurrentListForm
    Case "Main":
      Me.Hide
      frmSecondary.Show
      RetValue = SetParent(cboMyList.hWnd, frmSecondary.hWnd)
      frmSecondary.txtName = cboMyList.Text
    Case "Secondary":
      frmSecondary.txtName = cboMyList.Text
    Case Else
  End Select

End Sub
```

We used a *Select Case* statement to check for the form containing the cboMyList control. The text box txtName is loaded on frmSecondary whether frmMain or frmSecondary is using the list. We could have placed this statement outside the *Select Case* statement, but that would make it more difficult to add the same list to a third or fourth form at some time.

NOTE Why do we use *SetParent* after the *Show* statement instead of before? Because any reference to a property or method of a form will cause that form to load. In this case, *SetParent* would trigger the form load when it moved the control, which would not have worked in our sample with the *Select Case* statement.

Form_Activate **event procedure and** *SetActiveForm* **method**

Most of the other procedures in frmMain are the same as those found in the first MoveList sample. One that is not is the *Form_Activate* event procedure. This procedure calls a method named *SetActiveForm,* which is also called in the *Form_Load* event procedure. We added *SetActiveForm* to handle setting the form name and make it easy to call the same code from several places.

```
Private Sub Form_Activate()
  SetActiveForm
End Sub

Sub SetActiveForm()
  sCurrentListForm = "Main"
End Sub
```

frmSecondary Form

The other form (frmSecondary) has a few modifications as well. There is now a button to allow us to move the list back to the main form. We also added a new method (*SetActiveForm*) to set the *sCurrentListForm* property. This method is called from the *Form_Activate* event procedure.

cmdClose_Click **event procedure**

The *cmdClose_Click* event procedure is used to move the list back to frmMain and to hide frmSecondary. We simply hide the form, rather than unloading it, in case it is needed again. Notice the housekeeping statements at the end to reset the Left and Top properties of the list back to their original settings.

```
Private Sub cmdClose_Click()

  RetValue = SetParent(frmMain!cboMyList.hWnd, frmMain.hWnd)
  frmMain.Show
  frmSecondary.Hide
  frmMain!cboMyList.Left = iOrigListLeft
  frmMain!cboMyList.Top = iOrigRight

End Sub
```

Form_Activate **event procedure and** *SetActiveForm* **method**

These two procedures are comparable to their counterparts in frmMain.

```
Private Sub Form_Activate()
  SetActiveForm
End Sub

Sub SetActiveForm()
  sCurrentListForm = "Secondary"
End Sub
```

Form_Load event procedure

The only action in the *Form_Load* event procedure is to call the *SetActiveForm* method. The method is executed from both the *Form_Load* and *Form_Activate* event procedures, forcing the action regardless of how the form gets loaded or activated. For instance, if the form loads but is not visible, *Form_Load* calls the method to correctly set the variable. If the list has been moved to the main form, then back to the secondary form, *Form_Activate* calls the method as soon as the form becomes visible.

```
Private Sub Form_Load()
   SetActiveForm
End Sub
```

Utilities as Components

Now it's time to look at some other components that are required in all client/ server development efforts. Every application requires lots of general-purpose procedures in addition to custom functions. One of the nice features that Visual Basic 4 introduces is the ability to create class libraries. We have created a class, CSUtilities, that contains a small sampling of utilities for use in a typical client/ server application.

Sample Program: Client/Server Utilities

The CSUtilities sample program, which you can find in the Utilities directory on the companion CD, creates the CSUtilities class. This class should always be built as a DLL and used as an in-process server. This provides optimum performance, reduces application load time (as long as you don't use any of the methods in this class during the *Form_Load* event procedure), and protects the class from accidental modification.

> **NOTE**   To build the DLL properly, choose Make OLE DLL File from the File menu. After the DLL is created the first time, choose Options from the Tools menu and click the Project tab. Click the ellipsis button (...) next to the Compatible OLE Server text box, select CSUtilities.dll, and click OK. Now rebuild the DLL by choosing Make OLE DLL File from the File menu again.

clsUtilities Class Module

The clsUtilities class module contains all of our utilities.

Declarations

This section declares the Win32 API functions used in this class and the properties that store values used by the class or by the client application.

```
Option Explicit

' Used by the INI file functions.
Private Declare Function APIGetPrivateProfileString _
   Lib "Kernel32" Alias "GetPrivateProfileStringA" _
   (ByVal lpAppName As String, ByVal lpKeyName As Any, _
   ByVal lpDefault As String, ByVal lpReturnedString As String, _
   ByVal nSize As Long, ByVal lpFileName As String) As Long

Private Declare Function APIWritePrivateProfileString _
   Lib "Kernel32" Alias "WritePrivateProfileStringA" _
   (ByVal lpAppName As String, ByVal lpKeyName As String, _
   ByVal lpString As String, ByVal lpFileName As String) As Long

' Type safe declare for section deletion.
Private Declare Function APIDeletePrivateProfileSection _
   Lib "Kernel32" Alias "WritePrivateProfileStringA" _
   (ByVal lpSection As String, ByVal lpEntry As Long, _
   ByVal lpString As Long, ByVal lpFileName As String) As Long

' Returns the current user system ID.
Private Declare Function WNetGetUser _
   Lib "mpr.dll" Alias "WNetGetUserA" _
   (ByVal lpName As String, ByVal lpUserName As String, _
   lpnLength As Long) As Long

Private Declare Function APISetWindowPos _
   Lib "user32" Alias "SetWindowPos" _
   (ByVal hwnd As Long, ByVal hWndInsertAfter As Long, _
   ByVal x As Long, ByVal y As Long, _
   ByVal cx As Long, ByVal cy As Long, _
   ByVal wFlags As Long) As Long

' Used to track our open log file number.
Private LogFileNumber As Long

' The path to Master.ini.
Public LogFilePath As String

' The full path to the application INI file, if it exists.
' This is useful if the INI file is in a different directory than
' the application itself. Set in the StartApplication method.
Public ApplicationINIPath As String

' The name of the application set in the StartApplication method.
Public ApplicationName As String
```

(continued)

```
' Current network user name set in the StartApplication method.
Public CurrentUserName As String

' Specifies the EntryClass parameter for the WriteLogEntry method.
' Set by the client application.
Public LastEntryClass As String

' Specifies the EntryText parameter for the WriteLogEntry method.
' Set by the client application.
Public LastEntryText As String

' Indicates the starting time for timing an action.
' Used by the StopTime Property Let procedure.
Public StartTime As Date
```

UT_OnTop method

This method is used to place a form on top of all other forms on a system. The form will remain on top until another form is specified to be on top. The parameters are the form object itself and a flag to indicate whether to place the form on top or return it to normal.

```
Sub UT_OnTop(frmCallingForm As Object, bFloatToTop As Boolean)

    Dim nReturnVal As Integer

' Constants defined in the Win32 SDK.
    Const SWP_NOMOVE = 2
    Const SWP_NOSIZE = 1
    Const FLAGS = SWP_NOMOVE Or SWP_NOSIZE
    Const HWND_TOPMOST = -1
    Const HWND_NOTOPMOST = -2

    If bFloatToTop = True Then
      nReturnVal = APISetWindowPos(frmCallingForm.hwnd, _
        HWND_TOPMOST, 0, 0, 0, 0, FLAGS)
    Else
      nReturnVal = APISetWindowPos(frmCallingForm.hwnd, _
        HWND_NOTOPMOST, 0, 0, 0, 0, FLAGS)
    End If

End Sub
```

SetMousePointer method

Do you ever get tired of typing the statements to set and reset your mouse pointer over and over? You can use this little method to set the mouse pointer to any icon you want. It will save the current pointer in a form-level property,

named iFormLastMousePointer, in the form where you are changing the
pointer. It also returns the pointer number as the return value of the method.
The comments at the end of the method demonstrate how to use it. The
CSUtilitiesTester application on page 153 also demonstrates how to use the
method and how to declare the form-level property.

```
Public Function SetMousePointer(FormName As Object, _
  PointerNumber As Integer) As Integer

  On Error Resume Next

  FormName.iFormLastMousePointer = FormName.MousePointer
  SetMousePointer = FormName.iFormLastMousePointer
  FormName.MousePointer = PointerNumber
  Exit Function

  ' Sample calls to this method
  ' i = objUtilities.SetMousePointer me, vbArrowHourglass
  ' ... code goes here
  ' i = objUtilities.SetMousePointer me, i

End Function
```

FixSQLString method

When a user enters a single quote character (') into a text box that is the same
as the quote character used to delimit your SQL statements, your application
usually blows up with some type of ODBC or SQL error.

We wrote the *FixSQLString* method to solve this problem. *FixSQLString* takes
the string to check as its one parameter. The method returns the string with the
correct formatting to handle single quotes. Every single quote in the input
string is replaced with two single quotes ('') in the output string, which trans-
lates correctly when Visual Basic parses the string.

```
Public Function FixSQLString(sStringName As String) As String

  Dim i As Integer, sTemp As String, sTempIn As String

  sTempIn = sStringName
  i = InStr(sTempIn, "'")
  While i > 0
    sTemp = Left$(sTempIn, i) & "'"
    sTempIn = Mid$(sTempIn, i + 1, Len(sTempIn) - i)
    i = InStr(sTempIn, "'")
  Wend
  FixSQLString = sTemp & sTempIn

End Function
```

UT_IniRead method

Do you ever need to read or write to an INI file but hate to dig out the API call and work through setting up the parameters again? Been there, done that! Here is a utility that reads any INI file.

The method takes four parameters:

- **tSectionName** Name of the section to read

- **tItemName** Name of the item to read

- **tItemType** Type of the item:
  ST=String, IN=Integer, LO=Long, DO=Double, SI=Single, BO=Boolean, CU=Currency

- **tFileName** Name of the INI file, including the file path if the file is not in the PATH environment variable (set using "PATH=C:\;C:\WINDOWS;" in Autoexec.bat, for example)

The method returns a variant that contains the value read. The return value will be blank or zero (depending on the value of tItemType) if no value was found.

```
Public Function UT_IniRead(tSectionName As String, _
  tItemName As String, tItemType As String, _
  tFileName As String) As Variant

  Dim tReturnStr As String * 256
  Dim lReturnSize As Long
  Dim nBufferSize As Integer
  Dim tTempStr As String

  nBufferSize = 255

  lReturnSize = APIGetPrivateProfileString(tSectionName, _
    tItemName, "", tReturnStr, nBufferSize, tFileName)
  tTempStr = Trim$(Left$(tReturnStr, lReturnSize))
```

```
Select Case Left$(UCase$(tItemType), 2)
  Case "ST"                       ' String
    If Len(tTempStr) <> 0 Then
      UT_IniRead = tTempStr
    Else
      UT_IniRead = ""
    End If

  Case "IN", "LO", "SI", "DO"     ' Integer, Long, Single, Double
    If Len(tTempStr) <> 0 Then
      UT_IniRead = CVar(tTempStr)
    Else
      UT_IniRead = 0
    End If

  Case "BO"                       ' Boolean (True/False)
    If Left$(UCase$(tTempStr), 1) = "T" Then
      UT_IniRead = True
    Else
      UT_IniRead = False          ' Defaults to false
    End If

  Case "CU"                       ' Currency
    UT_IniRead = CVar(tTempStr)
End Select

End Function
```

UT_IniWrite method

The *UT_IniWrite* method is the same as the *UT_IniRead* method, except that it is used to store a value in an INI file. If the item and header do not exist, they will be created. The method returns *True* if it succeeds, *False* if it fails.

```
Public Function UT_IniWrite(tSectionName As String, _
  tItemName As String, vntItemValue As Variant, _
  tItemType As String, tFileName As String) As Boolean

  Dim tNewValue As String
  Dim tTempStr As String
  Dim nResult As Integer

  If UCase$(Trim$(tItemType)) = "KILLSECTION" Then
    nResult = APIDeletePrivateProfileSection(tSectionName, _
      0&, 0&, tFileName)
    Exit Function
  End If
```

(continued)

```
    If Len(tItemType) < 2 Then Exit Function

    Select Case UCase$(Left$(tItemType, 2))
      Case "ST"                       ' Strings
        tTempStr = vntItemValue
      Case "IN", "LO", "SI", "DO"     ' Integer, Long, Single, Double
        tTempStr = Format$(vntItemValue, "General Number")
      Case "BO"                       ' Boolean (True/False)
        If vntItemValue = True Then
          tTempStr = "True"
        Else
          tTempStr = "False"
        End If
      Case "CU"                       ' Currency
        tTempStr = Format$(vntItemValue, "Currency")
      Case "HE"                       ' Hex
        tTempStr = "&H" & Hex$(vntItemValue)
      Case "OC"                       ' Octal
        tTempStr = "&O" & Oct$(vntItemValue)
      Case "DA"                       ' Date
        tTempStr = Format$(vntItemValue, "Short Date")
      Case "TI"                       ' Time
        tTempStr = Format$(vntItemValue, "Short Time")
    End Select
    tTempStr = Trim$(tTempStr)

    nResult = APIWritePrivateProfileString(tSectionName, _
      tItemName, tTempStr, tFileName)

    If nResult = 0 Then UT_IniWrite = False Else UT_IniWrite = True

End Function
```

UT_NetUserID method

The *UT_NetUserID* method retrieves the current network user ID from the user's workstation. You can use this ID for a SQL login ID or any other task your application needs to perform, such as stamping transactions with the user's name.

The method takes no parameters and returns the user ID of the current user.

```
Public Function UT_NetUserID() As String

  Dim tName As String
  Dim tUser As String
  Dim nStatus As Integer
  Dim nReturn As Integer
  Dim tTempStr As String
```

```
Dim tNetType As String
Dim hNetwork As Integer
Dim bWFW As Integer

tTempStr = ""              ' Assume the user is not logged in
tUser = Space$(256)        ' Allocate return buffer space

nStatus = WNetGetUser(tName, tUser, 255) ' Check for a user name
If nStatus = 0 Then                      ' Valid call so move data
  tTempStr = Left$(tUser, InStr(tUser, Chr(0)) - 1)
End If

If tTempStr <> "" Then
  UT_NetUserID = tTempStr
  Exit Function
End If

UT_NetUserID = tTempStr

End Function
```

CreateDatasource method

You can use the *CreateDatasource* method to create a new entry for an ODBC data source or to update an existing data source. The code is essentially the same as in the application discussed on page 63, so we will not go into the details again here. The major differences are the parameters we pass to the method. The parameters for this version are the following:

- **dsName** Specifies the name for the data source

- **dsServer** Specifies the name of the server if the database is a remote database; otherwise should contain an empty string

- **dsDescription** Specifies the description for the data source

- **dsDatabase** Specifies the name of the database the data source will use

```
Sub CreateDatasource(dsName As String, _
  dsServer As String, dsDescription, dsDatabase As String)

  Dim strAttributes As String

  strAttributes = "Description=" & dsDescription & Chr(13)
  strAttributes = strAttributes & "Server=" & dsServer & Chr(13)
  strAttributes = strAttributes & "Database=" & dsDatabase & Chr(13)
  strAttributes = strAttributes & "FastConnectOption=Yes" & Chr(13)
  strAttributes = strAttributes & "UseProcForPrepare=Yes" & Chr(13)
```

(continued)

```
strAttributes = strAttributes & "OEMTOANSI=No" & Chr(13)
strAttributes = strAttributes & "Language=" & Chr(13)

rdoEngine.rdoRegisterDataSource DSN:=dsName, _
  Driver:="SQL Server", Silent:=True, Attributes:=strAttributes

End Sub
```

StopTime Property Let procedure

The StopTime Property Let procedure is called to stop the timing of an event and write the event entry to the log file. The timing methods are used in the Asynchronous Query Sample beginning on page 178.

This procedure is passed the current time when it is called and uses the LastEntryText property for the class of the log entry. (The log class can be used later to filter events from the log database by type. For instance, you could query the database for all events where the class is set to Initialize, which could tell you a lot about the problems your applications experience during the initilization process. By using LastEntryText, we do not have to pass the class entry every time we stop the timer. We can just set the property once and forget it until we change the class.) This demonstrates a good way to use a property, by setting it only when it changes and reusing it repeatedly within the class.

The *WriteLogEntry* method updates the log file.

```
Property Let StopTime(dTime As Date)

  If Len(LastEntryText) > 0 Then
    WriteLogEntry EntryText:=LastEntryText, _
      EntryClass:="MethodTime", _
      EntryStartTimeValue:=StartTime, EntryStopTimeValue:=dTime
  Else
    MsgBox "You must set the LastEntryText property " & _
      "before using StopTime"
  End If

End Property
```

StartApplication method

The *StartApplication* method is used to set the CSUtilities properties (found in the declarations section) for an application:

- ApplicationName stores a string to identify the application. This property can be set by passing the method a text string or by using one of the properties of the App object (Title, EXEName, FileDescription, or Product-Name). You might also want to append the version number of the application to its name using the Major and Minor properties of the App object.

■ CurrentUserName stores the current network user name.

The first thing this method does is attempt to read the LogFilePath entry in the Master.ini file located in the application's current directory. If the entry exists, we use that path for the location of the log file. If the entry does not exist, the log file goes in the current application's directory. In a real application, you would almost always want to locate the log file on a network share by specifying an entry in Master.ini.

```
Sub StartApplication(sApplicationName As String)

  Dim sApplicationINIPath As String, sBuffer As String

' Create the path to Master.ini, if it exists.
  sApplicationINIPath = App.Path & "\" & "Master.ini"

  Read the entry from Master.ini using UT_IniRead,
' another method in this class.
  sBuffer = UT_IniRead(tSectionName:="Setup", _
    tItemName:="LogFilePath", tItemType:="ST", _
    tFileName:=sApplicationINIPath)
  If Len(sBuffer) > 0 Then
    LogFilePath = sBuffer
  Else
    LogFilePath = App.Path
  End If

' Set the ApplicationINIPath property (in the declarations section)
' with the ApplicationINIPath entry from Master.ini, if it exists.
  sBuffer = UT_IniRead(tSectionName:="Setup", _
    tItemName:="ApplicationINIPath", tItemType:="ST", _
    tFileName:=sApplicationINIPath)
  If Len(sBuffer) > 0 Then
    ApplicationINIPath = sBuffer
  Else
    ApplicationINIPath = App.Path
  End If

' Set the ApplicationName and CurrentUserName properties
' (found in the declarations section).
  ApplicationName = sApplicationName
  CurrentUserName = UT_NetUserID

' Open the log file. After this method ends,
' the application can use any method in CSUtilities.
  OpenLogFile

End Sub
```

WriteLogEntry method

The *WriteLogEntry* method places the entry in the log file. Notice the use of the optional parameters and the use of the *IsMissing* function to detect whether the parameters are passed or not. *WriteLogEntry* can be used by itself and is also called automatically by the StopTime Property Let procedure in this class. This method can be used to write any type of information to the log, including failure messages (such as "cannot find INI file" or "update transaction failed"), general success messages (such as "transaction completed on time"), security messages (such as "user KKL tried to access financial records"), or timing events (such as "The process update event executed, started at: 3/14/96 10:22PM, stopped at 3/14/96 11:34PM"). *WriteLogEntry* takes four parameters:

- **EntryText** Specifies the text to write in the log entry. If the text contains an error message, it should also direct the user to a source for resolving the error.

- **EntryClass** (optional) Specifies the class name for this particular error. The class name should be descriptive for this type of error, not specific to a particular error.

- **EntryStartTimeValue** (optional) Specifies the start time for an event. This parameter and the next are used mainly for timing events.

- **EntryStopTimeValue** (optional) Specifies the time the event completes.

```
Sub WriteLogEntry(EntryText As String, Optional EntryClass, _
  Optional EntryStartTimeValue, Optional EntryStopTimeValue)

  Dim dStartTimeValue As Date, dStopTimeValue As Date

  If Not IsMissing(EntryClass) Then
    EntryClass = LastEntryClass
  End If

  If IsMissing(EntryStartTimeValue) Then
    dStartTimeValue = 0
    dStopTimeValue = 0
  Else
    dStopTimeValue = EntryStopTimeValue
    dStartTimeValue = EntryStartTimeValue
  End If
```

```
   If Len(EntryClass) = 0 And IsMissing(LastEntryClass) Then
     MsgBox "You cannot use WriteLogEntry without a valid EntryClass"
     Exit Sub
   End If

   Write #LogFileNumber, ApplicationName, LastEntryClass, _
     Now(), EntryText, dStartTimeValue, dStopTimeValue

End Sub
```

OpenLogFile method

OpenLogFile either opens a log file or creates a new one if a log file for the current user does not exist. It creates the log filename by appending ".tmp" to the value of the CurrentUserName property. Before implementing the CSUtilities class, you probably would want to change this method to create a new file even if one did exist. To do this, you could use CurrentUserName and keep appending a counter to the name before creating the file. Creating a new file is the only way to make sure you do not run into sharing problems with the file.

```
Sub OpenLogFile()

  Dim sFound As String

  If Len(LogFilePath) > 0 Then

' FreeFile returns a valid free file number.
     LogFileNumber = FreeFile
     If Right(LogFilePath, 1) = "\" Then
       LogFilePath = LogFilePath & CurrentUserName & ".tmp"
     Else
       LogFilePath = LogFilePath & "\" & CurrentUserName & ".tmp"
     End If

' If the file is found, set sFound to the filename.
' (The first part of the If statement is where you would
' place the code to create a unique filename. The Else
' section would then become part of the general method.)
     sFound = Dir(LogFilePath)
     If sFound <> "" Then
       Open (LogFilePath) For Append As LogFileNumber
     Else
       Open (LogFilePath) For Output As LogFileNumber
```

(continued)

```
' Every time we create a new log file, we write a header to the file.
    Write #LogFileNumber, "Database Log - Created ", _
      Now(), " ", Now(), Now()
  End If

' Write the header entry in the log file,
' indicating the application is starting.
    Write #LogFileNumber, ApplicationName, _
      "Application Started", Now(), " ", Now(), Now()
  End If

End Sub
```

ShutdownApplication method

If we have a *StartApplication* method, there must be a method to stop the application, right? The current implementation of the *ShutdownApplication* method just closes the log file and changes the file extension from "tmp" to "log". The reason we do this is to prevent sharing problems with the file. We originally created the file as a LOG file, but our ReadLogAgent application (also found in the Utilities directory) would occasionally try to grab the file while we were writing it. Our solution was to create the file as a TMP file and then rename it. We also placed some error checking for file conflicts in both this method and in the ReadLogAgent application (described beginning on page 184).

```
Sub ShutdownApplication()

  Dim i As Integer, tmpFileName As String

  On Error GoTo ShutdownApplicationError

  Close LogFileNumber
  tmpFileName = LogFilePath
  i = InStr(LogFilePath, ".tmp")
  If i > 0 Then
    LogFilePath = Left(LogFilePath, i - 1) & ".log"
    Name tmpFileName As LogFilePath
  End If
  Exit Sub

ShutdownApplicationError:
  If Err = 58 Then
    Kill LogFilePath
    Resume
  End If
  Sleep (1000)
  Resume

End Sub
```

Sample Program: Testing the Methods in CSUtilities

The CSUtilitiesTester sample program, which you can find in the Utilities directory on the companion CD, uses the frmUtilityTester form to test some of the methods in our class library. It also shows how these methods can be used.

Figure 7-7 shows the interface of this extremely simple application just after we have tested the two methods used in the application.

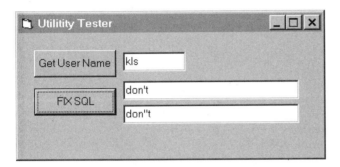

Figure 7-7. *The CSUtilitiesTester application interface.*

Notice how the last text box shows the word *don't* with two quotes ('') replacing the original single quote ('). This keeps the SQL engine happy when you use the text in a SQL statement.

frmUtilityTester Form

This form contains all of our testing code.

Declarations

This section defines one object reference (objUtil) to use for the clsUtilities class and a property to hold the last mouse pointer. You must define the iFormLastMousePointer property in every form that will use the *SetMouse-Pointer* method.

```
Option Explicit
Dim objUtil As New clsUtilities
Dim iFormLastMousePointer As Integer
```

cmdButton_Click event procedure

The *cmdButton_Click* event procedure sits behind our control array for both command buttons on the form.

```vb
Private Sub cmdButton_Click(Index As Integer)

  Dim i As Integer

' Set the mouse pointer to an hourglass.
  i = objUtil.SetMousePointer(FormName:=Me, _
    PointerNumber:=vbArrowHourglass)

' Determine which command button was clicked.
  Select Case cmdButton(Index).Caption

    Case "Get User Name":
      objUtil.LastEntryText = "UT_NetUserID"
      objUtil.StartTime = Now()
      txtUserName = objUtil.UT_NetUserID
      objUtil.StopTime = Now()

' Check the length of the text in txtSQLIn before
' executing the FixSQLString method, so we don't
' waste time processing an empty string.
    Case "FIX SQL":
      If txtSQLIn > "" Then
        txtSQLOut = objUtil.FixSQLString(sStringName:=txtSQLIn)
      End If

    Case Else
  End Select

  i = objUtil.SetMousePointer(FormName:=Me, PointerNumber:=i)

End Sub
```

8

Developing for Performance

Performance is frequently the Achilles' heel of a client/server database application. The raw transaction speed might be fine, but users often complain about the time it takes to perform particular tasks. For instance, many applications take so long to load that users think the application has stopped and either kill the application or start another copy. A simple splash screen can often fix this problem. Other times users think that the application has stopped when it is performing a query. This situation can often benefit from a switch to an asynchronous method of retrieving data, where the user can get back to work while the database application cranks on the query.

This chapter introduces a number of things that you can do to improve the performance of your application. Instead of examining issues such as the speed of RDO vs. ODBC, we look at a number of issues that affect real-world applications that users must run daily. This chapter covers the following topics:

- Building a splash screen as an OLE server
- Managing relatively static lists you can use to fill list boxes and grids
- Using transactions with a client/server database
- Using cursors to improve performance
- The impact of connections on the performance that a user experiences
- Using the ODBC trace facility
- Gaining performance advantages using asynchronous features of RDO and tracking the performance using our performance log sample application

Performance Perceptions—Splash Screens

Users' first impressions of an application are vitally important. No matter how fantastic the application's ultimate performance, a difficult installation or a baffling interface might leave such a bad aftertaste that your users will never be satisfied.

Your application makes its first impression during installation, regardless of whether you construct commercial applications or design them for in-house use. Don't make the mistake of having users manually install your application. It will take longer than an automatic installation, and if things go poorly, the users' machines could be rendered unusable for several days.

After installation, application startup is the next area to examine for performance. At startup, the application might take several seconds to establish a connection with its remote data source, issue the first query, and wait for the result. If you've implemented the suggestions in this book for maximizing performance of your applications, you probably can't do much more about the time it takes to retrieve that initial data. But that doesn't mean that you can't provide the impression that your application is responsive. Like a magician producing a coin out of thin air, you can create the illusion of a responsive application.

One common and effective way to accomplish this feat is through the use of a splash screen. Traditionally, splash screens contain the name of the application and copyright information (although this information should also be available from the About item on the Help menu) and can also include graphics and animations. As with most facets of application programming with Visual Basic, splash screens are a snap. There are a few little tricks to successfully pulling off the illusion, however.

Timers

If your application is well written, it will likely be used for years. (We have select pieces of software that we routinely use that are over 10 years old. Boy, do they run fast now!) During that time, several generations of new processors and technology will appear, and something that takes 30 seconds today might take only a second in 2 years. If your splash screen removes itself immediately upon the loading of the first "real" form, it might become nothing more than an annoying flash as the application loads. A timer provides a simple solution.

Using a timer ensures that the splash screen remains on the screen for a specified time regardless of advances in technology. Simply place the timer on your splash screen form, and set its Interval property to the minimum length of time you want the form to be displayed. After the specified time has elapsed, the splash screen can be unloaded.

Two conditions must be met before you unload the splash screen: the timer must complete its countdown, and the startup code must finish executing. To ensure both conditions have been met, some coordination is in order.

When the Timer event fires, the startup code might or might not have finished executing. If the startup code is finished, you can unload the splash screen. If it hasn't, you need to wait for the startup code to finish. Conversely, when the startup code is finished executing, the timer might or might not have reached its terminal count. If it has, the splash screen should be unloaded. If it hasn't, it shouldn't.

There are several ways to coordinate this activity. One that is both effective and straightforward uses a global Boolean variable—let's call it gbLoadHalfDone—to indicate when either the specified time has elapsed or the load activity has finished. (In other words, either half of the initial load process is done.) When the application starts, set this variable to *False*. When the Timer event occurs or the load activity is finished, check gbLoadHalfDone. If it is *True*, you should unload the splash screen. If gbLoadHalfDone is *False*, set it to *True* to cause the splash screen to unload when the other half of the initial load process is done.

Animations and Graphics

Applications that have exceptionally long startup times can benefit from simple animation on the splash screen. There are many ways to accomplish this, but no matter how you do it, make sure that the animation has a minimal effect on load time. Animation is neat the first time you see it, but sooner or later, it's old hat. Because the user might associate the load time with the animation, you might want to offer a Registry setting to turn it off. Better yet, display it only the first time the software is loaded, and provide a switch to turn it on all the time.

Your splash screen should have an eye-catching graphic—without it there won't be much of a "splash." Rather than placing the graphic directly in the Image or PictureBox control on the form, consider using a resource file, which offers two advantages. First, by placing all graphics and other resources in a resource file, they are easy to locate if you need to update them. Second, if the image is used elsewhere in your application, the overall size of the executable is reduced because both locations can draw on the same binary data, as opposed to each having its own copy. A resource file also makes localization easier if you need to export your application.

While the application loads, the mouse pointer should indicate that something is happening. Most users wait a little more patiently when they see that hourglass. More important, the hourglass offers visual feedback that the application is actually started so users are less likely to start a second instance unintentionally.

Additional Splash Screen Tips

Of course, you will want to center your splash screen. As you might not know the resolution of the user's system, use the *Form_Load* event procedure on page 159 to ensure that the splash screen is always centered.

Under some circumstances, you might want the user to be able to terminate the splash screen. This can be accommodated by unloading the splash form if the user clicks any control on the form or the form itself. You can also check for all keystrokes and unload the splash screen whenever the user presses a key. This is useful if the application completes its loading process before the timer expires.

A polite splash screen exhibits one additional characteristic: it does not interfere with the execution of other applications. As users take better advantage of the multitasking capabilities offered by Microsoft Windows NT and Microsoft Windows 95, they will expect to be able to use other software while your application is loading.

Sample Program: Using Splash Screen Objects

Now for the fun! The sample Splash application included in the Splash directory on the companion CD is actually an OLE server. Creating the splash screen as an OLE server allows you to use it in different applications without ever changing one line of code. This sample is actually an out-of-process server, which was the only way to create the splash screen because in-process servers don't allow you to have forms in them. Now let's look at the details of our splash screen project.

Before you can build or run Splash.exe, you need to make sure that the reference to CSUtilities points to CSUtilities.dll, which is found in the Utilities directory on the companion CD. (Choose References on the Tools menu.)

Furthermore, you need to make sure that the Compatible OLE Server option in the CSUtilities project is set correctly. Open CSUtilities.vbp, choose Options from the Tools menu, and click the Project tab. The Compatible OLE Server option should point to the CSUtilities.dll file on your system. If the path is incorrect, click the ellipsis button (...) to display the Compatible OLE Server dialog box. Select CSUtilities.dll, click Open, and then click OK in the Options dialog box. You will then need to rebuild CSUtilities.dll by choosing Make OLE DLL File from the File menu.

frmSplash Form

The frmSplash form uses only five controls: an Image control holds a graphic for the form, a Timer control determines when the form unloads, and three Label controls contain the text.

Form_Load **event procedure**

The *Form_Load* event procedure centers the form on the screen.

```
Private Sub Form_Load()
  Me.Left = (Screen.Width - Me.Width) \ 2
  Me.Top = (Screen.Height - Me.Height) \ 2
End Sub
```

The integer division performed in this code is slightly faster than floating-point division and yields the same results because fractional display units are not supported.

tmrSplash_Timer **event procedure**

The *tmrSplash_Timer* event procedure is the heart of our splash screen OLE server.

```
Public Sub tmrSplash_Timer()

  tmrSplash.Enabled = False
  If gbLoadHalfDone Then
    frmSplash.MousePointer = vbDefault
    Unload frmSplash
  Else
    gbLoadHalfDone = True
  End If

End Sub
```

modSplash Module

This module contains the global property gbLoadHalfDone and the *Main* method. *Main* is the startup method for the application.

Declarations

In this section we declare one property. The gbLoadHalfDone property works just like the one we mentioned earlier.

```
Option Explicit
Public gbLoadHalfDone As Boolean
```

Main **method**

This method is fired whenever the Splash sample application starts executing and is required in an OLE server even if it doesn't contain any code.

clsSplash Class

This class provides the properties and methods that are exposed to other applications and also contains several private properties that are used internally by the class. The properties for the class are shown in the following table.

Property Name	Value
Instancing	Creatable SingleUse
Name	clsSplash
Public	True

Declarations

This section defines several private properties to hold various pieces of information. We also define an object reference (objUtil) to our clsUtilities project. (See page 183 for more information.)

```
Option Explicit
Private intCopyRight As String
Private intTitleMessage As String
Private intTextMessage As String
Private intPicturePath As String
Private intTimerValue As Long
Private objUtil As New clsUtilities
```

Property Let procedures

A Property Let procedure fires when you set a property, enabling us to do several things each time the property's value changes. For instance, in the TimerValue Property Let procedure, we set the internal property intTimerValue to hold our timer setting, and then we update the actual timer setting on the frmSplash form. Every time TimerValue changes, the form's timer gets updated. All of the Property Let procedures in this class work this way.

```
Public Property Let TimerValue(lTimerSetting As Long)
   intTimerValue = lTimerSetting
   frmSplash!tmrSplash.Interval = lTimerSetting
End Property
```

The Property Let procedure below sets the PicturePath property. This property holds the full path to the file to be displayed in our Image control on the frmSplash form.

```
Public Property Let PicturePath(sMsg As String)
   intPicturePath = sMsg
   frmSplash.imgSplash = LoadPicture(sMsg)
End Property
```

The code below shows the TitleMessage, TextMessage, and CopyRight Property Let procedures.

```
Public Property Let TitleMessage(sMsg As String)
  intTitleMessage = sMsg
  frmSplash.lblSplashTitle = sMsg
End Property

Public Property Let TextMessage(sMsg As String)
  intTextMessage = sMsg
  frmSplash.lblTextMessage = sMsg
End Property

Public Property Let CopyRight(sMsg As String)
  intCopyRight = sMsg
  frmSplash.lblSplashCopyright = sMsg
End Property
```

Splash method

The *Splash* method actually causes the splash screen to display.

```
Public Sub Splash()

  gbLoadHalfDone = False
  frmSplash.MousePointer = vbArrowHourglass
  frmSplash.Show

' The UT_OnTop method from our clsUtilities class forces the
' frmSplash form to the top of all forms.
  objUtil.UT_OnTop frmCallingForm:=frmSplash, bFloatToTop:=True

' Start the splash screen timer countdown.
  frmSplash!tmrSplash.Enabled = True

' DoEvents caps off our Splash method and allows the Splash
' application to perform any tasks. (This line is redundant
' in this case because we are ending the procedure and
' processing would continue within the application anyway.)
  DoEvents

End Sub
```

SplashStop method

A call to the *SplashStop* method is one of the two events that must occur for the splash screen application to terminate. (The other one is the *Timer* event.)

```
Public Sub SplashStop()

  If gbLoadHalfDone = True Then
    Unload frmSplash
  Else
    gbLoadHalfDone = True
  End If

End Sub
```

Sample Program: Using a Splash Screen with a Real Application

At this point, we have not tested our splash screen application. We do this in the Test sample application, which you can find in the Splash directory on the companion CD.

Before you can use the splash screen OLE Server, you need to create a reference (called Splash Screen) to Splash.exe in the References dialog box. (Choose References from the Tools menu.)

Form1 Form

The Form1 form displays when you start the Test application. It lets you test the splash screen server in both of its modes of operation. (See Figure 8-1.)

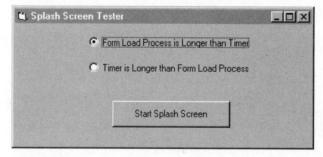

Figure 8-1. *This form displays when you start the Test application.*

Command1_Click event procedure

Clicking the Command1 button starts the splash screen server. Notice that we didn't set the graphic for the splash screen object but simply placed a default graphic directly on the splash screen form. This is handy if your organization wants to use the same logo for all of its applications.

```
Private Sub Command1_Click()

' Decide whether the timer or the form load process will be longer.
  If Option1 Then
    tmrFormShow.Interval = 10000
  Else
    tmrFormShow.Interval = 1000
  End If

' Establish the messages for the splash screen.
  objSplash.TitleMessage = "Ken's New Program"
  objSplash.TextMessage = "I hope this program works for you"
  objSplash.CopyRight = "Copyright 1996 My Software Co."

' Set the splash screen timer.
  objSplash.TimerValue = 5000

' Display the splash screen.
  objSplash.Splash

' Display the form to simulate a form load process.
  Form2.Show
  tmrFormShow.Enabled = True
  DoEvents

End Sub
```

tmrFormShow_Timer event procedure

The *tmrFormShow_Timer* event procedure calls the *SplashComplete* method to shut down the splash screen.

```
Private Sub tmrFormShow_Timer()
  tmrFormShow.Enabled = False
  SplashComplete
End Sub
```

modSplashTester Module

The modSplashTester module contains the code that works in conjunction with the Form1 form.

Declarations

The first thing we need to do is create an object reference to our clsSplash object. We almost always use the *New* keyword to create a new reference the first time we reference the object.

```
Option Explicit
Public objSplash As New clsSplash
```

SplashComplete method

This method is used to shut down the splash screen. It is called from the timer on Form1.

```
Sub SplashComplete()

' Kill the splash screen.
  objSplash.SplashStop

' Release the resources used by object reference.
  Set objSplash = Nothing

End Sub
```

List Boxes and Grids and Local Databases

Lists boxes and grids are both the best and worst features of Windows. A list box or grid makes it easy for a user to retrieve information from a system, but, with the most benign action, it can also pull an unbelievable amount of information over the network. How can you overcome the limitations of list boxes and grids and still provide the benefits to the user? Some solutions to this problem are simple but not obvious. We have created a little sample application to demonstrate some concepts surrounding the use of both list boxes and grids.

Sample Program: Managing Lists of Information Using List Boxes and Grids

Let's say you have a list of countries or a list of states that you want to display. The number of countries or states changes, but not very often. It is fairly safe to store these lists in a local Microsoft Access database with a little creative coding to synchronize the local lists with the master lists stored on the server. We demonstrate this in the Country sample application, which is located in the ListAndGridDemo directory on the companion CD.

When you created the ClientServerBook database in SQL Server using the procedure described in the section "Building Your Database Schema in SQL Server" on page 84, you created master lists of countries and states in SQL Server. The key to making the synchronization of the local database with the server painless is twofold. First we created update, insert, and delete triggers on the server for the Country and State tables. Whenever the user makes changes in one of these tables, the appropriate trigger fires, updating the StatusDate column in the StaticTableStatus table. This table is an indicator for all clients that shows whether the Country or State table has changed.

The syntax for both triggers (in BuildIndexProcedure.sql) is shown below. The only thing that changes for the State table is the *CREATE TRIGGER* statement.

```
CREATE TRIGGER CountryChange ON dbo.Country
FOR INSERT,UPDATE,DELETE
AS update StaticTableStatus set StatusDate = GETDATE()
GO
```

Second we created a Visual Basic method (*CheckStaticTableStatus*, shown in the code on page 169) that checks the StaticTableStatus column. If the value in this column in the remote database is different from the value in the same column in the local database, *CheckStaticTableStatus* updates the Country and State tables by executing the appropriate queries in the Access database.

You can use the local or remote Country and State tables for your reports. It is best, however, to use the remote tables in this case because you have no guarantee that a user has updated the local database recently.

Before you can build or run the Country application, you need to make sure that the paths are correct for your system in three places. First the project needs a reference called Splash Screen that points to Splash.exe. (Choose References from the Tools menu.) Second you need to check all occasions of the text *"Country.mdb"* in the code. Third the DatabaseName property for the two data controls on the frmListAndGridDemo form must also contain the correct path. (There is one data control for the Country table and one for the State table.)

Figure 8-2 shows the interface for the application.

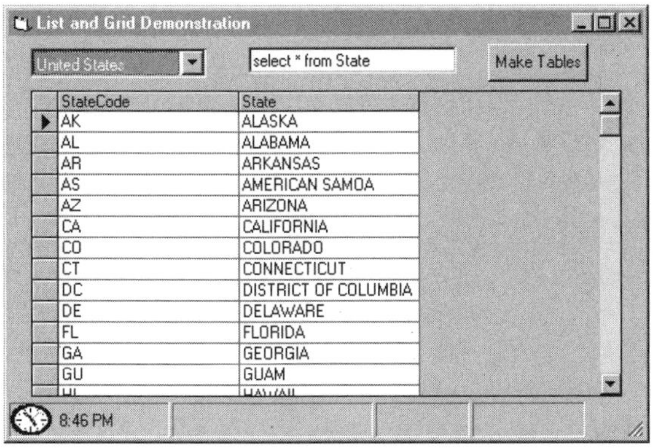

Figure 8-2. *The Country sample application.*

The Country application uses a DBCombo control and a DBGrid control plus some DAO and RDO functions. It also uses an array of PictureBox controls, two Data controls, and a Timer, Textbox, StatusBar, and CommandButton control. The list and grid functions are fairly simple. The list box displays the list of countries from which a user makes a selection. If the user selects the United States, the states are displayed in the grid.

The only magic in this application is in the functions used to update the local database. Some manuals and books suggest updating the local list each time an application loads; however, this approach can delay the application load each time it starts. Add a few more static tables, and the load time can go up dramatically, leading to lots of additional support calls. We solved the problem by using a timer to periodically check the status of a status field on the server. If the status has not changed, there is no need to update the local tables, and if the tables do need updating, they only get updated once.

This example also illustrates a few of the new controls included in Visual Basic 4. Some of the features of these controls are different from similar third-party or built-in controls. Other controls, such as the StatusBar control, are totally new. Let's take a look at the code for this application.

frmListAndGridDemo Form

The frmListAndGridDemo form is the only form in our application. It also contains some of the application's source code.

Declarations

The declarations section for the form defines two objects as status bar panels. Each panel displays a piece of status information.

```
Option Explicit
Dim pnlCurrentTime As Panel
Dim pnlStatus As Panel
```

cboCountry_Click event procedure

The *cboCountry_Click* event procedure for the DBCombo control illustrates one of the features you must understand to effectively use the new list controls included with Visual Basic 4. The Area parameter is passed to the procedure when it fires to indicate the area of the control clicked by the user. Notice that we check for *Area = 2* to determine if the user clicked an item in the list.

The heart of this procedure is the *If* statement that checks whether the user selected *United States*. When this condition is *True*, dcState.RecordSource is reset to select all records from the State table. After the RecordSource property is set, the SQL statement is passed to the text box txtSQLStuff and the Data control is refreshed. At this point, we set the Visible property of the grdStates DBGrid control to *True*.

```
Private Sub cboCountry_Click(Area As Integer)

  If Area = 2 Then      ' the user clicked an item in the list
    If cboCountry.Text = "United States" Then
      dcState.RecordSource = "select * from State"
      txtSQLStuff = dcState.RecordSource
      dcState.Refresh
      grdStates.Visible = True
    Else
      grdStates.Visible = False
    End If
  Else
    grdStates.Visible = False
  End If

End Sub
```

cboCountry_GotFocus event procedure

The *cboCountry_GotFocus* event procedure is an important part of the operation for the DBCombo control. Whenever the focus shifts to the cboCountry control, we reset the grdStates control's Visible property to *False*. This keeps the user from getting confused by trying to select another country with the states from the United States displayed.

```
Private Sub cboCountry_GotFocus()
  grdStates.Visible = False
End Sub
```

cmdMakeTables_Click event procedure

The *cmdMakeTables_Click* event procedure calls the *MakeCountryTable* and *MakeStateTable* methods.

```
Private Sub cmdMakeTables_Click()

  frmListAndGridDemo.MousePointer = vbArrowHourglass
  DoEvents
  MakeCountryTable
  MakeStateTable
  frmListAndGridDemo.MousePointer = vbDefault

End Sub
```

Form_Load event procedure

The *Form_Load* event procedure is used to perform some general setup functions that occur only once. The *Set* statement simply creates an object variable to use as a shortcut for the panel in the StatusBar control.

167

```
Private Sub Form_Load()
   Set pnlStatus = StatusBar1.Panels("Status")
End Sub
```

tmrCheckStaticTableStatus_Timer event procedure

The following *Timer* event procedure checks the status of our static tables. We have placed all the code to check the status and perform the update in the *CheckStaticTableStatus* method. Notice how easy it is to access the status panel and reset its text.

```
Private Sub tmrCheckStaticTableStatus_Timer()
   pnlStatus.Text = "Checking Static Tables Status"
   CheckStaticTableStatus
   pnlStatus.Text = ""
End Sub
```

modListAndGrid Module

The modListAndGrid module contains the startup *Main* method and several other methods.

Declarations

The modListAndGrid module begins by defining objects for our local database and Recordset. It then defines an object for the startup splash screen.

```
Option Explicit
Public dbStatus As Database, rsStatus As Recordset
Public objSplash As New clsSplash
```

Main method

The application starts by executing the *Main* method.

```
Sub Main()

' Set the text for the splash screen.
   objSplash.TextMessage = "List and Grid Demonstration Program"
   objSplash.CopyRight = "List and Grid Inc., 1996"
   objSplash.TitleMessage = "List and Grid Demo"

' Set the path for the picture to be used in the splash screen.
   objSplash.PicturePath = App.Path & "\" & "Apptbook.wmf"

' Because the application might take a long time to load,
' set the timer interval for the splash screen to approximately
' 10 seconds.
   objSplash.TimerValue = 10000
```

```
' Show the splash screen, load and show our form,
' and shut down the splash screen.
  objSplash.Splash
  DoEvents·
  Load frmListAndGridDemo
  frmListAndGridDemo.Show
  DoEvents
  objSplash.SplashStop

End Sub
```

CheckStaticTableStatus method

The next method checks the status of the remote static tables. This procedure does not assume that any connections to the local database or the remote database exist.

```
Sub CheckStaticTableStatus()

  Dim ConnectString As String
  Dim cnStaticTableStatus As rdoConnection, _
    enStaticTableStatus As rdoEnvironment
  Dim rsStaticTable As rdoResultset
  Dim i As Integer, StartTime As Date, _
    StopTime As Date, TotalTime As Date

' Set the mouse pointer to an hourglass.
  frmListAndGridDemo.MousePointer = vbArrowHourglass

' Create our connection information.
  ConnectString = "DSN=ClientServerBook;UID=sa;PWD=;"

' Create a reference to our environment.
  Set enStaticTableStatus = rdoEnvironments(0)

' Open a connection.
  Set cnStaticTableStatus = enStaticTableStatus.OpenConnection _
    ("", rdDriverNoPrompt, False, ConnectString)

' Create the result set for the remote database
' based on the StaticTableStatus table.
  Set rsStaticTable = cnStaticTableStatus.OpenResultset _
    ("Select * from StaticTableStatus", , rdConcurRowver)
  Set dbStatus = Workspaces(0).OpenDatabase _
    ("C:\Kens\ListAndGridDemo\Country.mdb")
```

(continued)

```
' Create a Recordset from the local StaticTableStatus table.
  Set rsStatus = dbStatus.OpenRecordset _
    ("Select * from StaticTableStatus", dbOpenDynaset)

' Check whether the local database needs to be updated.
' If the StatusDate field is the same on each table, the update
' process is skipped. If the two do not match, the StatusDate
' field in the local table is set to the StatusDate field in the
' remote table and all local tables are updated.
  If rsStaticTable("StatusDate") <> rsStatus("StatusDate") Then
    rsStatus.Edit
    rsStatus("StatusDate") = rsStaticTable("StatusDate")
    rsStatus.Update
    MakeCountryTable
    MakeStateTable
  End If

' Close the local database and the remote connection.
  dbStatus.Close
  cnStaticTableStatus.Close
  frmListAndGridDemo.MousePointer = vbDefault
  DoEvents

End Sub
```

MakeCountryTable and *MakeStateTable* methods

The *MakeCountryTable* and *MakeStateTable* methods are simple but contain one interesting feature. The *DeleteCountry* and *MakeCountryTableFromServer* queries in the *MakeCountryTable* procedure demonstrate how to execute a query in a local Access database. Executing the query directly in the database is fast and efficient. You can also change the query without changing your application by opening the Access MDB file and modifying the query. When you reexecute the Visual Basic application, it runs with the modified query.

```
Sub MakeCountryTable()

  Dim CountryDb As Database
  Dim CountryInTable As Recordset

  Set CountryDb = Workspaces(0).OpenDatabase _
    ("C:\Kens\ListAndGridDemo\Country.mdb")
  CountryDb.Execute "DeleteCountry"
  CountryDb.Execute "MakeCountryTableFromServer"
```

```
   CountryDb.Close
   frmListAndGridDemo.dcCountry.Refresh

End Sub

Sub MakeStateTable()

   Dim CountryDb As Database
   Dim CountryInTable As Recordset

   Set CountryDb = Workspaces(0).OpenDatabase _
     ("C:\Kens\ListAndGridDemo\Country.mdb")
   CountryDb.Execute "DeleteState"
   CountryDb.Execute "MakeStateTableFromServer"
   CountryDb.Close
   frmListAndGridDemo.dcState.Refresh

End Sub
```

These modules' performance can be improved to an extent. For instance, we could declare the database objects at the module level and then leave them open until the update is completed. We could also open the database objects when the form loads and leave them open.

Using Transactions

Transactions are extremely valuable in database operations. A *transaction* is a series of changes made to a database's data. We most often think of transactions as useful for creating blocks of items that should be executed as a single group. If one transaction fails, the entire group fails and all other actions that were performed are reversed. Transactions are also useful for improving the performance of certain database actions on some systems. For instance, when using Access, transactions can dramatically improve the performance of a database when you are using a loop to write information to a database. Access will buffer all code within a set of transactions and write it at one time to the database instead of writing each action separately.

> **NOTE** The operation of transactions can differ in different databases. For instance, ODBC databases support only one level of transactions, whereas Access supports multiple levels of nested transactions. You might be able to use SQL code to create nested transactions on an ODBC database. Check your database documentation to determine how many levels of transactions your database supports.

The Visual Basic documentation *Building Client/Server Applications with Visual Basic* includes a section called "Locking Strategies," which has more information on using transactions and how their use applies to database locks.

RDO supports three transaction methods:

- *BeginTrans* begins a new transaction.

- *CommitTrans* ends the current transaction and saves the changes to the . database.

- *RollbackTrans* ends the current transaction and restores the databases in the rdoEnvironment object to the state they were in when the current transaction began.

These methods can operate at either the connection or environment level. Transactions used on a connection object are limited in scope to either the result set or the prepared statement objects they are used on. Transactions used on an environment object cover all open connections in the environment.

RDO transactions are created in Visual Basic by using the following syntax:

```
object.BeginTrans
  <Database code goes here>
object.CommitTran
```

You can undo all your changes since *BeginTrans* by using the *RollbackTrans* method:

```
object.RollbackTrans
```

You should make sure that your database supports transactions. The methods just mentioned might appear to work in your database but actually have no effect. You can check the Transactions property of an rdoConnection or rdoResultset object to determine whether the object supports transactions:

```
If object.Transactions Then
```

A return value of *True* indicates transactions are supported; a return value of *False* indicates they are not.

Transactions in some databases can also be nested. That is, after beginning one transaction you can begin a second (and third, fourth, and fifth) transaction within that transaction. There are two constraints to this nesting: transactions cannot overlap, and they can be nested only five levels deep. Make sure that if you need to roll back a nested transaction, you do so in reverse order.

Queries and Cursors

The type of query you use can also have an impact on network performance. For instance, server-side cursors have a minimum impact on the network because the server manages the cursor and the data, returning only necessary data to the client. Client-side cursors, on the other hand, require passing everything over the network. For instance, using DAO to issue a request to the Jet database engine for a snapshot-type Recordset will move the entire result set to the client, causing maximum network traffic.

If you have bulk operations to perform, you should use a stored procedure, an rdoPreparedStatement object, or a SQL *Update* statement to update the database. These techniques can move all of the processing to the server, where it is most efficient. If you were to perform the update by retrieving a result set and then doing the update in Visual Basic, the entire result set would have to be moved to the client, updated, and then moved back to the server.

Connections to the Database

Believe it or not, database connections might actually be the most problematic part of your application if you do not manage them carefully, as each connection requires memory and network resources on both the client and the server. Most databases will limit the number of transactions that can be open at one time. Many database operations might open an implicit connection when certain actions are performed. For instance, retrieving rows of a result set using DAO might use an existing connection, create one new connection, or create several connections. The specific action depends on how many rows are returned, whether an existing connection can be used, and whether the result set can be updated.

Jet manages a cache of active connections that it checks for a match on DSN and database parameters before opening a new connection. The cache usually contains at least one or two connections. Jet automatically closes connections if they have not been used for a specific period of time.

The *OpenDatabase* method automatically opens a connection that remains open even after the database object is closed. Jet can hold a connection open, anticipating future use, unless there is already a cached connection open.

The *OpenRecordset* method, on the other hand, tries to share an existing connection or reuse an existing cached connection before opening a new connection. Jet will also open additional connections to improve performance as needed. The first connection remains open until the Recordset is closed, or fully populated in the case of a read-only Recordset.

RDO provides more explicit control over connections. RDO supports the *Open-Connection* method, which creates a separate connection for each object you create with it. You can close a connection with the *Close* method, as it is not automatically closed. Connections are also closed if the object using the connection goes out of scope. For instance, if you open a connection and populate a result set inside a procedure, the result set is released when the procedure terminates and its connection is closed.

The RemoteData control creates and closes connections automatically. There is at least one connection for each RemoteData control. If you are using this type of control to handle all of the database interface, you will not have much control over its connections. You can use RDO to populate the RemoteData control result set and gain some degree of control over its connections and other aspects of its operation.

Tracing and Tuning for Performance

Tuning any system has long required the ability to trace its performance. Tracing allows you to record what is occurring and then go back and review the details. The tracing information should help you pinpoint any problems and arrive at a solution.

ODBC Trace Logs

ODBC automatically traces every ODBC function used on a particular system. The tracing options are set using the ODBC application in Control Panel.

Figure 8-3 shows the ODBC Options dialog box, which is used to configure ODBC logging. You access this dialog box by clicking the Options button in the Data Sources dialog box in the ODBC application.

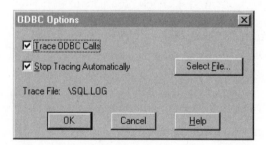

Figure 8-3. *The Windows 95 ODBC Options dialog box.*

When the Trace ODBC Calls box is checked, any applications that use ODBC are logged to the Trace File shown in the dialog box. Keep in mind that logging does slow down each application. The log file will also continue to grow as long as the Trace ODBC Calls box is checked, further affecting the performance of the client system.

Check the Stop Tracing Automatically option to allow ODBC to turn off logging automatically. If this box is checked when you run the first application that uses ODBC, that application's ODBC functions will be logged. As soon as that application terminates, the Trace ODBC Calls box will be cleared.

The trace file will contain every ODBC statement that is executed on behalf of your application. For instance, executing two RDO statements might trigger 15 or 20 ODBC function calls. To effectively use the data in the trace file, you must understand what ODBC does. A detailed discussion of ODBC is outside the scope of this book, so we suggest that you review the ODBC information on the Microsoft Developer Network (MSDN) CD for more information.

Application Performance Logs

Custom logs that are generated by your application are usually more useful than delving into the depths of ODBC. A custom log can record information on every login or query, or any level in between. You might even want to enable levels of logging that can be turned on and off when the system is used for production. Our CSUtilities class (page 153) has both custom log methods and a simple timer function that works with the log file to store information in the standard log file.

A log file should contain information on the application writing to the log, the date and time the event occurred, a text message describing the event, an event identifier, and any discrete information on the event, such as data or timing information. Our sample event procedures actually consist of methods to open the log file and store information in the file, plus another miniapplication to pick up log files and store them in the database. The client and server portions of this utility are explained in the next section, "Asynchronous Operations."

Code Profiler is a Visual Basic Add-In that tracks which code is being used in your application and how long it takes to execute. It is not installed by default, but you can find it on the Visual Basic CD in the Tools\Vbcp directory. To use the Code Profiler, copy the appropriate executable—there are both 16-bit and 32-bit versions—and the help file to your hard drive and run the executable once to add it to Visual Basic's Add-Ins menu. The next time you run Visual Basic, Code Profiler will be available. Help for the Visual Basic Code Profiler is available from the Profiler's Help menu.

Capturing More Accurate Time Between Operations

The CSUtilities class uses the *Now()* function to retrieve the time between operations. This function is accurate to one second. In most client/server implementations, one second is precise enough to capture most timing issues on queries and other similar operations, although it might not be accurate enough for capturing time in tight loops or other places where time must be captured in milliseconds.

The *timeGetTime* function from the multimedia library (Winmm.dll) of the Microsoft Win32 SDK returns the number of milliseconds since Windows started. Declare the function as follows:

```
Declare Function timeGetTime Lib "Winmm.dll" Alias "timeGetTime" ()
  As Long
```

To use the function, use this format:

```
Dim lElapsedTime as Long, lStartTime as Long

lStartTime = timeGetTime
<Executing code goes here>
lElapsedTime = timeGetTime - lStartTime
```

After running this code, lElapsedTime will contain the number of milliseconds that have elapsed.

Bruce McKinney discusses this function in detail in his book, *Hardcore Visual Basic* (Microsoft Press, 1995). He also uses it in the sample library that is included on the book's CD. You can also use the Visual Basic Code Profiler to capture times in applications.

Asynchronous Operations

Most actions that take place in a Visual Basic application are synchronous: one action must complete before another can start. The idea behind asynchronous operations is exactly the opposite: start one action, and continue on to the next before the first completes. The beauty of the asynchronous approach is that we can actually begin to simulate multithreading in our Visual Basic applications.

Multithreading is a feature of the Windows 32-bit operating systems that is primarily intended to take advantage of multiprocessor systems, but even if your computer doesn't have multiple processors, you can use multithreading to your advantage.

For instance, let's say we have a SQL statement to execute that takes 20 or 30 minutes to complete. When it is done, we would like the application that started the process to be notified. You can accomplish this type of action in one of at least four ways:

- Remote Automation, which supports using callback functionality to allow one application to asynchronously start methods on remote systems

- RDO, which supports asynchronous queries

- The RemoteData control, which supports asynchronous queries

- ODBC, which supports asynchronous queries through the ODBC API

Of the four, Remote Automation is the most powerful because it not only provides the ability to run queries but also can perform any task imaginable on a remote system. Remote Automation also allows you to construct your remote application so that it can actually execute methods in your client application. For instance, let's take the problem of monitoring a database. Using Remote Automation, our client program can request a graph of some particular data, using a method that executes on another system. When the query is completed on the remote system, the remote application actually executes the method on the client to update the graph.

RDO and the RemoteData control are also powerful, and both are easier to implement than the ODBC API functions. Both RDO and the RemoteData control allow you to start an asynchronous query, continue with another task, and then access the results of the query when it finishes. In either case, you must have logic in your application to check the StillExecuting property of the rdoResultset object until it returns *False*. When the return value is *False*, you can access the result set in the normal manner. A Timer control is useful to trigger the monitoring of the StillExecuting property.

There are two other useful properties of the rdoResultset object that you might want to use with asynchronous operations. The RowsAffected property returns the number of rows affected by the query. The AsyncCheckInterval property specifies the amount of time between checks by RDO to determine if the query is still executing.

How do you start an asynchronous operation with RDO or the RemoteData control? Using RDO, simply set the Options argument to *rdAsyncEnable* when you create the result set with either the *OpenResultset* or *Execute* methods:

```
Set variable = connection.OpenResultset _
  (SQLConnect,rdOpenDynamic, _
  rdConcurRowver, rdAsyncEnable)
```

The RemoteData control option is even easier. Set the Options property of the RemoteData control to *rdAsyncEnable* before executing a query.

Let's look at a sample program that uses RDO and an asynchronous query.

Sample Program: Using RDO to Execute an Asynchronous Query

This sample application, called AsyncStuff, is located in the AsynchronousStuff directory on the companion CD. Before you can build or run the application, you need to make sure that the project contains a valid reference to CSUtilities.dll, located in the Utilities directory on the companion CD. (Choose References from the Tools menu.)

frmAsyncStuff Form

The entire application is contained in the frmAsyncStuff form. Figure 8-4 shows the interface.

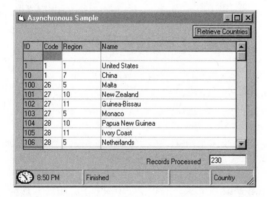

Figure 8-4. *The simple interface of the AsyncStuff sample application.*

Click the Retrieve Countries button to execute the asynchronous query. As in most of our applications, the grid is not visible until there is something to show.

Declarations

```
Option Explicit

' Objects to use as references to sections of the StatusBar control.
Dim pnlTableToProcess As Panel
Dim pnlStatus As Panel

' An object for our CSUtilities class.
Dim objUtil As New clsUtilities
```

```
' A string to hold our SQL statement.
Dim ConnectString As String

' Object references for our RDO objects.
Dim cnCountry As rdoConnection, enCountry As rdoEnvironment
Dim rsCountryIn As rdoResultset

' An integer to use as a record counter.
Dim i As Integer
```

StartQuery method

The *StartQuery* method kicks off the start of our query execution.

```
Private Sub StartQuery()

' Update the status bar with the name of the table we're using.
  pnlTableToProcess.Text = "Country"

' Set the mouse pointer.
  frmAsyncStuff.MousePointer = vbArrowHourglass

' Initialize the text box that tracks
' the number of records processed.
  txtRecordsProcessed = 0

' Update the status bar.
  pnlStatus.Text = "Executing Query"
  DoEvents

' Create a new result set object from Recordset object.
' The rdAsyncEnable argument specifies an asynchronous query.
  Set rsCountryIn = cnCountry.OpenResultset _
    ("Select * from Country", , rdConcurRowver, rdAsyncEnable)

' Show in the status bar that the query is still executing.
  pnlStatus.Text = "Query Executing"
  DoEvents

' Enable the timer and set the interval
' to approximately five seconds.
  tmrCheckExecuting.Enabled = True
  tmrCheckExecuting.Interval = 5000

End Sub
```

You might want to inspect the SQL syntax specified for the query and determine how long to set the timer interval (at the end of the method). For instance, if the query will ask for all records from a large table, use your past experience to determine that the interval should be set to a longer period of time. A request for 10 records might dictate a short interval. It would also be useful to store the results of how long each query takes to return in a database on the server. A simple analysis program could run daily and set the timer interval for each table in a central INI file.

RetrieveQuery method

The *RetrieveQuery* method is executed from the *tmrCheckExecuting_Timer* event procedure and retrieves the rows from the result set.

```
Sub RetrieveQuery()

' Holds each row returned from the result set.
  Dim sBuffer As String

' Loop through the entire result set.
  i = 1
  Do While Not rsCountryIn.EOF

' Place each column followed by a tab in the property in sequence.
    sBuffer = rsCountryIn("UniqueCountryCode") & Chr(9) _
      & rsCountryIn("CountryCode") & Chr(9) _
      & rsCountryIn("RegionCode") & Chr(9) _
      & rsCountryIn!Country & Chr(9)

' Add the entire row to the grid at once.
    grdCountry.AddItem sBuffer

' Move to the next record and update the counters.
    rsCountryIn.MoveNext
    txtRecordsProcessed = i
    DoEvents
    i = i + 1
  Loop

' Place a message in the status bar.
  pnlStatus.Text = "Closing Database"
  DoEvents

' Display the grid with its contents.
  grdCountry.Visible = True

' Close the database.
  cnCountry.Close
  pnlStatus.Text = "Finished"
```

```
' Reset the mouse pointer.
  frmAsyncStuff.MousePointer = vbDefault
  DoEvents

End Sub
```

cmdRetrieveCountries_Click event procedure
This event procedure simply executes the *StartQuery* method.

```
Private Sub cmdRetrieveCountries_Click()
  StartQuery
End Sub
```

Form_Load event procedure
The *Form_Load* event procedure initializes the references to the StatusBar control and executes the *Init* method.

```
Private Sub Form_Load()
  Me.Show
  Set pnlStatus = StatusBar1.Panels("Status")
  pnlStatus.Text = "Initializing Application"
  DoEvents
  Set pnlTableToProcess = StatusBar1.Panels("TableToProcess")
  DoEvents
  Init
End Sub
```

Init method
The *Init* method contains all of our startup code for both the grid and the database.

```
Sub Init()

' Set the parameters for the grid.
  grdCountry.Row = 0
  grdCountry.Col = 0
  grdCountry.Text = "ID"
  grdCountry.Col = 1
  grdCountry.Text = "Code"
  grdCountry.Col = 2
  grdCountry.Text = "Region"
  grdCountry.Col = 3
  grdCountry.Text = "Name"
  grdCountry.ColWidth(0) = 500
  grdCountry.ColWidth(1) = 500
  grdCountry.ColWidth(2) = 1000
  grdCountry.ColWidth(3) = 3500
```

(continued)

```
' Open a log file and set the application's properties in the
' CSUtilities class. Once StartApplication is executed, we can
' use the WriteLogEntry method and the StartTime and StopTime
' properties. The only argument to StartApplication is the
' application name, which is recorded in the log file when the
' application starts (now) and each time a log entry is written.
  objUtil.StartApplication sApplicationName:="AsyncStuff"

' Inform the user we are connecting to the database.
  pnlStatus.Text = "Connecting"
  DoEvents

' Set up the string for the connection.
  ConnectString = "DSN=ClientServerBook;UID=sa;PWD=;"

' Create a reference to the environment.
  Set enCountry = rdoEnvironments(0)

' Open a connection to the database.
  Set cnCountry = enCountry.OpenConnection _
    ("", rdDriverNoPrompt, False, ConnectString)

' Update the status bar.
  pnlStatus.Text = "Ready"
  DoEvents

End Sub
```

tmrCheckExecuting_Timer event procedure

The *tmrCheckExecuting_Timer* event procedure occurs each time the timer triggers.

```
Private Sub tmrCheckExecuting_Timer()

' Disable the timer to prevent reentry into this procedure.
  tmrCheckExecuting.Enabled = False

' Update the status bar.
  pnlStatus.Text = "Checking Results"
  DoEvents

' If the query is still executing, reenable the timer;
' if it's complete, execute the RetrieveQuery method.
  If rsCountryIn.StillExecuting Then
    tmrCheckExecuting.Enabled = True
```

```
Else
  pnlStatus.Text = "Retrieving Results"
  DoEvents
  objUtil.LastEntryText = "RetrieveQuery"
  objUtil.StartTime = Now()
  RetrieveQuery
  objUtil.StopTime = Now()
End If

End Sub
```

Notice that we set the StartTime and StopTime properties of objUtil near the end of the event procedure. (We discussed how these properties worked in Chapter 7.) This timer is extremely simple, but the basic logic is OK. You can easily extend the timer to handle multiple queries in a single application: add a Boolean property for each asynchronous query, and then check for which queries to return, using a simple *If* statement in the *Timer* event procedure.

Tracking Performance Data

Let's look at what our application has stored for us in the log file to record performance information. The name of the log file is <network login ID>.log, and the file is stored in the Utilities directory. The login ID is picked up by the *StartApplication* method (in CSUtilities.dll) and used to either open an existing log file or create a new one. A sample log (Sample.log in the Asynchronous-Stuff directory) from our AsyncStuff application is shown in Figure 8-5.

```
"Database Log - Created ",#1996-05-14 17:41:01#," ",#1996-05-14 17:41:01#,#1996-05-14 17:41:01#
"AsyncStuff","Application Started",#1996-05-14 17:41:01#," ",#1996-05-14 17:41:01#,#1996-05-14 17:41:01#
"AsyncStuff","MethodTime",#1996-05-14 17:41:17#,"RetrieveQuery",#1996-05-14 17:41:10#,#1996-05-14 17:41:17#
```

Figure 8-5. *An application log for AsyncStuff.*

To learn when the application started, look at the lines with *Application Started* as the second field (the name of our application is always in the first field). The lines with *MethodTime* as the second field contain timing information. The method or module we are timing is indicated in the fourth field in the lines with timing information.

To use this information, we'll load it into a tracking database using SQL Server. This will let us analyze any queries we want, including graphing the information to show performance trends. Notice that we track the start time and stop time, not the elapsed time, for each timing entry. Tracking start and stop times allows us to analyze the times in any format we want. If we stored the elapsed time in a particular format, we would be limited to that format during analysis.

Sample Program: Sending Logs to the Server

How do we get this data into SQL Server if the information is written to an ASCII log file? We are going to use a little sample application called ReadLog-Agent (located in the Utilities directory on the companion CD), which looks for LOG files on a network drive and loads each file into the database.

Using a log file and not a direct connection to the database might seem strange. If we tried to write directly to the database, we would add lots of overhead to the process at first. We might even hang up the application while writing to a log file. Writing to a small file on a network drive is usually faster. We could even keep the log files locally on the client and then move them to the network drive when the application ends.

Figure 8-6 shows the simple interface to this application.

Figure 8-6. *The interface of the ReadLogAgent application provides status at a glance.*

A system manager can change the log file timer interval by changing the value in the Check Log File Timer Interval box and clicking the Apply Now button that will appear. This application uses only one form, frmLogStorageAgent.

frmLogStorageAgent Form

frmLogStorageAgent is the main form in this application. It provides a simple status display of its progress and also includes the timer that drives the application.

cmdApplyNow_Click event procedure

The *cmdApplyNow_Click* event procedure illustrates two actions. First we hide the cmdApplyNow button when a user clicks the button. The button is visible only after the user changes the value in the txtCheckForLogTimerInterval control. Second we execute the *SetTmrCheckForLogFilesInterval* method to update the timer interval.

```
Private Sub cmdApplyNow_Click()
  cmdApplyNow.Visible = False
  objUtil.SetTmrCheckForLogFilesInterval txtCheckForLogTimerInterval
End Sub
```

Init method

The *Init* method is called from the *Form_Load* event procedure and performs all the necessary startup tasks. The object references to the StatusBar control and the database references are created here.

We also set the initial value for the Timer control (tmrCheckForLogFiles) and update the display in the txtCheckForLogTimerInterval control. Notice that we always divide the timer interval by 1000 to obtain the number of seconds to display, which makes the interface a little more understandable for the user. We also turn off the display of the cmdApplyNow button.

```
Sub Init()

  Set pnlStatus = StatusBar1.Panels("Status")
  Set pnlFiles = StatusBar1.Panels("FilesProcessed")
  Set pnlRecords = StatusBar1.Panels("RecordsProcessed")
  pnlStatus.Text = "Connecting"
  DoEvents

  ConnectString = "DSN=ClientServerBook;UID=sa;PWD=;"
  Set enPerformanceLog = rdoEnvironments(0)
  Set cnPerformanceLog = enPerformanceLog.OpenConnection _
    ("", rdDriverNoPrompt, False, ConnectString)

  pnlStatus.Text = "Waiting"

  If tmrCheckForLogFiles.Interval > 1000 Then
    txtCheckForLogTimerInterval = tmrCheckForLogFiles.Interval / 1000
  Else
    txtCheckForLogTimerInterval = 0
    tmrCheckForLogFiles = 0
  End If

  cmdApplyNow.Visible = False

End Sub
```

Form_Unload event procedure

We use the *Form_Unload* event procedure to close our log file.

```
Private Sub Form_Unload(Cancel As Integer)
  enPerformanceLog.Close
End Sub
```

tmrCheckForLogFiles_Timer method

The *Timer* method executes the *LookForLogFiles* method. We like to place common code where we can reuse it rather than bury it in a *Timer* event procedure.

```
Private Sub tmrCheckForLogFiles_Timer()

tmrCheckForLogFiles.Enabled = False
  LookForLogFiles
  tmrCheckForLogFiles.Enabled = True

End Sub
```

txtCheckForLogTimerInterval_Change method

The *txtCheckForLogTimerInterval_Change* method shows the cmdApplyNow button whenever the value in the control changes.

```
Private Sub txtCheckForLogTimerInterval_Change()
  cmdApplyNow.Visible = True
End Sub
```

modLogStorage Module

This module contains the common methods for the application. Check out the clsLogFileAgent class to see some other ways to quickly extend functionality.

Declarations

```
Option Explicit

Public pnlStatus As Panel
Public pnlFiles As Panel
Public pnlRecords As Panel

Public LogFileName As String
Public LogDirectoryName As String
Public TotalNumberOfLogFilesRead As Long
Public TotalNumberOfEntriesProcessed As Double

' Use these properties internally to track various
' pieces of information read from the log file.
Private sApplicationName As String
Private sClassDescription As String
Private sEventText As String
Private dEventTime As Date
Private dStartTime As Date
Private dStopTime As Date
Private sUserName As String
```

```
Public ConnectString As String
Public cnPerformanceLog As rdoConnection, _
  enPerformanceLog As rdoEnvironment
Public rsPerformanceLog As rdoResultset
```

ReadLog method

The *ReadLog* method opens and reads the log file and writes the information to the database. It also opens and closes our result set. (For your own applications, it would probably make more sense to open the result set at the application level and leave it open, rather than opening and closing it for each log file.) The one parameter to the method is the log filename. The method returns *True* if it is successful or *False* if an error occurs.

```
Function ReadLog(LogFileName As String) As Boolean

   Dim sBuffer As String, iTotalNumberOfEntriesProcessed As Integer

   On Error GoTo ReadLogError
   frmLogStorageAgent.MousePointer = vbArrowHourglass

' Extract the user name from the log filename.
' Change this if you change the way log files are named.
   sUserName = Left(LogFileName, InStr(LogFileName, ".") - 1)
   sUserName = ParseName(sLineIn:=sUserName)

' Open the log file.
   pnlStatus.Text = "Opening Log File"
   pnlRecords = sUserName & ".log: "
   DoEvents
   Open LogFileName For Input As #1

' Open the result set.
' (The SQL statement requests a result set from
' the PerformanceLog table that is guaranteed to
' have zero records. We're going to update the
' result set, so why retrieve anything now?)
   pnlStatus.Text = "Opening Result Set"
   DoEvents
   Set rsPerformanceLog = cnPerformanceLog.OpenResultset _
     ("Select * from PerformanceLog where UserName = '????'", _
     , rdConcurRowver)

' Read each line.
   pnlStatus.Text = "Processing "
   DoEvents
   TotalNumberOfLogFilesRead = TotalNumberOfLogFilesRead + 1
```

(continued)

187

```
    pnlFiles = "Log Files: " & TotalNumberOfLogFilesRead
    DoEvents
    iTotalNumberOfEntriesProcessed = 0
    ReadLog = True

' Split out the parts of each line and place
' them in the module-level properties.
    Do While Not EOF(1)
      Line Input #1, sBuffer
      If InStr(sBuffer, "Database Log") = 0 Then
        ParseLine sBuffer

' Add the entry to the database.
        WriteLogToDatabase

        iTotalNumberOfEntriesProcessed = _
          iTotalNumberOfEntriesProcessed + 1
      End If
    Loop

' Close the log file and the result set.
    pnlStatus.Text = "Closing File & Resultset"
    DoEvents
    Close #1
    rsPerformanceLog.Close
    TotalNumberOfEntriesProcessed = iTotalNumberOfEntriesProcessed
    pnlRecords = sUserName & ".log: " & "Records: " & _
      iTotalNumberOfEntriesProcessed
    DoEvents
    pnlStatus.Text = "Completed " & sUserName & ".log"

' Cleanup.
ReadLogExit:
    frmLogStorageAgent.MousePointer = vbDefault
    DoEvents
    Exit Function

' Error.
ReadLogError:
    ReadLog = False      ' Prevent deleting the log file.
    pnlStatus.Text = "Skipped "
    GoTo ReadLogExit
```

```
' You could use a Select statement such as this to trap
' for "55 File Open" or "75 Path/File Access Error":
'   Select Case Err
'     Case 55, 75:
'     Case Else
'   End Select

End Function
```

WriteLogToDatabase method

The *WriteLogToDatabase* method does exactly what its name implies. It sets the various columns in the database table to the values in the properties for this module. It would make a lot more sense here to use either a SQL *Update* statement or a stored procedure, as opposed to executing the *AddNew* and *Update* methods. A stored procedure would work best because we know that this particular function probably will be executed more than any other on our system.

```
Sub WriteLogToDatabase()

  Dim i As Integer

  rsPerformanceLog.AddNew
  rsPerformanceLog!ApplicationName = sApplicationName
  rsPerformanceLog!ClassDescription = sClassDescription
  rsPerformanceLog!EventText = sEventText
  rsPerformanceLog!EventTime = dEventTime
  rsPerformanceLog!StartTime = dStartTime
  rsPerformanceLog!StopTime = dStopTime
  rsPerformanceLog!DateAdded = Now()
  rsPerformanceLog!UserName = sUserName
  rsPerformanceLog.Update

End Sub
```

ParseLine method

The *ParseLine* method splits the sLineIn parameter into the various properties. The *For* loop provides an interesting example of how to generically split a comma-delimited string.

```
Sub ParseLine(sLineIn As String)

  Dim i As Integer, iStop As Integer
  Dim sTemp As String
```

(continued)

```
   sTemp = sLineIn
   For i = 1 To 6
     iStop = InStr(sTemp, ",")
     Select Case i
       Case 1: sApplicationName = Mid$(sTemp, 2, iStop - 3)
       Case 2: sClassDescription = Mid$(sTemp, 2, iStop - 3)
       Case 3: dEventTime = Mid$(sTemp, 2, iStop - 3)
       Case 4: sEventText = Mid$(sTemp, 2, iStop - 3)
       Case 5: dStartTime = Mid$(sTemp, 2, iStop - 4)
       Case 6: dStopTime = Mid$(sTemp, 2, Len(sTemp) - 2)
       Case Else
     End Select
     sTemp = Mid$(sTemp, iStop + 1, Len(sTemp) - iStop)
   Next i

End Sub
```

ParseName method

The *ParseName* method is another general string method we use to extract the filename from its full pathname. This one is a good candidate for a class module method. In fact, while its name is *ParseName*, it can pull the last item from any list delimited by backslashes (\).

```
Function ParseName(sLineIn As String) As String

   Dim i As Integer, iStop As Boolean
   Dim sTemp As String

   sTemp = sLineIn
   iStop = False
   Do While iStop = False
     i = InStr(sTemp, "\")
     If i = 0 Then
       iStop = True
       ParseName = sTemp
     End If
     sTemp = Mid$(sTemp, i + 1, Len(sTemp) - i)
   Loop

End Function
```

LookForLogFiles method

The *LookForLogFiles* method is the master controller for processing log files. It retrieves all the log files it can find and places them in an array (LogFiles). After we have retrieved all the files, we can process them one by one.

```
Sub LookForLogFiles()

  Dim LogFiles() As String, i As Integer

' Start the LogFiles array with one dimension.
  ReDim LogFiles(1)

' Create the full path for the log file.
  SetLogFileName

' Find the first log file.
  LogFileName = Dir(LogFileName)

' Retrieve the balance of the log files in the directory.
  i = 0
  Do While LogFileName <> ""
    If Len(LogFileName) > 0 Then
      LogFileName = LogDirectoryName & LogFileName
      LogFiles(i) = LogFileName

' Increase the size of the array by one
' while keeping current contents intact.
      ReDim Preserve LogFiles(UBound(LogFiles) + 1)

      i = i + 1
    End If
    LogFileName = Dir
  Loop

' Process each log file;
' if ReadLog fails, do not delete the log file.
  For i = 0 To UBound(LogFiles) - 1
    If ReadLog(LogFiles(i)) Then Kill LogFiles(i)
  Next i

End Sub
```

SetLogFileName method

The *SetLogFileName* method builds the log filename. (We should change this method to extract the log file directory name from Master.ini. It will fail if we use the Master.ini file to indicate the location of the log files.)

```
Sub SetLogFileName()
  LogDirectoryName = App.Path & "\"
  LogFileName = LogDirectoryName & "\" & "*.log"
End Sub
```

clsLogFileAgent Class

This small class module is a great illustration of how to take an application that was not designed for OLE automation and add that functionality without extensive modifications. As we worked on the performance log monitor discussed later in this chapter, we thought, Wouldn't it be nice to retrieve the statistics from the ReadLogAgent program and display them? So we modified our class module.

Property Get procedures

This Property Get procedure simply returns the value from the TotalNumberOfLogFilesRead property of the application.

```
Public Property Get TotalNumberOfLogFiles() As Long
   TotalNumberOfLogFiles = TotalNumberOfLogFilesRead
End Property
```

This Property Get procedure returns the value of the TotalNumberOfEntriesProcessed property.

```
Public Property Get TotalNumberOfEntries() As Long
   TotalNumberOfEntries = TotalNumberOfEntriesProcessed
End Property
```

This Property Get procedure returns the value of the TextBox control from the frmLogStorageAgent form. Wow! Can we really use a property procedure to return a "virtual" property that is actually a control? Yep!

```
Public Property Get CurrentTimerInterval() As Long
   CurrentTimerInterval = _
     frmLogStorageAgent!txtCheckForLogTimerInterval
End Property
```

StartLogStorageAgent method

You would be almost right to think this method does nothing. While it does not perform any actions, it serves one useful purpose: we call this method from a client application to start the ReadLogAgent application. It works fine because any reference to a method or property in an OLE server starts the server.

```
Public Sub StartLogStorageAgent()

End Sub
```

SetTmrCheckForLogFilesInterval method

This method can be executed by a client application to change the timer interval.

```
Public Sub SetTmrCheckForLogFilesInterval _
  (CheckForLogTimerInterval As Long)

' Make sure the timer value is valid.
  If CheckForLogTimerInterval <= 10 Then
    CheckForLogTimerInterval = 10
  ElseIf CheckForLogTimerInterval > 60 Then
    CheckForLogTimerInterval = 60
  End If

' Set the text box to the CheckForLogTimerInterval parameter.
  frmLogStorageAgent!txtCheckForLogTimerInterval = _
    CheckForLogTimerInterval

' Calculate the number of ticks for the timer.
  CheckForLogTimerInterval = CheckForLogTimerInterval * 1000

' Update the timer interval.
  frmLogStorageAgent!tmrCheckForLogFiles.Interval = _
    CheckForLogTimerInterval

' Hide the cmdApplyNow button.
' (How did the Visible property change? Remember the
' Change event procedure for the TextBox control?)
  frmLogStorageAgent!cmdApplyNow.Visible = False
  DoEvents

End Sub
```

Sample Program: A Performance Log Monitor

No performance monitoring system would be worth much if you did not have a method to review the information. Same thing for our simple approach here. We created the PerformanceLogMonitor application (in the PerformanceLog-Monitor directory on the companion CD) to display information from the Performance Log database and provide a bit of control over the ReadLog server.

This application and the associated log management tools are a subset of an application that our company is going to market commercially. The application will be extended to provide remote hooks into SQL Server, as well as provide lots of other information from applications running on the server.

In order to build the PerformanceLogMonitor application, you must have a licensed copy of First Impression by Visual Components, Inc. If you don't have First Impression and you open the project in design mode, Visual Basic will change the form—so don't save the project when you close it!

You must also make sure that the project's references have the correct paths. Choose References from the Tools menu, and make sure that the path is correct for LogFileAgent (which should point to ReadLogAgent.tlb in the Utilities directory) and for CSUtilities (which should point to CSUtilities.dll in the Utilities directory).

Figure 8-7 shows the default view of the form. Clicking a different graph type in the list updates the graph.

NOTE Because the *Click* event procedure of the combo box control actually retrieves the data, you must select a class by clicking the combo box, even if a class is already selected.

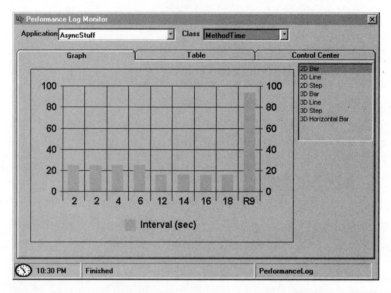

Figure 8-7. *The graphics are provided using the First Impression OCX control (Vcfi32.ocx), by Visual Components, Inc., which is very powerful and provides an excellent interface.*

Figure 8-8 shows the Table tab, which contains a Grid control that displays the columns used in our graph plus some additional information.

The Control Center tab is shown in Figure 8-9. This tab provides a way to see what the ReadLogAgent program is doing and to have some degree of control over it. Clicking the Start LogFileAgent button will start the remote server if it is not already running. The button is redundant because the performance log monitor will automatically start the ReadLogAgent application the first time it accesses one of its properties. (The button is included with this sample, however, to illustrate how to accomplish the task of starting the server. In production applications, you might not need the button.)

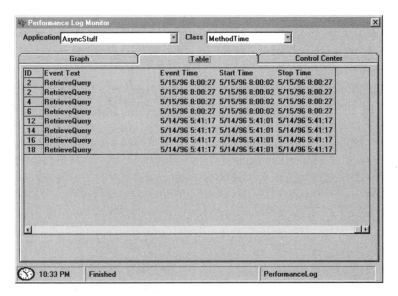

Figure 8-8. *This view shows detailed data from the database.*

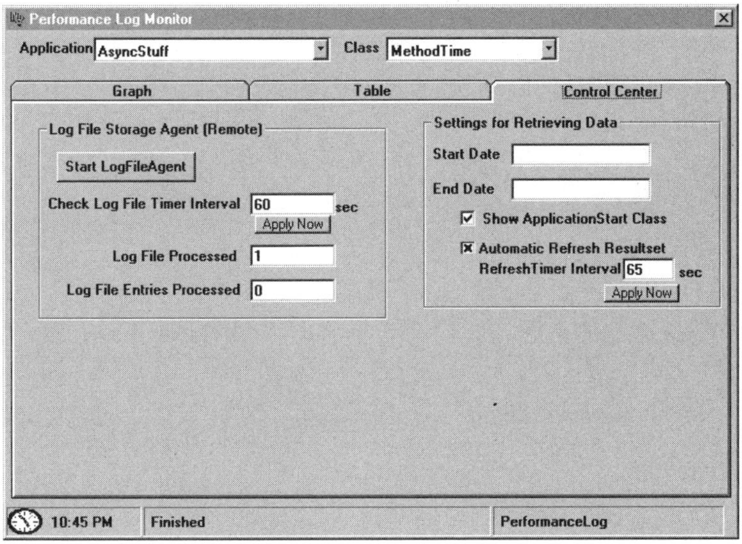

Figure 8-9. *This tab allows us to control the ReadLogAgent program as well as certain criteria for our database query.*

The Settings For Retrieving Data frame on the right allows us to specify the start and end dates for a query. We can also turn off display of the ApplicationStart class, which is entered whenever an application starts. The Automatic Refresh Resultset check box allows us to refresh our query based on a timer value.

These settings provide the start of a friendly interface for system managers. Also notice the status bar on the bottom of the form.

Now let's dig into this application and see how it works.

frmPerformanceLogMonitor Form

The frmPerformanceLogMonitor form displays statistics from the database. This form allows us to control the process of the performance log system to some degree and to filter the data that is retrieved.

Declarations

The first part of the declarations section contains the normal declarations, plus declarations for our two class libraries.

```
Option Explicit
Dim objLogFileAgent As New clsLogFileAgent
Dim pnlTableToProcess As Panel
Dim pnlStatus As Panel
Dim objUtil As New clsUtilities

' Tracks the status of a query.
' Set to False by Form_load; Set to True by StartQuery.
Dim bQueryInProgress As Boolean

Dim ConnectString As String
Dim cnPerformanceLog As rdoConnection, _
  enPerformanceLog As rdoEnvironment
Dim rsPerformanceLog As rdoResultset

Dim i As Integer
```

StartQuery method

The *StartQuery* method begins a new query. We have isolated it here to be able to call it easily. The only parameter is the SQL statement that retrieves the result set.

```
Private Sub StartQuery(SQLStatement As String)

   pnlTableToProcess.Text = "PerformanceLog"
   pnlStatus.Text = "Executing Query"
   StatusBar1.Refresh

' Make the grid and graph controls invisible because this
' method runs only when a user starts a new query. Also set
' the grid to one row to delete all of the current data.
   grdPerformanceData.Visible = False
   chrtPerformanceData.Visible = False
   grdPerformanceData.Rows = 1
```

```
      If bQueryInProgress Then
         rsPerformanceLog.Close
      End If

   ' Indicate that a query has been started.
      bQueryInProgress = True

   ' Execute the OpenResultset method.
      Set rsPerformanceLog = cnPerformanceLog. _
         OpenResultset(SQLStatement, , rdConcurRowver, rdAsyncEnable)
      pnlStatus.Text = "Query Executed, Waiting for Completion"
      StatusBar1.Refresh

   ' Enable the Timer control, and set its interval. This timer
   ' rechecks the status of the query. When the query is
   ' finished executing, the timer fires the RetrieveQuery
   ' method to retrieve the result set.
      tmrCheckExecuting.Enabled = True
      tmrCheckExecuting.Interval = 5000

End Sub
```

RetrieveQuery method

The *RetrieveQuery* method retrieves the result set. This method is executed by the tmrCheckExecuting Timer control when the query finishes executing.

```
Sub RetrieveQuery()

   Dim sBuffer As String, TimeInterval As Long

   i = 1

   ' Retrieve the result set.
   Do While Not rsPerformanceLog.EOF

   ' Calculate the interval between the start
   ' and stop times retrieved from the database.
      TimeInterval = DateDiff _
         ("s", rsPerformanceLog!StartTime, rsPerformanceLog!StopTime)

   ' Load sBuffer with the fields to load into the grid.
   ' Then use AddItem to load the next row of the grid with the data.
      sBuffer = Str(rsPerformanceLog!ID) & Chr(9) _
         & TimeInterval & Chr(9) _
         & rsPerformanceLog!UserName & Chr(9) _
         & rsPerformanceLog!EventText & Chr(9) _
```

(continued)

197

```
         & rsPerformanceLog!EventTime & Chr(9) _
         & rsPerformanceLog!StartTime & Chr(9) _
         & rsPerformanceLog!StopTime
      grdPerformanceData.AddItem sBuffer
      rsPerformanceLog.MoveNext
      DoEvents
      i = i + 1
   Loop

   pnlStatus.Text = "Updating Graph"
   StatusBar1.Refresh

' Move the data from the grid to the First Impression grid.
   GridToDataGrid

' Make the grid and chart visible. These lines are effective
' only after the user has started a new query. On requeries,
' the grid and chart will already be displayed.
   grdPerformanceData.Visible = True
   chrtPerformanceData.Visible = True

   If chkAutoRefreshResultSet.Value = 1 Then
      tmrRefreshResultSet.Enabled = True
   End If

   pnlStatus.Text = "Finished"
   frmPerformanceLogMonitor.MousePointer = vbDefault

End Sub
```

cboClassDescription_Click event procedure

This event procedure executes when the user selects a class from the cboClass-Description control. It drives the query process by setting up the SQL statement and executing the *StartQuery* method.

```
Private Sub cboClassDescription_Click(Area As Integer)

   Dim SQLStatement As String, DateRestriction As String

' If Area = 2 then the user clicked an item in the list.
   If Area = 2 Then

' Process the query only if the user
' selected a valid application name.
      If Len(cboApplicationName.Text) > 0 Then
         DateRestriction = ""
```

```
' If the user specified start and end dates, use them in
' the Where clause to bracket the date range for the query.
      If Len(txtStartDate) > 0 And Len(txtEndDate) > 0 Then
         DateRestriction = " and (EventTime >= '" & txtStartDate
         DateRestriction = DateRestriction _
            & "' and EventTime <= '" & txtEndDate & "') "
      End If
      SQLStatement = "select ID, EventText, EventTime, " _
         & "UserName, StartTime, StopTime from PerformanceLog " _
         & "Where (ApplicationName = '" & cboApplicationName.Text _
         & "' and ClassDescription = '" & cboClassDescription.Text _
         & "')"
      If Len(DateRestriction) > 0 Then
         SQLStatement = SQLStatement & DateRestriction
      End If

' Attach the Order By clause to the SQL statement,
' and execute the StartQuery method.
      SQLStatement = SQLStatement & " order by ApplicationName"
      StartQuery SQLStatement

   End If
 End If

End Sub
```

At this point, we have started the query, but it has not returned any data. Check out the *tmrCheckExecuting_Timer* event procedure on page 201 to see how we get the data back.

tmrCheckLogFileParameters_Timer **event procedure**

This timer is used routinely to retrieve properties from the ReadLogAgent application and provides a useful example of OLE automation and Remote Automation. This event procedure pulls three parameters from the objLogFileAgent object and places the values in corresponding Text controls. This is most useful when the server is running remotely, because you are continually getting status updates.

```
Private Sub tmrCheckLogFileParameters_Timer()

   tmrCheckLogFileParameters.Enabled = False
   txtLogFilesProcessed = objLogFileAgent.TotalNumberOfLogFiles
   txtLogFileEntriesProcessed = objLogFileAgent.TotalNumberOfEntries
   txtCheckForLogTimerInterval = objLogFileAgent.CurrentTimerInterval
   tmrCheckLogFileParameters.Enabled = True

End Sub
```

tmrRefreshResultSet_Timer event procedure

The *tmrRefreshResultSet_Timer* event procedure is used to periodically refresh our result set. This keeps the graph in a continual update mode for the user so it is always current.

```
Private Sub tmrRefreshResultSet_Timer()

  tmrRefreshResultSet.Enabled = False
  pnlStatus.Text = "Refreshing Results"
  StatusBar1.Refresh

' Enable or disable the timer depending on the value
' of the Automatic Refresh Resultset check box.
  If chkAutoRefreshResultSet.Value = 1 Then
    tmrRefreshResultSet.Enabled = True
  Else
    tmrRefreshResultSet.Enabled = False
  End If

' Check for a valid result set to be able to execute
' the second If statement without an error.
  If bQueryInProgress = True Then

' Check the Restartable property of the result set to
' determine if the query can be reexecuted without
' closing the result set. Requery updates the result
' set just as if we had used OpenResultset again.
    If rsPerformanceLog.Restartable Then
      rsPerformanceLog.Requery

' Set the timer to check the result set in 5 seconds,
' and retrieve it if the query is complete.
      tmrCheckExecuting.Enabled = True
      tmrCheckExecuting.Interval = 5000

    End If
  End If

End Sub
```

Text change event procedures

These two event procedures use a technique that is handy for lots of different controls. Whenever the user enters anything in the control, it makes the appropriate Apply Now button visible. This alerts the user to click that button to apply the change. As you will see in the *ApplyNow* event procedures below, we make the button invisible.

```
Private Sub txtCheckForLogTimerInterval_Change()
  cmdApplyNow.Visible = True
End Sub

Private Sub txtRefreshTimerInterval_Change()
  cmdApplyNowRefreshTimerInterval.Visible = True
End Sub
```

ApplyNow_Click event procedures

The first event procedure updates the timer interval in the ReadLogAgent application. We accomplish this by executing the *SetTmrCheckForLogFilesInterval* method in the objLogFileAgent object and pass it the new timer interval in seconds.

```
Private Sub cmdApplyNow_Click()

  cmdApplyNow.Visible = False
  objLogFileAgent.SetTmrCheckForLogFilesInterval _
    txtCheckForLogTimerInterval

End Sub
```

The next event procedure updates the tmrRefreshResultSet Interval property. Notice that we only set the timer for 10 seconds or longer.

```
Private Sub cmdApplyNowRefreshTimerInterval_Click()

  cmdApplyNowRefreshTimerInterval.Visible = False
  If txtRefreshTimerInterval > "10" Then
    tmrRefreshResultSet.Interval = txtRefreshTimerInterval * 1000
  End If

End Sub
```

Form_Unload event procedure

This event procedure executes the *ShutdownApplication* method of the objUtil object, which closes the log file opened by CSUtilities in the *StartApplication* method.

```
Private Sub Form_Unload(Cancel As Integer)
  objUtil.ShutdownApplication
End Sub
```

tmrCheckExecuting_Timer event procedure

This event procedure is used to determine whether the query for the rsPerformanceLog result set is still executing. If the query has completed, we can retrieve the result set from the database.

```
Private Sub tmrCheckExecuting_Timer()

  tmrCheckExecuting.Enabled = False
  pnlStatus.Text = "Checking Results"
  StatusBar1.Refresh

' If the query is still executing, enable the timer because
' the result set is not yet available for retrieval.
  If rsPerformanceLog.StillExecuting Then
    tmrCheckExecuting.Enabled = True

' If the query is finished, retrieve the result set by
' executing the RetrieveQuery method. Notice the timer
' properties before and after RetrieveQuery.
  Else
    pnlStatus.Text = "Retrieving Results"
    StatusBar1.Refresh
    objUtil.LastEntryText = "RetrieveQuery"
    objUtil.StartTime = Now()
    RetrieveQuery
    objUtil.StopTime = Now()
  End If

End Sub
```

cboApplicationName_Click event procedure

The *cboApplicationName_Click* event procedure fires when a user selects an application from the cboApplicationName control. If we have a valid selection, we make the grid and chart visible and then execute the *SetClassDescriptionFilter* method to fill the second Combo control. Notice that we make the SSTab1 control visible before we end the procedure.

```
Private Sub cboApplicationName_Click(Area As Integer)

  Dim SQLStatement As String

' If Area = 2 then the user clicked an item in the list.
  If Area = 2 Then
    If Len(cboApplicationName.Text) > 0 Then
      grdPerformanceData.Visible = False
      chrtPerformanceData.Visible = False
      SetClassDescriptionFilter cboApplicationName.Text
      SSTab1.Visible = True
    End If
  End If

End Sub
```

Form_Load event procedure

The *Form_Load* event procedure performs a number of routine startup tasks. The only line of real interest here is *bQueryInProgress = False*. This property is used as a flag showing whether or not we have a valid query in progress, which is useful information in the *RetrieveQuery* method.

Init method

The *Init* method is used to set most of the startup values for the application, with the following tasks:

- Setting a few chart parameters

- Loading the lstChartType control with valid chart types

- Setting up the grid control

- Executing the *StartApplication* method of the objUtil object

- Enabling the rdcPerformanceLogList control and creating the RDO environment and connection

- Other general functions, such as setting up a timer and setting visible properties for some controls

Using a startup method such as *Init* is handy. You can use it normally as we do here and also give the user a button that resets the application to its startup configuration when clicked. For even greater control, this type of routine can also be broken up into several smaller methods, each called from a master method.

SetClassDescriptionFilter method

This method sets the SQL statement for the rdcPerformanceLogClass-DescriptionList control and then refreshes the control. This displays the correct class information for the selected application.

```
Sub SetClassDescriptionFilter(ApplicationName As String)

  Dim SQLStatement As String

' If chkShowApplicationClass is True, restrict the
' SQL statement with a Where clause to retrieve all
' classes except the Application Started class.
  If chkShowApplicationClass.Value = 0 Then
    rdcPerformanceLogClassDescriptionList.SQL = _
      "select distinct ClassDescription " _
      & "from PerformanceLog order by ClassDescription"
  Else
```

(continued)

203

```
          SQLStatement = "select distinct ClassDescription "
          SQLStatement = SQLStatement & "from PerformanceLog "
          SQLStatement = SQLStatement & "where (ApplicationName = '"
          SQLStatement = SQLStatement & ApplicationName & "' "
          SQLStatement = SQLStatement & "and ClassDescription not like "
          SQLStatement = SQLStatement & "'Application Started') "
          SQLStatement = SQLStatement & "order by ClassDescription"
          rdcPerformanceLogClassDescriptionList.SQL = SQLStatement
       End If

   ' Enable the rdcPerformanceLogClassDescriptionList control,
   ' and execute the Refresh method to build the result set.
       rdcPerformanceLogClassDescriptionList.Enabled = True
       rdcPerformanceLogClassDescriptionList.Refresh

       cboClassDescription.Visible = True

   End Sub
```

lstChartType_Click event procedure

This event procedure changes the type of chart displayed by the lstChartType control, by using a *Select Case* statement to pick the type of chart chosen and reset the chart to the new type using the ChartType property.

The procedure also sets some default chart values.

```
Private Sub lstChartType_Click()

   Dim ind%, colCount%, i%
   Dim j%

   chrtPerformanceData.Plot. _
      Axis(VtChAxisIdZ).AxisScale.Hide = False
   chrtPerformanceData.Plot. _
      SeriesCollection.Item(1).SeriesMarker.Show = False

   Select Case lstChartType.Text
      Case "2D Bar"
         chrtPerformanceData.ChartType = VtChChartType2dBar

      Case "2D Line"
         chrtPerformanceData.ChartType = VtChChartType2dLine

      Case "2D Step"
         chrtPerformanceData.ChartType = VtChChartType2dStep

      Case "3D Bar"
         chrtPerformanceData.ChartType = VtChChartType3dBar
```

```
  Case "3D Line"
    chrtPerformanceData.ChartType = VtChChartType3dLine

  Case "3D Step"
    chrtPerformanceData.ChartType = VtChChartType3dStep

  Case "3D Horizontal Bar"
    chrtPerformanceData.ChartType = VtChChartType3dHorizontalBar
    chrtPerformanceData.Plot. _
      Axis(VtChAxisIdZ).AxisScale.Hide = True

  End Select

End Sub
```

GridToDataGrid method

This method takes the data in our standard Grid control (grdPerformanceData) and copies it to the chart's data grid.

```
Private Sub GridToDataGrid()

  Dim i As Integer, j As Integer

  grdPerformanceData.Col = 0
  chrtPerformanceData.RowCount = grdPerformanceData.Rows

' Load the labels.
  For i = 1 To chrtPerformanceData.RowCount - 1
    grdPerformanceData.Row = i
    chrtPerformanceData.Row = i
    chrtPerformanceData.RowLabel = grdPerformanceData.Text
  Next i

' Load the chart grid from the standard grid.
  For i = 1 To chrtPerformanceData.RowCount - 1
    For j = 1 To chrtPerformanceData.ColumnCount
      grdPerformanceData.Row = i
      grdPerformanceData.Col = j
      chrtPerformanceData.DataGrid.SetData i, j, _
        Val(grdPerformanceData.Text), False
    Next j
  Next i

' It probably isn't necessary to refresh
' the grid, but it doesn't hurt.
  grdPerformanceData.Refresh

End Sub
```

Prepared Statements and Stored Procedures

This section discusses one of the best parts of RDO: using *prepared statements* with stored procedures. You implement a prepared statement by defining an rdoPreparedStatement object, which allows you to create a prepared query definition—you can think of it as creating a compiled SQL statement. Because you use the properties of an rdoPreparedStatement object to define a query, you can create a definition for a prepared statement on the fly and change the parameters later during the execution of your program.

Sample Program: Using Prepared Statements with RDO

The PreparedStatements sample application, which you can find in the PreparedStatements directory on the companion CD, uses RDO to execute a stored procedure that runs on SQL Server. This particular stored procedure takes one parameter and returns one result set. However, RDO allows you to execute stored procedures that return more than one result set.

Figure 8-10 shows the interface for the application. Enter the application name you want to find in the Application Name box, and then click the Search Now button. Nothing new here. In fact, it looks just like any other application. Only behind the scenes can you see how this application is different.

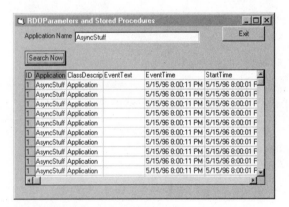

Figure 8-10. *The PreparedStatements application.*

There are basically three steps to follow when using this application:

1. Creating the prepared statement in the *Form_Load* event procedure of frmMain.

2. Setting the parameter to search for.

3. Executing the prepared statement.

frmMain Form

The frmMain form is the only form in this application and contains some of the application source code.

cmdRetrieveStatistics_Click event procedure

The *CmdRetrieveStatistics_Click* event procedure calls the *GetStatistics* method, which executes the stored procedure. We pass the text contained in the TextBox control (named txtApplicationName) to *GetStatistics*.

```
Private Sub cmdRetrieveStatistics_Click()


  Me.MousePointer = vbArrowHourglass
  lblStatus = "Retrieving Data"

  GetStatistics sApplicationName:=txtApplicationName

  Me.MousePointer = vbDefault
  lblStatus = ""

End Sub
```

Form_Load event procedure

The *Form_Load* event procedure executes the *ConnectDatabase* method. This attaches to the database and sets up the prepared statement.

```
Private Sub Form_Load()
  ConnectDatabase
End Sub
```

ModRDOStuff Module

This module contains most of the real database code in the application. The public properties for the application are also defined here.

Declarations

The declarations section is pretty simple. Notice the standard definitions of objects for RDO. The only line that is unique to this example is the third statement, which creates an object variable for the prepared statement.

```
Option Explicit
Public cn As rdoConnection, en As rdoEnvironment
Public psPerformanceLog As rdoPreparedStatement
Public sConnect As String
Public rs As rdoResultset
Dim ResultSetActive As Boolean
```

ConnectDatabase method

This method performs all of the initialization logic for our application. Notice the strange format of the SQL statement near the middle of the routine. The braces ({ }) around the statement are part of the ODBC SQL syntax that allows you to specify particular features of a SQL statement. The braces should surround the entire statement. The *Call* operator must be used to execute stored procedures that return any values or result sets. The parameter for a SQL statement is identified by the *?* placeholder.

```
Sub ConnectDatabase()

Dim sSQL As String

' Create an object reference to the RDO environment
    Set en = rdoEnvironments(0)

    sConnect = "DSN=clientserverbook;UID=sa;pwd=;"
    Set cn = en.OpenConnection("", rdDriverNoPrompt, False, sConnect)

' Create the proper SQL statement
    sSQL = "{ call spperformancelogstandardquery (?)}"

' Create the prepared statement. The first parameter normally
' contains a string that names the prepared statement. This
' example only creates one prepared statement and leaves the
' name blank. You might need to set the Direction property of
' the prepared statement to indicate whether a parameter is a
' return value (rdParamReturnValue), input parameter
' (rdParamInput), or a result set output parameter.
    Set psPerformanceLog = cn.CreatePreparedStatement("", sSQL)

' Indicate that a result set is not active.
    ResultSetActive = False

End Sub
```

GetStatistics method

This method executes our prepared statement.

```
Sub GetStatistics(sApplicationName As String)

  Dim i As Integer, sTemp As String

  frmMain!grid1.Rows = 1
  frmMain!grid1.Visible = False
  frmMain!grid1.Refresh
```

```
' Set parameter 0 to the incoming parameter sApplicationName.
  psPerformanceLog.rdoParameters(0) = sApplicationName

' If a result set is active, use the Requery method
' to reexecute the query. This will update the result
' set if any values in the underlying data have changed.
' It will also use any new values in the query parameters.
  If ResultSetActive Then
     rs.Requery

' If a result set is not active, execute the prepared statement.
  Else
     Set rs = psPerformanceLog.OpenResultset()
     ResultSetActive = True
  End If

' Retrieve the number of rows in the result set; the For loop below
' uses this value for the number of iterations it performs.
  frmMain!grid1.Cols = rs.rdoColumns.Count

  frmMain!grid1.Row = 0

' Retrieve the column names from the result set, and set the title
' of each grid column to the corresponding name from the result set.
' (This is not as efficient as setting the grid column names at
' startup, but it is more flexible. You should use this approach when
' you do not know the column names before you execute the SQL code.)
  For i = 0 To rs.rdoColumns.Count - 1
     frmMain!grid1.ColWidth(i) = (frmMain.TextWidth(rs(i)) + 60)
     frmMain!grid1.Col = i
     frmMain!grid1.Text = rs(i).Name
  Next

  sTemp = ""

' Retrieve the data from the result set.
  Do While Not rs.EOF
     For i = 0 To rs.rdoColumns.Count - 1
        frmMain!grid1.ColWidth(i) = (frmMain.TextWidth(rs(i)) + 60)
        If Len(sTemp) = 0 Then
          sTemp = rs(i)
        Else
          sTemp = sTemp & Chr(9) & rs(i)
        End If
     Next
```

(continued)

```
' Load the next row of the grid.
  If Len(sTemp) > 0 Then
     frmMain!grid1.AddItem sTemp
  End If

  rs.MoveNext
Loop

  frmMain!grid1.Visible = True

End Sub
```

CloseResultSet method

This method sets our ResultSetActive flag to *False* and closes the result set. It is always a good idea to clean up when you have finished using a resource.

```
Sub CloseResultSet()

  ResultSetActive = False
  rs.Close

End Sub
```

dbo.spPerformanceLogStandardQuery Stored Procedure

The stored procedure is shown below. This procedure runs on SQL Server, and we used SQL Enterprise Manager to export the SQL script into BuildIndex-Procedure.sql in the root directory on the companion CD.

This procedure is simple and straightforward, taking only one parameter and returning a single result set.

```
if exists (select * from sysobjects where id =
  object_id('dbo.spPerformanceLogStandardQuery')
  and sysstat & 0xf = 4)

  drop procedure dbo.spPerformanceLogStandardQuery

GO
```

The next line creates the procedure using the Transact-SQL *CREATE PROCE-DURE* statement. The parameter for the procedure is defined as @Application-Name with a type of varchar and a length of 255. The equal sign (=) and asterisk (*) define the default value for the parameter if it is not included. This means that if we leave off the parameter, we will get all records.

```
CREATE PROCEDURE spPerformanceLogStandardQuery
  @ApplicationName varchar(255) = '*'
```

```
AS
```

The action of our query takes place in the next line. The @ApplicationName parameter is used in the *Where* clause.

```
SELECT *
  FROM PerformanceLog
  WHERE ApplicationName like @ApplicationName
  ORDER BY ApplicationName
```

```
GO
```

9

Cool Database and Application Tips

This chapter is devoted to showing you how to do things that developers demand these days and how to use some of the nifty new features in Microsoft Visual Basic 4 that will make your life much easier. These tips will ultimately translate into useful tools for your users. For example, we will explore how to create a user-friendly interface with a drill-down metaphor that lets users point and click their way through the data. This example uses objects and collections behind the scenes to implement the drill-down effect.

In this chapter, we are going to look at two sample programs that illustrate the use of objects. The first program, called ObjectsGalore, does not use a database but illustrates the encapsulation principle with two simple methods. The interesting part of this application is its use of a collection to hold the data objects built as we enter information.

The second sample, called PublisherClient, is somewhat more sophisticated, pulling data from a database to load the collection.

Many users also like an application to store their individual, applicationwide preferences and options. Of course, when you have multiple people using the same system this becomes more difficult. We show you how to use the Registry and a few simple Visual Basic statements to accomplish this task in your applications.

This chapter also includes a pool manager application, which is in great demand by many developers. This application allows you to dynamically load and unload OLE servers from a pool of servers. The application uses many of the features of Visual Basic 4 to illustrate how to accomplish this task.

Smart Data Objects

Now let's look at some cool stuff we can do with the new object technology in Visual Basic. We hear a lot about placing business rules in a middle tier that our applications talk to, but how does that really work? What advantage does it have for us?

One of the neat uses of object technology is to encapsulate data and code (methods) in an object, instead of calling a subroutine and passing a parameter to it. For instance, the traditional way to print a document is to create a procedure called *PrintSomething* and pass the name of the document to it. To use the procedure to print something about an individual named Ken, you would call the function using the following syntax:

```
PrintSomething Ken
```

This syntax is the traditional manner of application programming. You always need to know what you want to do and to what you want to do it. What if the method (*PrintSomething*) and the data were embedded in the same object? If we had a *PrintSomething* method in an object called Ken, we could call it by using the following:

```
Ken.PrintSomething
```

Other advantages of object technology arise from some of the tools that come with Visual Basic:

- The Object Browser browses objects when you're working in Visual Basic. It displays not only true object classes but also your forms, modules, and built-in constants. You can access the Object Browser by pressing F2 while in design mode.

- Regclean.exe cleans up the Registry, removing and updating invalid entries. You can copy it from the Tools\Pss directory on the Visual Basic CD.

- Ole2vw32.exe displays information about OLE servers. You can copy it from the Tools\Pss directory on the Visual Basic CD.

Sample Program: Using Objects to Encapsulate Data and Code

The ObjectsGalore sample application, which you can find in the Objects-Galore directory on the companion CD, uses one form, as shown in Figure 9-1.

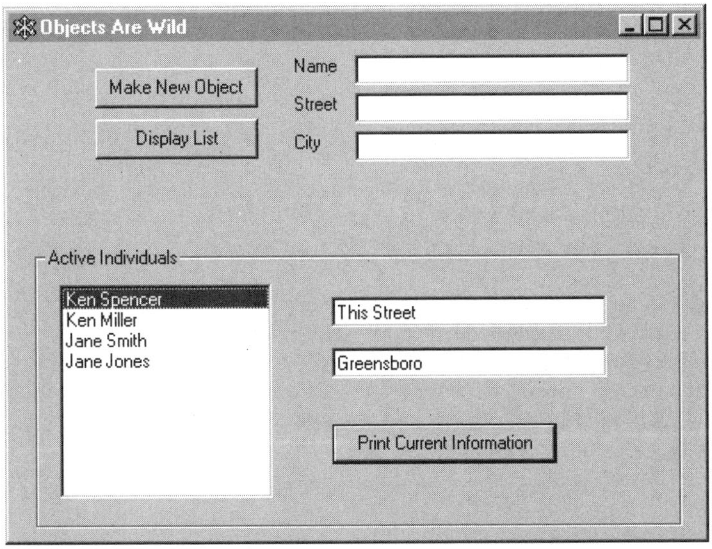

Figure 9-1. *This simple application shows how data objects work.*

Each time the user enters a name, street, and city in the upper right corner, clicking the Make New Object button creates an instance of the clsPerson class and places the individual's name in the list in the Active Individuals frame. The application is actually placing each individual's information in a collection as soon as the object instance is created. Clicking a name in the list retrieves the object from the collection and displays the street and city in the text boxes to the right of the list.

frmObjectsAreWild Form

This form provides the main interface for our application.

Declarations

The only thing we declare in this section is nPersons as a collection object. This is the master collection that will contain all the names.

```
Option Explicit
Dim nPersons As New Collection
```

cmdMakeNewObject_Click event procedure

This event procedure occurs when the user clicks the Make New Object button.

```
Private Sub cmdMakeNewObject_Click()

  Dim rPerson As clsPerson

' Create a new instance of the clsPerson class. We use the New
' keyword here because we did not create the object using New
' when we declared it (called early binding). The following
' statement is an example of late binding.
  Set rPerson = New clsPerson

' Store the name, street, and city information
' in the corresponding properties of the class.
  rPerson.Name = txtNameIn
  rPerson.Street = txtStreetIn
  rPerson.City = txtCityIn

' Load the entire class into the nPersons collection.
' The Name property is used as the index.
  nPersons.Add rPerson, rPerson.Name

' Add the individual name to the list on the form.
  lstIndividualList.AddItem rPerson.Name

' Clean up the input text boxes.
  txtNameIn = ""
  txtStreetIn = ""
  txtCityIn = ""

End Sub
```

cmdPrintCurrent_Click event procedure

This event procedure illustrates how we ask the class to print itself.

```
Private Sub cmdPrintCurrent_Click()

  Dim s As String

' Create a reference object to use with the clPerson class.
' We do not use the New keyword because this reference will
' be set to an existing instance.
  Dim rPerson As clsPerson

' Make sure the user has clicked a valid entry in the list.
  If lstIndividualList.ListIndex >= 0 Then

' Retrieve the name from the list, and place it in the variable s.
    s = lstIndividualList.List(lstIndividualList.ListIndex)
```

```
' Set a reference that points to the object stored in the
' nPersons collection. The name just retrieved (contained
' in the variable s) is used as the index to the
' collection to retrieve the object.
      Set rPerson = nPersons(s)

' Tell the object (rPerson) to print its information
' on the form (frmObjectsAreWild).
      rPerson.PrintAddress frmObjectsAreWild

   End If

End Sub
```

lstIndividualList_Click **event procedure**

This event procedure uses the *DisplayAddress* method of the clsPerson class to display the information on our form. It is similar in functionality to the *cmdPrintCurrent_Click* event procedure.

```
Private Sub lstIndividualList_Click()

   Dim s As String
   Dim rPerson As clsPerson

   s = lstIndividualList.List(lstIndividualList.ListIndex)
   Set rPerson = nPersons(s)

' Pass DisplayAddress the names of the controls to use
' for displaying the street and city data. DisplayAddress
' sets the Text property of these two controls directly.
   rPerson.DisplayAddress txtStreet, txtCity

' Make visible the Print Current Information button.
   cmdPrintCurrent.Visible = True

End Sub
```

txtNameIn_LostFocus **event procedure**

This event procedure checks the current name in the txtNameIn text box against the nPersons collection. If the name is already in the collection, a message box is displayed, warning you that you have entered a name that already exists.

Notice the error handling. In every procedure that uses a collection, you should include an error handling routine. The collections in Visual Basic 4 do not return error codes when you perform an invalid action, such as asking for an item with an index that does not exist. Instead, Visual Basic just pops an error and throws it to the user if you don't have an error handler.

```
Private Sub txtNameIn_LostFocus()

  On Error GoTo txtNameInContinue

  If nPersons(txtNameIn).Name > "" Then
    MsgBox "You have entered a duplicate name in the Name box"
  End If
  Exit Sub

txtNameInContinue:
  Exit Sub

End Sub
```

clsPerson Class

The clsPerson class is used to store information about an individual. This class is simple but serves as a good illustration. The properties for this class are set as shown in Figure 9-2. The Instancing property does not need to be set, unless you make this an out-of-process server. Make sure the Public property is set to *True*.

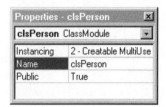

Figure 9-2. *The clsPerson class properties.*

Declarations
The following properties hold the information on a person.

```
Option Explicit
Public Name As String
Public Street As String
Public City As String
```

DisplayAddress method
This is about as simple as a method gets. Just pass the objects that will display the information to the method, and the method will pass the data back. The example passes text box objects to the method, but some other controls would work as well (such as a combo box or list box), as long as the default action of the control is to display data.

```
Sub DisplayAddress(StreetA As Object, CityA As Object)
  StreetA = Street
  CityA = City
End Sub
```

PrintAddress method

The *PrintAddress* method is also extremely simple: pass it a form, and it will print the information on the form.

```
Sub PrintAddress(FormA As Object)

  FormA.Print Street
  FormA.Print City
  FormA.Print Name

End Sub
```

Implementing the Drill-Down Metaphor

One of the most usable features found in many systems is the ability to "drill down" from one object to another. This usually involves looking at some type of parent information and then delving into the details at a lower level. For instance, users might look at information on total sales for a particular product and then want to know what sales look like by customer. Double-click the product, and it should explode into details by customer. There's only one problem. This time they wanted detailed customer information, but what if next time they want to see product details by region? Furthermore, what if some users need to routinely view customer details, while others need to routinely view region details? The list of possibilities goes on and on.

The first item to consider when developing a solution for managing these issues is how to allow the user to select which view to use for drill-down operations. We have several choices:

■ Right-click pop-up menus. Just right-click the object to set preferences for drill-down operations.

■ A list box with preference options. This implementation requires more screen real estate.

■ Radio buttons. Like list boxes, this implementation works well but also takes up more screen real estate.

Sample Program: A Drill-Down Application

The PublisherClient sample application (in the BusinessRules1 directory on the companion CD) uses the object techniques from the previous sample to demonstrate how they can be used for a simple drill-down application. It uses business rule capabilities to retrieve data from a database encapsulated in a simple OLE server. Most of you have probably built an application that takes a value from one control and uses it to look up related data. Taking data from a grid or chart and displaying the detailed information can work in the same manner.

The user can enter either an asterisk (*) or a name in the Publisher Name text box. Clicking the Find Now button will display the names from the resulting SQL query in the grid. Double-clicking a name will display the details for that publisher name.

Figure 9-3 shows the application with the main form (Publishers Information) in the background and the detail form (Publisher Details) displayed over it.

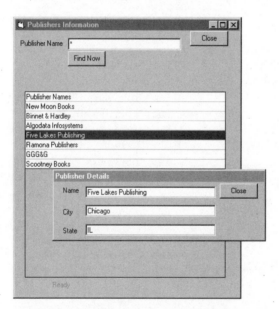

Figure 9-3. *The Publishers Information and Publisher Details forms.*

While this example uses the methods in our class to do some simple database lookups, think how easy it would be to hide all the nasty SQL code in an object layer for your organization. (We did not say application because a correctly constructed object layer will be used again and again for many different applications. Most developers will actually be insulated from all the SQL stuff going on underneath.)

This example also illustrates the concept of using objects to locally cache information and provide the methods to operate on it. Imagine encapsulating the code to perform calculations on someone's account in an object that also contains the account details. Just reference the object, and ask it to do the calculation for itself!

Before you can build or run the PublisherClient application, you need to make sure that the paths for the project's references are correct for your system. Choose References from the Tools menu, and make sure that the Publisher reference points to Publisher.exe in the BusinessRules1 directory. The Splash Screen reference should point to Splash.exe in the Splash directory, and CSUtilities should point to CSUtilities.dll in the Utilities directory.

This application also includes two batch files for registering (Register.bat) and unregistering (UnRegister.bat) your OLE server. You must run Register.bat before you run PublisherClient for the first time. The batch files are easy to understand and are patterned after the files of the same names in the Rental Car application in Chapter 10.

Register.bat contains the application name and the /regserver parameter. This parameter will cause your application to execute, register itself, and then terminate:

```
REM This assumes you have built all
REM servers/EXEs in the same directory.
"Publisher" /unregserver
"Publisher" /regserver
```

Notice how the first line has a comment regarding the location of the servers. This is because there is no path specified for the server name. The second line tries to unregister the server using the /unregserver parameter. The last line actually registers the server using the /regserver parameter. The name of the application is surrounded in quotes just in case the name was changed to include spaces.

The UnRegister.bat program is exactly like Register.bat except that there is no /regserver line.

```
REM This assumes you have built all
REM servers/EXEs in the same directory.
"Publisher" /unregserver
```

Now let's see how this sample application works.

frmPublishersInformation Form

This form is used to obtain the query text from the user.

cmdFindNow_Click event procedure

This event procedure executes the method in our server to process the query and load the names in the grid. All the action takes place on the line that executes the *AddNames* method. We added a simple check to make sure the user does not click the button without first defining the search criteria.

```
Private Sub cmdFindNow_Click()

  If Len(txtPublisherQuery) > 0 Then
    AddNames (objPublisher.LoadPublishers(sName:=txtPublisherQuery))
  Else
    MsgBox "You must enter a search string before " _
      & "the search can begin" & Chr(13) & _
    "Enter a * if you wish to retrieve all records"
  End If

End Sub
```

Form_Load event procedure

The *Form_Load* event procedure sets the properties for our grid.

```
Private Sub Form_Load()

  grdPublisher.Row = 0
  grdPublisher.Text = "Publisher Names"
  grdPublisher.ColWidth(0) = 6000

End Sub
```

Form_QueryUnload event procedure

This event procedure cleans up our object by setting it to *Nothing* when the application begins to shut down.

```
Private Sub Form_QueryUnload(Cancel As Integer, _
  UnloadMode As Integer)
  Set objPublisher = Nothing
End Sub
```

grdPublisher_DblClick event procedure

This drill-down event procedure fires when the user double-clicks a name in the grid. Note that there is no check to ensure that the user did not double-click Row 0, which contains our header. In a real application, you need to make sure the user can't run a query trying to use header information to retrieve data, unless, of course, that is your intention. Some drill-down applications do exactly that when pulling information by region or some other criterion.

```
Private Sub grdPublisher_DblClick()

  Dim sName As String
  Dim rPublisher As clsPublisherDetails

' Set the current column in the grid to 0.
  grdPublisher.Col = 0

' Get the publisher's name in the current row of the grid.
  sName = grdPublisher.Text

' Execute the LoadPublisher method (in modClientMaster), which
' puts the publisher's information in the gaPublishers collection.
  If CheckIndex(sName:=sName) Then
    LoadPublisherRecord sName
  End If

' Set the reference to the object in the gaPublishers collection.
' To simplify the example, we violate our own rule about using
' an error handler whenever using a collection. In the real
' world, always use one.
  Set rPublisher = gaPublishers(sName)

' Display the publisher's address.
  rPublisher.DisplayAddress frmPublisherDetails!txtState, _
    frmPublisherDetails!txtCity, frmPublisherDetails!txtName

' Show the form.
  frmPublisherDetails.Show

End Sub
```

The *DisplayAddress* method, called near the end of the routine, was also used in the ObjectsGalore application on page 214. This example is slightly different because we pass not only the name of the control but also the complete reference including the form name. We do this because the controls are located on a different form.

tmrLoadPublisherServer_Timer event procedure

The *Timer* event procedure in this application is used only at startup, and the interval is set to about 2 seconds. This event procedure allows our application to load very quickly and then load the OLE server Publisher. The server is loaded when we reference the City property.

```
Private Sub tmrLoadPublisherServer_Timer()

  Dim sTemp As String

  tmrLoadPublisherServer.Enabled = False
  lblStatus = "Loading Publisher Server"
  DoEvents
  sTemp = objPublisher.City
  lblStatus = "Ready"

End Sub
```

clsPublisherDetails Class

The clsPublisherDetails class contains the properties and methods for a publisher. When an object is created from this class, the object contains both the information about the publisher (name, state, and city) and the methods to print and display the publisher's address.

Declarations

The declarations section declares the properties for our clsPublisherDetails class.

```
Option Explicit
Public Name As String
Public State As String
Public City As String
```

DisplayAddress method

The *DisplayAddress* method is almost the same as the one in our clsPerson class in the ObjectsGalore sample, described on page 214. The only differences are that we changed the Street property in this class to State and added the Name property.

```
Sub DisplayAddress(StateA As Object, CityA As Object, _
  NameA As Object)

  StateA = State
  CityA = City
  NameA = Name

End Sub
```

PrintAddress method

This method is also similar to the one used earlier in the clsPerson class. Here we changed Street to State.

```
Sub PrintAddress(FormA As Object)

  FormA.Print State
  FormA.Print City
  FormA.Print Name

End Sub
```

modMasterClient Module

This module contains the object declarations, the startup method (*Main*), and other assorted methods.

Declarations

Here we declare a new instance of a collection to hold our clsPublisher class, and we declare a clsPublisher object.

```
Option Explicit
Public gaPublishers As New Collection
Public objPublisher As New clsPublisher
```

Main method

The only unusual thing we do in this method is use a multiline message on our splash screen. We use sMessage to hold the title message and insert a carriage return (*chr(13)*) between the two lines.

It is good programming practice to explicitly destroy the splash screen object (objSplash) when the procedure is completed, as we do here. The object should disappear when the method goes out of scope, but what happens if we move the *Dim* statement to the Declarations section of our module? By explicitly destroying the object, we don't have to worry about the scope of the property.

```
Sub Main()

  Dim objSplash As New clsSplash
  Dim sMessage as string

  With objSplash
    .CopyRight = "My Computer Company, Inc."
    sMessage = "Publisher information demonstration " _
      & Chr(13) & "using the Publisher business rule server"
    .TextMessage = sMessage
    .TextMessage = "Publisher Information demonstration"
    .TitleMessage = "Publisher Information "
    .Splash
  End With
```

(continued)

225

```
    frmPublishersInformation.Show
    DoEvents

    objSplash.SplashStop
    Set objSplash = Nothing

End Sub
```

AddNames method

This method adds the names of the publishers to the grid.

```
Sub AddNames(sNames As String)

    Dim tNameList As String, i As Integer, tName As String

' Force grid size to one row, which is the title row.
' Otherwise, every time you execute this method the rows
' will be added to the rows already in the grid.
    frmPublishersInformation!grdPublisher.Rows = 1

' Loop through the name list until it is blank.
    tNameList = sNames
    Do While tNameList > ""

' Each name in the list is delimited by a carriage return.
' Find the location of the next carriage return in the list.
        i = InStr(tNameList, Chr(13))

' If the carriage return isn't found, exit the loop.
        If i = 0 Then Exit Do

' Add the name to the grid.
        tName = Left$(tNameList, i - 1)
        frmPublishersInformation!grdPublisher.AddItem tName

' If at the end of the list, exit the loop.
        If i >= Len(tNameList) - 1 Then Exit Do

' Delete the name just retrieved from the list.
        tNameList = Mid$(tNameList, i + 1, Len(tNameList) - (i + 1))

    Loop

End Sub
```

LoadPublisherRecord method

This method is called when the user double-clicks the grid. It retrieves one publisher and stores the city and state information for that publisher in the gaPublishers collection.

```
Sub LoadPublisherRecord(sName As String)

' Create object to hold the publisher information.
  Dim rPublisher As clsPublisherDetails

  On Error GoTo LoadPublisherRecordError

  frmPublishersInformation.MousePointer = vbArrowHourglass

' Create a new instance of the clsPublisherDetails class.
  Set rPublisher = New clsPublisherDetails

' Execute the LoadDemographics method of the Publisher class.
' The name of the publisher to retrieve is passed to the method.
  objPublisher.LoadDemographics sName:=sName

' Retrieve the demographics information and
' store it in our new object (rPublisher).
  rPublisher.Name = objPublisher.Name
  rPublisher.State = objPublisher.State
  rPublisher.City = objPublisher.City

' Add the object to the collection. We do not have any error
' handling here because we used the CheckIndex method before
' we called this method to validate the collection.
  gaPublishers.Add rPublisher, rPublisher.Name

  frmPublishersInformation.MousePointer = vbDefault
  Exit Sub

LoadPublisherRecordError:
  MsgBox "Error occurred when retrieving data" & Error$

End Sub
```

CheckIndex method

CheckIndex is used to determine if a publisher is already loaded in the collection. If a publisher exists, *CheckIndex* returns *False;* otherwise, it returns *True.* This might be the opposite of what you would expect, but in this case it makes sense. The caller will generally want to take action for publishers that don't already exist in the collection.

```
Public Function CheckIndex(sName As String) As Boolean

  On Error GoTo CheckIndexError

  CheckIndex = True
  If gaPublishers.Count > 0 Then
    If gaPublishers(sName).Name > "" Then
      CheckIndex = False
      Exit Function
    End If
  End If

  Exit Function

CheckIndexError:
  Exit Function

End Function
```

Sample Program: Encapsulating the Retrieval of Data from a Database in an OLE Server

The interface for the Publisher application (in the BusinessRules1 directory on the companion CD) is shown in Figure 9-4. Typically, we do not use a form in a server application, but in some cases it is useful. In this application, we use the App object to determine when we should display a form.

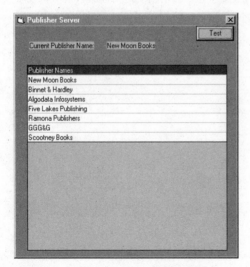

Figure 9-4. *The Publisher interface.*

This interface is used for testing the server only. The form does not display when the application is started from another application. Clicking the Test button executes all methods in the server.

Before you can build or run the Publisher application, you need to make sure that the paths for the project's references are correct for your system. Choose References from the Tools menu, and make sure that the Splash Screen reference points to Splash.exe in the Splash directory. Next make sure that the CSUtilities reference points to CSUtilities.dll in the Utilities directory.

This application's class module has two methods:

- *LoadPublishers* retrieves a result set from the Publishers table and returns it in a carriage-return–delimited string.

- *LoadDemographics* retrieves demographic information for a particular publisher from the Publishers table.

frmPublisherServer Form

The frmPublisherServer form is used only to test the OLE server.

cmdLoadTest_Click event procedure

The *cmdLoadTest_Click* event procedure executes both methods in the clsPublisher class. The *LoadDemographics* method is tested with a hard-coded name.

```
Private Sub cmdLoadTest_Click()

  Dim objPublisher As New clsPublisher

  objPublisher.LoadDemographics "New Moon Books"
  lblCurrentName = objPublisher.Name
  AddNames (objPublisher.LoadPublishers(sName:=""))
  Set objPublisher = Nothing

End Sub
```

AddNames method

The *AddNames* method is virtually the same as the one in our PublisherClient application.

Form_Load event procedure

This event procedure sets the parameters for the grid.

```
Private Sub Form_Load()

  grdPublisher.Row = 0
  grdPublisher.Text = "Publisher Names"
  grdPublisher.ColWidth(0) = 6000

End Sub
```

229

CLIENT/SERVER PROGRAMMING WITH MICROSOFT VISUAL BASIC

clsPublisher Class

This class is the guts of the server application. Notice how much code is buried in the methods.

Declarations

The declarations section contains no surprises.

```
Option Explicit

Public ConnectString As String
Public objUtilities As New clsUtilities

Public Name As String
Public City As String
Public State As String
Public PublisherError As String
```

LoadPublishers method

The *LoadPublishers* method encapsulates a SQL lookup to retrieve a result set from the Publishers table.

```
Public Function LoadPublishers(sName As String) As String

  Dim i As Long, j As Integer, tNameList As String

  On Error GoTo LoadPublishersError

' If sName is anything but blank or an asterisk (*), run
' it through the FixSqlString method in the objUtilities
' class. If it is blank or an asterisk (*), use a simple
' SQL query with no Where clause to retrieve all records.
' Failure to perform these actions can cause the
' application to crash if sName is an asterisk (*).
  If Not (sName = "" Or sName = "*") Then
    sName = objUtilities.FixSQLString(sName)
    ConnectString = "Select pub_name from Publishers "
    ConnectString = ConnectString & "where pub_name = "
    ConnectString = ConnectString & "'" & sName & "'"
  Else
    ConnectString = "Select pub_name from Publishers "
  End If

' Open a result set.
  Set rsPublisher = cnPublisher.OpenResultset(ConnectString, , _
    rdConcurRowver)
```

```
' If any rows are returned in the result set, add the name to
' the name list. (If you are not using SQL Server, be sure to
' check out your database's help information on the RowCount
' property. It might not work in the same manner.)
  If rsPublisher.RowCount <> 0 Then
    Do Until rsPublisher.EOF
      tNameList = tNameList & rsPublisher("pub_Name") & Chr(13)
      rsPublisher.MoveNext
    Loop
  End If

' Set the return value for the method.
  LoadPublishers = tNameList
  Exit Function

LoadPublishersError:
  PublisherError = "Error occurred when retrieving data" _
    & vbCrLf & Error$

End Function
```

LoadDemographics method

The *LoadDemographics* method also encapsulates a SQL lookup. This one retrieves demographic information about a particular publisher.

```
Sub LoadDemographics(sName As String)

  On Error GoTo LoadDemographicsError

' Run sName through FixSQLString to clean it up.
  sName = objUtilities.FixSQLString(sName)

' Build the SQL query.
  ConnectString = "Select * from Publishers where pub_name = "
  ConnectString = ConnectString & "'" & sName & "'"

' Open the result set for this publisher only.
  Set rsPublisher = cnPublisher.OpenResultset(ConnectString, , _
    rdConcurRowver)

' If any row is returned (there should be only one),
' then set the properties of the method.
  If rsPublisher.RowCount <> 0 Then
    Name = rsPublisher("pub_Name")
    State = rsPublisher("State")
```

(continued)

```
      City = rsPublisher("City")
   End If

   Exit Sub

LoadDemographicsError:
   PublisherError = "Error occurred when retrieving data" _
      & vbCrLf & Error$

End Sub
```

modMaster Module

This module contains the startup method (*Main*) and a few declarations for our RDO database objects.

Declarations

This section declares properties for our database connect string, connection, and environment, as well as for a result set.

```
Option Explicit
Dim ConnectString As String
Public cnPublisher As rdoConnection, enPublisher As rdoEnvironment
Public rsPublisher As rdoResultset
```

Main method

Main is our startup method.

```
Sub Main()

' Build the connect string. In a real application, the
' user ID and password should be passed as parameters.
   ConnectString = "DSN=Publishers;UID=sa;PWD=;"

' Connect to the database.
   Set enPublisher = rdoEnvironments(0)
   Set cnPublisher = enPublisher.OpenConnection("", _
      rdDriverNoPrompt, False, ConnectString)

' Display the frmPublisherServer form if
' the application is started directly.
   If Not App.StartMode = vbSModeAutomation Then
      frmPublisherServer.Show
   End If

End Sub
```

Tracking User Preferences in the Registry

One way of tackling the storage of user preference data is to use the *Save-Setting* statement and *GetSetting* function in Visual Basic to store the user's preferences in the Registry. Both were mentioned earlier when we discussed using INI files or the Registry to track the location of Access database files.

Each time a user opens an application, you can set the preferences to the same settings used the last time the application was opened. You might want to consider using an INI file in the user's home directory, instead of the Registry, to store preference and configuration data. This approach allows the information to be available to the application every time the user logs in, regardless of the workstation used.

The following code snippet, which should run whenever the user moves the form, saves the Top and Left properties for a form named frmMain to the user's section of the Registry:

```
SaveSetting(appname:="RentalCar", section:="Last", _
  key:="Top", setting:=frmMain.Top)
SaveSetting(appname:="RentalCar", section:="Last", _
  key:="Left", setting:=frmMain.Left)
```

The next snippet of code retrieves the settings used in the example above and sets the appropriate properties for the form:

```
Dim iTop As Integer, iLeft As Integer

iTop = GetSetting(appname:="RentalCar", section:="Last", _
  key:="Top", default:="")
iLeft = GetSetting(appname:="RentalCar", section:="Last", _
  key:="Left", default:="")

If iTop > 0 And iLeft > 0 Then
  frmMain.Top = iTop
  frmMain.Left = iLeft
end if
```

You should also check out the *DeleteSetting* statement and the *GetAllSettings* function for more Registry tools. If you want to use more of the Registry than is available from the built-in functions and statements (such as storing settings for your application that affect all users), you must use either the Registry API functions or use an add-on product such as StorageTools from Desaware.

Pool Managers for Remote Automation

Here is a killer idea. A pool manager application typically runs on some type of server and keeps a "pool" of OLE servers running. Other applications can request services from this pool, and the pool manager passes the reference to one of the servers in the pool. The pool manager can populate the servers in the pool from both its own system and from servers running remotely using Remote Automation.

Visual Basic Enterprise Edition includes a sample pool manager. The Pmgr_cli.vbp application is located in VbSamples\Remauto\Poolmngr on the Visual Basic CD or, if you installed samples, in samples\remauto\poolmngr under the directory in which you installed Visual Basic. This sample application is not complete and uses a linked list system to track its servers. We considered extending this pool manager but decided to look at other options, which led us to create our PassPoolManager and PassPoolClient projects, which you can find in the PoolManagerPassthru directory on the companion CD. (We used the simple Pass Thru Visual Basic sample application as a starting point.)

These sample applications should give you lots of ideas on what the class and OLE automation/Remote Automation features in Visual Basic can really do. This technology is so powerful, it is absolutely amazing. All of the class projects in this book can be extended for different purposes—applications, management, utilities, and so on.

Sample Program: Managing a Pool of OLE Servers

The PassPoolManager application provides a simple interface, as shown in Figure 9-5. This is one of those cases where you need an interface even though the application is running on a server somewhere. The interface in this application continuously displays statistics on the OLE servers the pool manager is managing. Not only does the interface show how many instances of each server are running but also how many attachments to each object are active and how many more servers can be loaded. In fact, it would be handy to put hooks into this application to allow the PerformanceLogMonitor application to pull this information into its display.

NOTE   Before you can run the PassPoolManager and PassPoolClient applications, you must run the TimerServer.exe and Helo_svr.exe servers, which are located in the Utilities directory.

We can see from Figure 9-5 that one instance of HelloClass is active and two instances of clsTimeServer are active. We can also see that both classes have one client using them.

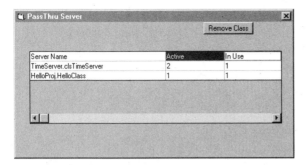

Figure 9-5. *The PassPoolManager application displays all OLE servers it is running and the number of applications using them.*

Three classes are the foundation of this application:

- clsServerDefinition is instanced once for each OLE server defined in the pool manager.

- clsServerInstance is instanced once for every instance of a server the pool manager creates. This class is created and maintained within the clsServerDefinition class.

- clsPassThruPoolManager contains general methods for the pool manager.

PassThruPoolManager Module

This module contains the startup method (*Main*) and several other general-purpose methods.

Main method

The *Main* method performs most of the startup actions for the pool manager. It reads the pool manager's INI file and loads the defined servers. When this method terminates, all servers and structures within the pool manager are up and running.

```
Sub Main()

    frmPassThruPoolManager.Show
    DoEvents
    objPoolManager.InitProjectArray
    DoEvents
    UpdateGrid

End Sub
```

UpdateGrid method

This simple method is executed periodically to update the information displayed on the active and used servers.

```
Sub UpdateGrid()

  Dim objServer As Object, strTemp As String

' Reset the number of rows in grid to 1.
  frmPassThruPoolManager!grdActiveServers.Rows = 1

' Move through entire collection of defined
' servers (colDefinedServers).
  For Each objServer In objPoolManager.colDefinedServers.

' Use objServer to retrieve information from the items in
' the collection for building the string to place in the grid.
    With objServer
      strTemp = .strProgID & Chr(9) _
        & .intCurActiveCount _
        & Chr(9) & .intCurUseCount
      frmPassThruPoolManager!grdActiveServers.AddItem strTemp
    End With
  Next

End Sub
```

IniStringGet method

The *IniStringGet* method retrieves a string from an INI file.

```
Function IniStringGet(KeyString As String) As String

  Dim strIniBuffer As String * 255

  On Error GoTo gisErr

  Dim lRetLen As Long
  lRetLen = GetPrivateProfileString(mstrINI_POOL_MNGR_KEY, _
    KeyString, "", strIniBuffer, 255, mstrINI_POOL_MNGR_FILE_NAME)
  If lRetLen > 0 Then IniStringGet = Left$(strIniBuffer, lRetLen)

  GoTo gisExit

gisErr:
  DisplayError
  Resume gisExit

gisExit:
End Function
```

IniStringSet method

The *IniStringSet* method updates an INI file.

```
Sub IniStringSet(KeyString As String, ValString As String)

  Dim sIniGroupKey As String

  On Error GoTo sisErr

  Dim lTmp As Long
  lTmp = WritePrivateProfileString(mstrINI_POOL_MNGR_KEY, _
    KeyString, ValString, mstrINI_POOL_MNGR_FILE_NAME)
  GoTo sisExit

sisErr:
  DisplayError
  Resume sisExit

sisExit:
End Sub
```

clsPassThruPoolManager Class

This class contains the bulk of the code for the pool manager.

Declarations

This section declares collections for our active and defined servers. These two collections are the master storage mechanisms for this application.

```
Option Explicit
Public colActiveServers As New Collection
Public colDefinedServers As New Collection
```

InitProjectArray method

The *InitProjectArray* method performs most of the startup tasks for the application. It retrieves the names of servers to initialize from the INI file, loads them, and updates the collections.

```
Sub InitProjectArray()

  Dim strPrjSettings As String
  Dim bDone As Integer
  Dim i As Integer
  Dim j As Integer
  Dim intPtr1 As Integer, intptr2 As Integer
```

(continued)

```
' Define a reference to the clsServerDefinition
' class to be used once for every server we define.
  Dim objCurrentServer As clsServerDefinition

' Defines a new instance of the clsServerInstance class to
' be instanced once for each instance of a server we create.
  Dim objCurrentInstance As New clsServerInstance

' Create the filename and path for the INI file.
  mstrAppPath = App.Path
  mstrINI_POOL_MNGR_FILE_NAME = mstrAppPath & "\" & "Poolmngr.ini"

  i = 0
  While Not bDone

' Retrieve an item from the INI file. The keys in the INI file
' are created in the format PoolSvr0, PoolSvr1, and so on.
' Use the counter i to increment the suffix to the key.
    strPrjSettings = IniStringGet(mstrINI_POOL_SVR_KEY & Format$(i))

' Check to see if we have a valid entry from the INI file
' (if the return value is blank). If so, we are done. Also
' check the counter to see if we loaded any servers. If not,
' execute InitPoolSvrList to at least give us something.
' (In a real production system, you would not place anything
' in the list if there are no servers defined.)
    If strPrjSettings = "" Then
      If i = 0 Then
        InitPoolSvrList
      Else
        bDone = True
      End If

' At this point, we have a valid entry from the INI file.
    Else

' Create an instance of the server definition class.
      Set objCurrentServer = New clsServerDefinition

' Parse the string from the INI file.
      intPtr1 = 1
      intptr2 = InStr(intPtr1, strPrjSettings, ",")
      If intptr2 > 0 Then objCurrentServer.strProgID _
        = Mid$(strPrjSettings, intPtr1, intptr2 - intPtr1)
      intPtr1 = intptr2 + 1
      intptr2 = InStr(intPtr1, strPrjSettings, ",")
```

```
        If intptr2 > 0 Then objCurrentServer.intMinUseCount _
          = Val(Mid$(strPrjSettings, intPtr1, intptr2 - intPtr1))
        intPtr1 = intptr2 + 1
        intptr2 = InStr(intPtr1, strPrjSettings, ",")
        If intptr2 > 0 Then objCurrentServer.intMaxUseCount _
          = Val(Mid$(strPrjSettings, intPtr1, intptr2 - intPtr1))
        intPtr1 = intptr2 + 1
        intptr2 = InStr(intPtr1, strPrjSettings, ",")
        If intptr2 > 0 Then objCurrentServer.intCloseDelay _
          = Val(Mid$(strPrjSettings, intPtr1, intptr2 - intPtr1))
        intPtr1 = intptr2 + 1
        intptr2 = InStr(intPtr1, strPrjSettings, ",")
        If intptr2 > 0 Then objCurrentServer.bLookAheadCreate _
          = Val(Mid$(strPrjSettings, intPtr1, intptr2 - intPtr1))
        If intptr2 > 0 Then objCurrentServer.bShutdownMethod _
          = Val(Mid$(strPrjSettings, intptr2 + 1))

' Create multiple instances of the server
' per the INI definition that we placed in
' objCurrentServer.intMinUseCount in the code above.
        For j = 0 To objCurrentServer.intMinUseCount - 1
          AddInstance objCurrentServer
        Next j

' Add the object to the collection of defined servers.
        colDefinedServers.Add objCurrentServer, _
          objCurrentServer.strProgID

' Remove the object.
        Set objCurrentServer = Nothing
        i = i + 1
      End If

  Wend

End Sub
```

AddInstance method

The *AddInstance* method creates an instance of an OLE server.

```
Function AddInstance(objServer As Object) As Boolean

  Dim objInstance As clsServerInstance

  On Error GoTo AddInstanceError

  AddInstance = True
```

(continued)

239

```vb
    ' Create a new instance of the clsServerInstance class.
      Set objInstance = New clsServerInstance

    ' Create the instance of our object. Place the
    ' reference to the object in the objHandle property.
      Set objInstance.ObjHandle = CreateObject(objServer.strProgID)

    ' Now that the OLE server is executing,
    ' update the properties of objInstance.
      With objInstance
        .strProgID = objServer.strProgID

    ' GetNewServerNode increments a counter
    ' and returns a new instance number.
        .InstanceIDNumber = GetNewServerNode()
        .bInUse = False
        If objServer.intCloseDelay > 0 Then
          .DeallocTime = DateAdd("n", objServer.intCloseDelay, Now)
        Else
          .DeallocTime = 0
        End If
      End With

    ' Update the objServer information by incrementing the
    ' intCurActiveCount property. Use AddInstanceNumber
    ' to add the instance information from objInstance.
    ' to objServer.
      With objServer
        .intCurActiveCount = .intCurActiveCount + 1
        .AddInstanceNumber objInstance.InstanceIDNumber
      End With

    ' Add the instance (objInstance) to the
    ' active servers collection (colActiveServers).
      colActiveServers.Add objInstance, _
        Str$(objInstance.InstanceIDNumber)

      gResetGridTimer = True
      Set objInstance = Nothing
      Exit Function

AddInstanceError:
      AddInstance = False

End Function
```

CloseOpenServers **method**

The *CloseOpenServers* method removes all active servers using a *For* loop.

```
Sub CloseOpenServers()

  Dim objCurrentInstance As Object

  On Error GoTo cosErr

  For Each objCurrentInstance In colActiveServers
    Set objCurrentInstance.ObjHandle = Nothing
  Next

  Exit Sub

cosErr:
  DisplayError
  Resume cosExit

cosExit:
End Sub
```

RequestServer **method**

The *RequestServer* method is used by a client application to request a server reference. The client passes the method a string identifying the server and a long integer to hold the instance number. The method returns the object ID as its return value, so we must use a parameter to return the instance number.

```
Public Function RequestServer(strProgID As String, _
  lngInstanceNumber As Long) As Object

  Dim objCurrentServer As Object

  lngInstanceNumber = -1
  On Error GoTo RequestServerError

' Set objCurrentServer to the server definition we are looking
' for with strProgID. (This is where the error handler comes in.
' If strProgID is not a valid index, an error occurs.)
  Set objCurrentServer = objPoolManager.colDefinedServers(strProgID)

' If we get to here, we have a valid object reference.
  With objCurrentServer
```

(continued)

```
' Exit if the number of instances
' exceeds the maximum (intMaxUseCount)
    If .intCurActiveCount >= .intMaxUseCount Then
       Exit Function
    End If

' Add a new instance if the maximum number of instances
' isn't exceeded and no servers are available.
    If .intCurActiveCount <= .intMaxUseCount And _
       .intCurActiveCount <= .intCurUseCount Then
       AddInstance objCurrentServer
    End If

' Execute the FindFreeInstance method
' to get a free instance reference.
    Set RequestServer = .FindFreeInstance(strProgID, lngInstanceNumber)

' If we have a valid instance number, use AddCurrentInUse
' to increment the counter in our class.
    If lngInstanceNumber >= 0 Then
       objCurrentServer.AddCurrentInUse
    End If

  End With

' Because you cannot update an item in a collection,
' you must remove the current object from the defined
' servers class, and then add it back.
  colDefinedServers.Remove objCurrentServer.strProgID
  colDefinedServers.Add objCurrentServer, objCurrentServer.strProgID

  Exit Function

RequestServerError:
  Exit Function

End Function
```

RemoveServer method

The *RemoveServer* method removes one server from the defined server collection and removes all instances of any executing servers.

```
Sub RemoveServer(strProgID As String)

  Dim objCurrentServer As Object

  On Error GoTo RemoveServerError

' Obtain an object reference to the server.
  Set objCurrentServer = objPoolManager.colDefinedServers(strProgID)

' Drop all instances.
  objCurrentServer.RemoveInstances

' Kill the server definition.
  Set objCurrentServer = Nothing

' Delete the server from the collection.
  objPoolManager.colDefinedServers.Remove strProgID

  Exit Sub

RemoveServerError:
  Exit Sub

End Sub
```

DropServer method

The *DropServer* method decreases the current in-use value in objCurrentServer.

```
Function DropServer(lngInstanceNumber As Long) As Boolean

  Dim objCurrentServer As Object
  Dim objCurrentInstance As Object
  Dim strProgID As String

  DropServer = False
  If lngInstanceNumber <= 0 Then Exit Function

  Set objCurrentInstance = objPoolManager.colActiveServers _
    (lngInstanceNumber)

  With objCurrentInstance
    .bInUse = True
    strProgID = .strProgID
  End With
```

(continued)

243

```
Set objCurrentServer = objPoolManager.colDefinedServers(strProgID)

With objCurrentServer
  objCurrentServer.DecreaseCurrentInUse
End With

objPoolManager.colDefinedServers.Remove _
  objCurrentServer.strProgID
objPoolManager.colDefinedServers.Add _
  objCurrentServer, objCurrentServer.strProgID

DropServer = True
Exit Function

DropServerError:

End Function
```

clsServerDefinition Class

This class is used to define each server.

Declarations

You can see that the declarations match the items we retrieved from the INI file.

```
Option Explicit

Public strProgID As String
Public intCurUseCount As Integer
Public intCurActiveCount As Integer
Public intMinUseCount As Integer
Public intMaxUseCount As Integer
Public intCloseDelay As Integer
Public bLookAheadCreate As Integer
Public bShutdownMethod As Integer

Dim colInstanceNumbers As New Collection
```

The last line declares a new collection to hold our instance numbers. This is pretty cool. Here we are in a class that is stored in a collection, and we are creating another collection in this class. Where does this power end? The beauty of object technology is that you can wrap stuff in an object and it is totally self-contained.

AddCurrentInUse and DecreaseCurrentInUse methods

The *AddCurrentInUse* and *DecreaseCurrentInUse* methods simply increment or decrement the intCurUseCount property.

```
Sub AddCurrentInUse()
  intCurUseCount = intCurUseCount + 1
End Sub

Sub DecreaseCurrentInUse()
  intCurUseCount = intCurUseCount - 1
End Sub
```

AddInstanceNumber method

The *AddInstanceNumber* method uses the *Add* method to place a new member in the collection. This collection (colInstanceNumbers) contains all of the instance numbers for a particular server. The instance number is used to index the active servers collection (colActiveServers).

```
Sub AddInstanceNumber(lInstanceNumber)
  colInstanceNumbers.Add Str(lInstanceNumber)
End Sub
```

FindFreeInstance method

The *FindFreeInstance* method retrieves a free instance number. The *For* loop is the heart of this method. The loop moves through the entire collection of instance numbers.

```
Function FindFreeInstance(strProgID As String, _
  lngInstanceNumber As Long) As Object

  Dim objIDCol, lngIDNumber As Long
  Dim objCurrentInstance As Object

  lngInstanceNumber = -1

  On Error GoTo FindFreeInstanceError

' Move through the entire collection of instance numbers.
  For Each objIDCol In colInstanceNumbers
    If Val(objIDCol) > 0 Then
      lngIDNumber = Val(objIDCol)
      Set objCurrentInstance = _
        objPoolManager.colActiveServers(objIDCol)
      lngInstanceNumber = lngIDNumber

' If the bInUse flag is False, we can use this instance.
' If it is True, the instance is already in use.
      With objCurrentInstance
        If Not .bInUse Then
          Set FindFreeInstance = .ObjHandle
```

(continued)

```
            .bInUse = True
            Exit For
         End If
      End With
   End If
Next

Exit Function

FindFreeInstanceError:
   Exit Function

End Function
```

RemoveInstances **method**

The *RemoveInstances* method removes all instances of all executing servers that are controlled by the pool manager. This method is useful when the pool manager is shutting down. We use a *For* loop again to walk through the instance numbers for a server.

```
Sub RemoveInstances()

   Dim objIDCol, lngIDNumber As Long
   Dim objCurrentInstance As Object
   Dim objCurrentServer As Object
   Dim objCurrentInstanceOfServer As Object
   Dim strProgID As String

   On Error GoTo RemoveInstancesError

' Move through the entire collection of instance numbers.
   For Each objIDCol In colInstanceNumbers
      If Len(objIDCol) > 0 Then
         lngIDNumber = Val(objIDCol)
         Set objCurrentInstance = _
            objPoolManager.colActiveServers(objIDCol)
         With objCurrentInstance
            Set objCurrentInstanceOfServer = .ObjHandle

' The next If statement illustrates a concept we implemented
' in some of our OLE servers. We created a shutdown method
' that could be executed to let a server know we wanted it to
' terminate. (This is most useful when you have an OLE server
' with an interface that will not automatically shut down
' when all connections to it have terminated.) We had to create
' a flag in our INI file to indicate whether a server supported
' the shutdown method. If it is supported, we execute it.
```

```
        If bShutdownMethod Then
            objCurrentInstanceOfServer.shutdown
        End If

        Set objCurrentInstanceOfServer = Nothing
    End With

' Remove the reference to the server from the collection.
        objPoolManager.colActiveServers.Remove (objIDCol)

    End If
  Next

  Exit Sub

RemoveInstancesError:
  Exit Sub

End Sub
```

clsServerInstance Class

This section defines the public properties for the application. This is a short class, consisting of nothing but the declarations for its properties.

Declarations

```
Option Explicit

Public strProgID As String
Public InstanceIDNumber As Long
Public ObjHandle As Object
Public DeallocTime As Date
Public bInUse As Boolean
```

frmPassThruPoolManager Form

The frmPassThruPoolManager form does not have any code that is noteworthy. For the most part, the form methods just execute methods in one of the classes or the module. The timer is used to continually update the grid with information about the defined and active servers.

Sample Program: A Pass Pool Client

Before you can build or run the PassPoolClient application, which is also in the PoolManagerPassthru directory on the companion CD, you need to make sure that the PassPoolManager reference points to PassPoolManager.tlb in the PoolManagerPassthru directory. (Choose References from the Tools menu.)

Figure 9-6 shows the simple PassPoolClient application we created from one of the original Visual Basic samples. This application uses the HelloClass and clsTimeServer classes. The real difference in this sample is that it asks the PassPoolManager application to hand it a reference to the application it wants.

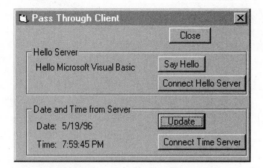

Figure 9-6. *The sample client application interface.*

The client interface uses two buttons for each possible action. The first button you must click is either Connect Hello Server or Connect Time Server. These buttons actually call the pool manager and ask it to pass a handle to the requested server. If the pool manager returns a valid reference, the appropriate action button (either Say Hello or Update) is displayed. When you click the action button, the actual method in the requested server is executed.

frmClient Form

This form contains all of the code in the application.

Declarations

The declarations in this form are created as generic objects, not as objects of a specific class.

```
Dim mobjPassThruSvr As Object
Dim mbPassThruSvrCreated As Integer
Dim objInterface  As Object
Dim bInterfaceOpen As Integer
Dim objServer As Object
Dim bServerOpen As Integer
Dim bSuccess  As Integer
Dim lngHelloInstanceNumber As Long
Dim lngTimeInstanceNumber As Long
```

cmdConnectServers_Click event procedure

The *cmdConnectServers_Click* event procedure is for the cmdConnectServers control array. We use the *RequestServer* method in the pool manager to request an object reference. You must pass the fully qualified class name to the method (for example, "TimeServer.clsTimeServer").

```
Private Sub cmdConnectServers_Click(Index As Integer)

  If cmdConnectServers(Index).Caption = "Connect Time Server" Then

' Ask the pool manager for a handle to the clsTimeServer class.
' If the statement is successful, the objInterface will contain
' a valid object reference to the clsTimeServer class and
' lngTimeInstanceNumber will be greater than zero.
    Set objInterface = mobjPassThruSvr.RequestServer _
      ("TimeServer.clsTimeServer", lngTimeInstanceNumber)
    bInterfaceOpen = True
    cmdUpdate.Visible = True

  Else

' Ask the pool manager for a handle to the HelloClass class.
    Set objServer = mobjPassThruSvr.RequestServer _
      ("HelloProj.HelloClass", lngHelloInstanceNumber)
    bServerOpen = True
    cmdSayHello.Visible = True

  End If

End Sub
```

cmdSayHello_Click event procedure

The *cmdSayHello_Click* event procedure checks the lngHelloInstanceNumber to make sure it has a valid object. If it does, it can execute any method in the server.

```
Private Sub cmdSayHello_Click()

  On Error GoTo shError

  If lngHelloInstanceNumber >= 0 Then lblHello = objServer.SayHello

  GoTo shExit

shError:
  MsgBox Error$
  Resume shExit

shExit:
End Sub
```

cmdUpdate_Click event procedure

The *cmdUpdate_Click* event procedure checks the lngTimeInstanceNumber and exits if it is not valid.

```
Private Sub cmdUpdate_Click()

  On Error GoTo cuError

  If lngTimeInstanceNumber = -1 Then GoTo cuError2

  labDate.Caption = objInterface.GetDate
  labTime.Caption = objInterface.GetTime

  GoTo cuExit

cuError:
  MsgBox Error$
  GoTo cuExit

cuError2:
  MsgBox "Unable to connect to server"
  GoTo cuExit

cuExit:
End Sub
```

Form_Load event procedure

The *Form_Load* event procedure creates the reference to our pool manager.

```
Private Sub Form_Load()

  Set mobjPassThruSvr = _
    CreateObject("PassPoolmanager.clsPassThruPoolManager")
  DoEvents
  mbPassThruSvrCreated = True

End Sub
```

Form_Unload event procedure

The *Form_Unload* event procedure executes the *DropServer* method for both the clsTimeServer and HelloClass classes by passing the instance number for each class to the method, which releases the server. If you do not execute *DropServer*, the pool manager will show one more usage of an object than is actually true.

```
Private Sub Form_Unload(Cancel As Integer)

    If bServerOpen Then _
        mobjPassThruSvr.DropServer lngHelloInstanceNumber
    If bInterfaceOpen Then _
        mobjPassThruSvr.DropServer lngTimeInstanceNumber

    Set objServer = Nothing
    Set objInterface = Nothing
    If mbPassThruSvrCreated Then Set mobjPassThruSvr = Nothing
    End

End Sub
```

10

Rental Car Demo from Microsoft

In this chapter, we use a neat sample application that Microsoft uses in many of their demonstrations. The Rental Car application illustrates a number of useful techniques that can be done with Microsoft Visual Basic 4. Some of the techniques in this application are really cool, but there are others we do not recommend using. We will critique the application as it stands, which affords us an opportunity to examine some of the real-world issues in migrating from Visual Basic 3 to Visual Basic 4.

In this chapter you'll learn how to use the following new features of Visual Basic in a client/server application:

- Using traditional batch files to register and unregister OLE servers
- Using either a Jet or SQL Server database with one application
- Creating a data source on the fly
- Running business rule objects on either the client or the server

You'll also learn about several other small tasks you can accomplish with Visual Basic, such as how to provide user feedback and how to make effective use of a few Visual Basic controls.

Using this application gives us an opportunity to describe how to use the surrounding and supporting technologies in interesting ways, although not every functional operation or method is discussed because of the size and complexity of the application. Occasionally, we discuss a method without showing the code in the book. However, all of the code is included on the companion CD.

Pay special attention to the Clerk and Manager classes in the RentalObjects project. These two classes encapsulate the business rules and methods for retrieving, updating, and deleting information in the database. They show how we can use three-tiered development to improve the development of applications. They also illustrate how to use *Connect* and *Disconnect* methods in a class to gracefully start and stop a connection to an application.

Setup Instructions

You can run the application using either Microsoft Access 7 (Jet 3.0) or Microsoft SQL Server 6 for your database engine. You must create a data source pointing to the database you will use. The setup process is similar for both. SQL Server is naturally a little more complicated to set up, and you must convert the Access 7 database included with the application (Rental.mdb) to SQL Server. The following sections explain both approaches in detail.

Files Included

The files for the Rental Car application are included on the companion CD in the RentalCarDemo directory. The subdirectories contain the following files:

Subdirectory	Description
Database	Rental.mdb is the database in Access 7 format. This database can be used directly with Jet 3.0 or Access 7.
Doc	The files in this directory are provided in both RTF (Rich Text Format) and Word 7 format. Demonstration Script.rtf and Demonstration Script.doc describe how to run the demonstration program. Troubleshooting.rtf and Troubleshooting.doc will help you if you have problems running the demo.
Exe	Executable versions of the Rental Car applications and support files. Rental Clerk and Rental Manager.exe are the client applications. Rental Connection and Rental Objects are both OLE Servers and should not be executed directly. The batch programs used to register the applications (Register.bat and UnRegister.bat) are also located in this directory.
Include	Resource file, resource source file, Visual Basic constants for resource files, and a batch file to compile the resource file.
Library – Connection	Source files for the Rental Connection OLE server.
Library – Objects	Source files for the Rental Objects OLE server.
Project – Clerk	Source files for the Rental Clerk application.
Project – Manager	Source files for the Rental Manager application.

The Rental Car application requires an ODBC data source that points to the database you will be using. The application was designed to be able to create the data source for you, or to allow you to create it ahead of time. However, because of a bug in the automatic creation process, you should always create the data source manually before running the program for the first time.

Using a Jet 3.0 Data Source

Perform the following steps on the client:

1. Create an ODBC data source for the Rental.mdb database using the ODBC application in Control Panel. Name the data source Car Rental DB.

2. Run Register.bat to register the applications. Register.bat can be found in the RentalCarDemo\Exe directory.

You now can run Rental Clerk.exe, selecting Car Rental DB from the Data Source list that appears, and Rental Manager.exe.

Using a SQL Server 6 Data Source

The first step in using the application with SQL Server 6 is to copy the Rental.mdb information to a SQL Server 6 database. To do so, first create a SQL Server database to hold the data, as described in the "Building Your Database Schema in SQL Server" section on page 84. (We used a 5-MB device to hold this database when testing the application for this book.) Next, perform the following steps on the client:

1. Create an ODBC data source for the database. Name the data source Car Rental DB.

2. Open the Rental.mdb database using Access 7.

3. Select the first table in the Tables tab.

4. Choose Save As/Export from the File menu to display the Save As dialog box, as shown in Figure 10-1.

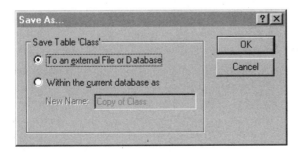

Figure 10-1. *The Save As dialog box.*

5. Choose the To An External File Or Database option and click OK to display the Save Table In dialog box, as shown in Figure 10-2.

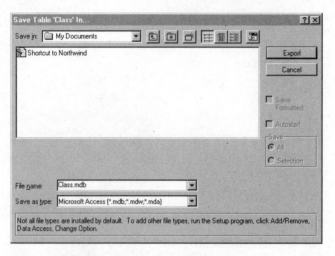

Figure 10-2. *The Save Table In dialog box.*

6. From the Save As Type drop-down list, select ODBC Databases ( ).

7. In the Export dialog box that appears, click OK to accept the default name for the table in SQL Server. The default name is the same as that of the current table.

8. In the SQL Data Sources dialog box that appears, choose the Car Rental DB data source from the list and click OK. (See Figure 10-3.)

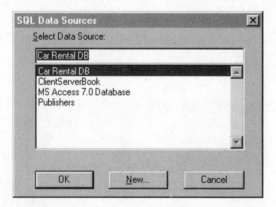

Figure 10-3. *The SQL Data Sources dialog box.*

9. The SQL Server Login dialog box appears, requesting login information for the selected data source. Enter your login name in the Login ID box, enter your password in the Password box, and then click OK.

10. Repeat this process for all tables in Rental.mdb and then close Access.

11. Run Register.bat.

You now can run Rental Clerk.exe, selecting Car Rental DB from the Data Source list that appears, and Rental Manager.exe.

Bypassing the Data Source Dialog Box on Startup

You can skip the Data Source startup dialog box by using a command line parameter that evaluates to a valid data source name. This is a nice feature to place in your own programs that require particular configuration information when they start. If the program doesn't find the information in an INI file or on the command line, ask the user for it.

To add a data source name to the command line, do the following:

1. Create a shortcut (or Program Manager icon in Microsoft Windows NT) for Rental Clerk.exe.

2. After the last quotation mark of the shortcut's target, enter the complete data source name, for example: *"C:\Kens\RentalCarDemo\EXE-\Rental Clerk.exe" Car Rental DB*. (You can also run this command from the DOS prompt.)

If the Clerk business object finds the data source, no dialog box will appear. If the data source is not found, a new data source will be created on the computer executing the Clerk object with the name given on the command line.

Local or Remote Execution of the Business Objects

Initially, the objects containing business rules will be configured to execute on the client, not the server. The Car Rental Watch form appears on the client whenever you execute the Rental Clerk or Rental Manager application. This form is created by the business rules in Rental Objects and appears on the computer running the objects.

Switching the Clerk and Manager objects to remote execution will cause the Car Rental Watch form to display on the server, not the client. This is a useful demonstration of how an object can run on one system and then, with a few clicks of the mouse, run on a different system.

To switch to remote execution of the objects, first make sure you have completed the steps in "Using a SQL Server 6 Data Source" on page 255. Then copy the RentalCarDemo\Exe subdirectory to the server, and perform the following steps on the server:

1. Create an ODBC data source for the Rental.mdb database using the ODBC application in Control Panel. Name the data source Car Rental DB.

2. Run Register.bat.

3. Start the Automation Manager. (An icon can be found in the Visual Basic 4.0 group.)

4. Start the Remote Automation Connection manager. (An icon can be found in the Visual Basic 4.0 group.) Click the Client Access tab, select the Allow All Remote Creates option, and then close the Remote Automation Connection Manager.

Perform the following steps on the client:

1. Start the Remote Automation Connection Manager (shown in Figure 10-4) from the Visual Basic 4.0 group.

2. From the OLE Classes list, select RentalObjects.Clerk and RentalObjects.Manager.

3. Enter the name of the server in the Network Address box.

4. Select a network protocol that both machines are running.

5. Select No Authentication from the Authentication Level list.

6. Choose Remote from the Register menu.

7. Close the Remote Automation Connection Manager dialog box.

8. Run Rental Clerk and Rental Manager to see the Car Rental Watch form appear on the server.

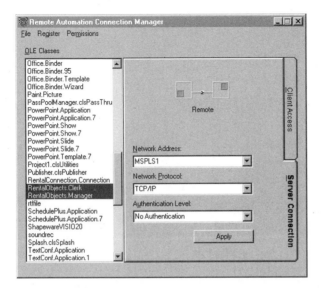

Figure 10-4. *Use the Remote Automation Connection Manager to control several parameters regarding the execution of Remote Automation applications.*

Switching back to local execution

Switching an OLE server back to local execution is even easier than changing it to remote execution. Perform the following steps on the client:

1. Start the Remote Automation Connection Manager (which you can find in the Visual Basic 4.0 group).

2. From the OLE Classes list, select RentalObjects.Clerk and RentalObjects.Manager.

3. Choose Local from the Register menu.

4. Close the Remote Automation Connection Manager dialog box.

5. Run Rental Clerk and Rental Manager to see the Car Rental Watch form appear back on the client.

You might have noticed at this point that some clients could be using the business objects locally and other clients could be using them remotely. This is just part of the incredible power of Remote Automation.

How Does the Rental Car Application Work?

Rental Clerk.exe and Rental Manager.exe are the end-user applications. When either is started, the Car Rental Watch form appears as shown in Figure 10-5.

Figure 10-5. *The Car Rental Watch form is a status form displayed by the OLE Server.*

The Car Rental Watch form will run locally on the client, or remotely on the server if the server is switched to Remote Automation. This form is displayed the entire time either the Rental Clerk or Rental Manager application is running. The form is updated continually to show the state of any activities the server is performing.

At some point during the display of the Car Rental Watch form, the Data Source dialog box appears as shown in Figure 10-6. It is interesting to note that all text on this form (including the labels) is created using a resource file.

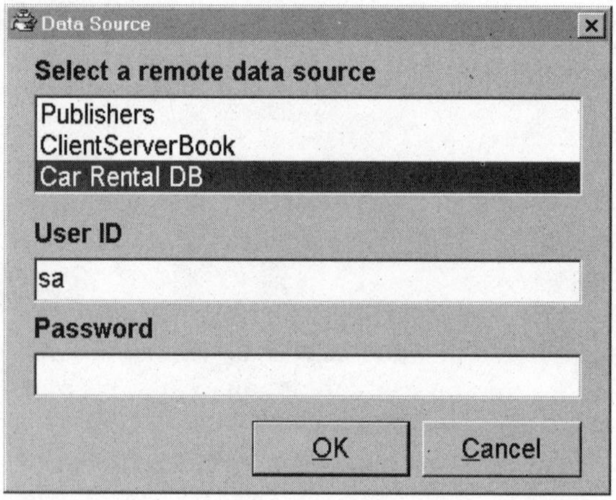

Figure 10-6. *The Data Source form.*

Rental Clerk Application

If you examine the code of the Rental Clerk application closely, you will find that some of the functionality is simulated. (The project file is Clerk.vbp and is located in the Project – Clerk directory.) The purpose of the application is to demonstrate the capabilities of Visual Basic 4, not to be a plug-in solution for a real-world problem. Keep this in mind as we examine some of its capabilities, including the following:

- Looking up a customer
- Verifying driver information
- Choosing the dates for the driver's trip
- Selecting the vehicle and rate
- Processing a credit card payment (fictitious, of course)

The main form for the Rental Clerk (Rent-A-Prize) is shown in Figure 10-7. The interface is built using the TabStrip control.

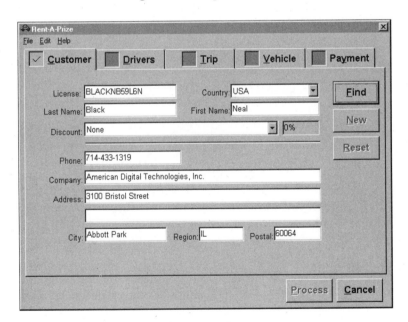

Figure 10-7. *The Rent-A-Prize main form.*

This program provides some useful feedback to users. Figure 10-8 on the next page shows the form after we have looked up a customer, switched to the

Drivers tab, and clicked the Verify button to check the status of drivers for the customer. The check mark in the Customer tab heading is actually green to signify success. The clock in the Drivers tab heading is yellow and indicates the verification is in progress. The user can continue to work with the application while the query processes and watch the graphic change to the green check mark if the verification is successful.

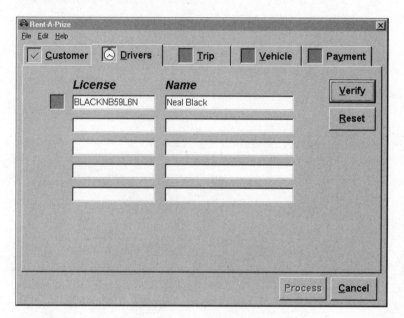

Figure 10-8. *The Drivers tab with verification of a driver query in process.*

Various status dialog boxes are also presented to the user during the execution of the application, providing constant feedback. You should always balance the display of graphic and feedback information with the performance of the application. Displaying information can generate significant overhead, often more than almost any other activity. Of course, if the client is waiting for an activity occurring on another machine, the display of status information is virtually free.

Let's see how this application works. We are not going to move line by line through this application, but instead we'll point out some of the more useful things you can accomplish.

frmMain Form

This is the main form for the Rental Clerk application shown in Figures 10-7 and 10-8.

Declarations

Every application module, form, and class library should have *Option Explicit* set as the first line in the declarations section. This forces you to declare every variable and property that you use. This line will be automatically inserted if you check Require Variable Declaration in the Options dialog box. (Choose Options from the Tools menu.)

The declarations section declares properties to track various activities in the application, including miMode, which tracks modes of operation, miKeep-Location, which tracks the current trip location, and miDateSelect, which is a Boolean that tracks whether or not a date has been selected.

ResetAll method

This method resets the various parts of the application to an initial state. Notice the use of a standard *Reset* method that can reset any of the options. This is a nice convention because you can reset everything as the *ResetAll* method does, or you can simply reset one particular option such as Customer. Also notice the last line in *ResetAll*, which resets the current tab to the Customer tab.

Reset method

The *Reset* method cleans up one option at a time. You pass the option to the method.

VTabClick method

The *VTabClick* method is executed in the tsMain_Click event procedure when the user clicks a tab.

```
VTabClick tsMain.SelectedItem.Index
```

Notice the use of the global constant HOURGLASS to reset the MousePointer property. This is an indicator either that the application was ported from Visual Basic 3 or that a Visual Basic 3 developer wrote this part of the application and was unfamiliar with the intrinsic constants in Visual Basic 4. Use the vbHour-glass intrinsic constant or the vbArrowHourglass intrinsic constant instead of a global constant. Neither one needs to be declared nor creates unnecessary additional code, and each offers greater forward compatibility. Of course, you should reset the MousePointer property to *vbDefault* instead of DEFAULT.

Notice the use of the *ZOrder* method in the sixth line of code: *garPics(iPick)-.Zorder*. This method changes the Z-order to place the object on top of other objects. Using the method with a parameter of 1 places the object at the back of the Z-order, while any other value or leaving out the parameter forces the object to the front.

This method uses the index (*iPick*) of the tab clicked to determine the action to take. This is basically the same logic we saw in the *Reset* method. Various methods are called in this method, depending on the value of *iPick*.

DoCarCalc method

This method calculates the car rates. Although it looks like a good candidate to move into a DLL, you do not necessarily want to move this method to an out-of-process server because all of the information it is using is local to this application.

chkAdditional_Click event procedure

This event procedure recalculates the payment when you select the Add Drivers checkbox on the Payment tab.

chkInsurance_Click event procedure

Like the *chkAdditional_Click* event procedure, this event procedure executes the *DoPmtCalc* method to recalculate the payment, including insurance.

cmdCancel_Click event procedure

The *cmdCancel_Click* event procedure resets the application by executing the *ResetAll* method.

cmdCarReserve_Click event procedure

This event procedure is executed when the user clicks the Reserve button. The sixth and seventh lines execute methods in the goClerk object.

```
iRet% = goClerk.AddRental(garRental)
iRet% = goClerk.ReserveVehicle(lboCar.ItemData _
    (lboCar.ListIndex), garRental(rtlRentalID, 0), _
    gsStartDate, gsEndDate)
```

The goClerk object happens to be an out-of-process server (Rental Objects.vbp).

Reset event procedures

These event procedures fire when the user clicks a Reset button (cmdCarReset, cmdCustReset, cmdTripReset, cmdPmtReset, or cmdDrvReset). The code for cmdPmtReset_Click is *Reset PIC_PMT*. This uses the common *Reset* method by passing it a constant (PIC_PMT) that defines which option to reset.

cmdCustGet_Click event procedure

This event procedure retrieves customer information. Notice the use of the general method *SetTabImage* at the beginning and end of the method.

A word about the keyword *Me* is also in order. The *Me* keyword refers to the form whose code is currently executing, which might be different from the top-most form onscreen. For example, it is possible for code to be executing that is contained in a form that is not visible. If another form is visible, you might erro-neously assume that the *Me* keyword refers to the visible form. *Me* always re-fers to the form from which the code is running.

```
SetTabImage PIC_CUST, TAB_WAIT
GetCustomerList Me
GetCustomerHistory garCustomer(rtlCustomerID, 0)
```

The next line shows how the garCustHist array is used to retrieve a particular element. The rtlCustHistClassID constant references the correct element of the array to retrieve the class ID. The 0 at the end of the line picks the first element in the array.

```
glClassID = garCustHist(rtlCustHistClassID, 0)
SetTabImage PIC_CUST, TAB_GREEN
```

cmdDrvVerify_Click event procedure
This event procedure verifies the driver. The *VerifyDriver* method is in the Rental Objects object.

cmdPmtVerify_Click event procedure
This event procedure verifies credit card payments by showing the frmCredit form. Credit verification is actually executed in the form when the credit card number is entered. The last two lines in this method make the txtCredit control on frmCredit blank and then set the focus to that control.

```
frmCredit!txtCredit = ""
frmCredit!txtCredit.SetFocus
```

cmdProcess_Click event procedure
This event procedure fires up the frmProcess form by executing the *Start* method.

```
frmProcess.Start
```

This code demonstrates how to execute a form's startup tasks without using the *Form_Load* event procedure. It also shows how you can control the startup of a form even if the form is already loaded.

Form_Load event procedure
Here is the infamous *Form_Load* event procedure again. Unlike most people, we prefer not to place too much startup code here but to move it to an *Init*

method instead. We also use a Timer control frequently (as you have seen earlier) to kick off some things in an orderly manner.

This particular event procedure performs lots of startup tasks. All of the variables are, of course, local to this method. They are used in the various calculations that occur during the method.

The event procedure also positions various controls, initializes picture arrays, retrieves initial lists of information from the server, initializes grids, and so on. What could we do differently here? For starters, many of the grids and other controls are located on a tab that is not displayed at startup. These initial settings could be placed in a separate method and executed from a timer, say, 2 seconds after startup. We could also delay retrieving the initial lists for a second or so. (Remember, it's easier to tear apart someone else's application than to create a perfect one yourself.)

Form_QueryUnload event procedure
This event procedure unloads all the forms and sets all the objects to *Nothing*. Notice that we also execute the *Disconnect* method in the goRental object to disconnect from the server application gracefully.

grdOut_Click event procedure
This event procedure is tied to the grdOut grid object, which displays the calendar on the Trip tab. The operation of the procedure is very simple. If miDateSelect evaluates to *True*, the Case True section is executed indicating the user has already selected a date out. If miDateSelect is *False*, the Case False section is executed indicating the user is selecting a date in. After the user selects either date out or date in, miDateSelect is reversed. (*True* becomes *False* and vice versa.)

All of the code in each Case section is pretty traditional. Notice how the colors of several controls are changed at the end of each Case section.

hsbMonth_Change event procedure
The hsbMonth control is a horizontal scrollbar that is used to change the month in our calendar display on the Trip tab. No magic here, except there is some good code for changing the display of a month incrementally. Notice the checks in the code to determine whether the month number has rolled forward (*giCurrentMonth = 13*) or backward (*giCurrentMonth = 0*). Also of interest is the execution of the *DoCalender* method at the end of this method. The control to use and the date built in this method are passed to *DoCalender*, which actually creates the calendar display.

lboClass_Click event procedure
This event procedure is triggered when a user chooses a vehicle class (for example, "Economy") from the first Combo control (lboClass) in the Vehicle

selection boxes. In the Rental History grid (grdCarHistory) of the Vehicle tab, the user can instantly see the types of cars a customer has rented before.

Once the user chooses a class, this method retrieves the rates for the class (GetRateList).

```
Me.MousePointer = HOURGLASS
glClassID = lboClass.ItemData(lboClass.ListIndex)
Me.MousePointer = HOURGLASS
GetRateList glClassID, glRateType
Me.MousePointer = HOURGLASS
```

Then the available vehicles are retrieved (*GetAvailableVehicleList*).

The txtCarRate text box is set using the *Format$* function and the garRate property. The rtlRateValue property is a constant used as an index into the garRate array.

Why does this method reset the mouse pointer to HOURGLASS after every action? You can usually see the mouse pointer flash intermittently in applications like this one. Placing a statement to reset the MousePointer after each method is called might cure some mouse pointer idiosyncrasies, but it isn't necessary in well-designed methods.

tsMain_Click event procedure

This event procedure occurs when the user clicks a tab. The method calls the *VTabClick* method and passes it the current Index for the tab strip.

txtDrvLicense_Change event procedure

This event procedure changes the color of the Drivers tab whenever the user enters anything into the txtDrvLicense control. This is a good use of low-overhead graphics to keep the user informed about the status of an application.

```
If txtDrvLicense(Index) = "" Then
    SetDriverImage Index, TAB_NONE
Else
    SetDriverImage Index, TAB_WHITE
End If
```

txtLicense_Change event procedure

This event procedure fires when the user enters anything in the License box (txtLicense) on the Customer tab. If there is anything in the control, the Find button (cmdCustGet button) is enabled. We always name controls to reflect their captions, if possible.

frmCredit Form

This is the credit card processing form.

txtCredit_Change event procedure

This event procedure does some cute work, depending upon the length of the text in the txtCredit box. At certain points (4, 9, and 14) it enters a dash (-) character. When the user enters the last character (19), the number is complete and the *VerifyPayment* method of the goClerk object is executed.

The automatic insertion of dashes can be disconcerting to the user. If you enter them automatically, you should add code in the KeyPress event for the control to ignore any dashes by setting the keyascii parameter to 0.

frmProcess Form

The code in this form does nothing but simulate the occurrence of an action.

Start method

The *Start* method is executed from the frmMain form and is a handy way to initiate action in a form before or after it is displayed. This method basically performs actions usually placed in the *Form_Load* event procedure. The *Me.Move* statement aligns this form with frmMain, which is good practice as users will get accustomed to seeing the form in the same relative place each time the application runs.

```
Me.Move frmMain.Left + _
    (frmMain.Width - Me.Width) \ 2, _
    frmMain.Top + (frmMain.Height - Me.Height) \ 2
```

Next we initialize several values for the ProgressBar1 control and then display the form. Notice that we turn on the timer in this routine to initiate the simulation.

Timer1_Timer event procedure

The *Timer1_Timer* event procedure simulates the actual processing of a car rental application. It increments a message counter (iNextmsg) until all messages have been processed. Once all messages have been processed, it hides the current form and then executes the *ResetAll* method in frmMain.

frmSplash Form

This is the splash screen for the application. It is a straightforward implementation in the traditional manner of splash screens. (For a discussion of splash screens, see Chapter 8.)

CallBackClass Class

The functionality of this class is pretty neat. It operates a little differently than the callback example that ships with Visual Basic. The class must be initiated in the client application by using the following steps:

1. Create an instance of the CallBackClass in the *Initialize* method:

```
Set goCallBack = New CallBackClass
```

2. Pass the newly created reference to the *Connect* method of the Connection class:

```
ret% = goRental.Connect(goCallBack)
```

Once these two actions are complete, the Rental Connection object has the handle (goCallBack) to the CallBackClass. Whenever an object method in the Rental Objects class completes an action, the method can invoke the *CallBack* method of the CallBackClass class. It is important to remember that both the Rental Connection object and the Rental Objects object are out-of-process (EXE) servers. When your application passes the object reference to the CallBackClass class to the Rental Connection object's *Connect* method, the *Connect* method passes the reference to the Rental Objects object. This allows methods in the Rental Objects object to directly access the *CallBack* method.

When the *CallBack* method is executed, it is passed two parameters: lContext and lReturn. lContext indicates which method invoked *CallBack*. lReturn indicates the status of the calling method.

There are default context constants (rtlCBVerifyDriver and rtlCBVerifyPayment) and return constants (rtlCBReturnOK, rtlCBReturnNotFound, and rtlCBReturnTelcomERR) in the basRentalConstants module.

CallBack method

This method is executed by methods in the Rental Objects class when they complete an action. You can easily extend the functionality of the *CallBack* method to handle many different tasks that must be executed by a remote server when it completes a process.

Notice the use of the two contexts in the *Select Case* statement. The return values are tested within each *Case* section by an *If* statement.

```
Public Sub CallBack(lContext As Long, lReturn As Long)
    Dim x%

    Debug.Print "CallBack Context = ";  _
        LoadResString(lContext + rtlCBContextOffset + rtlLangOffset)
    Debug.Print "CallBack Return = ";  _
        LoadResString(lReturn + rtlCBReturnOffset + rtlLangOffset)
    Select Case lContext
        Case rtlCBVerifyDriver
            If lReturn = rtlCBReturnOK Then 'Green driver tab
                SetTabImage PIC_DRV, TAB_GREEN
```

(continued)

```
                    SetDriverImages
                Else
                    'Change the driver tab to red
                    'Maybe display the error in sReturn
                End If
            Case rtlCBVerifyPayment
                If lReturn = rtlCBReturnOK Then
                    SetTabImage PIC_PMT, TAB_GREEN
                Else
                    'Change the payment tab to red
                    'Maybe display and error message
                End If
        End Select
End Sub
```

Global Module

This module is the catch-all module for our property definitions.

All the mouse pointer and color constants could most likely be replaced by the built-in constants in Visual Basic. The *Global* statement should also be replaced by the *Public* statement to bring the code in line with the new Visual Basic conventions.

basClerk Module

The basClerk module is the master module for the Rental Clerk application. It contains the startup method *Main*. A number of other general-purpose methods are also included in this module.

Main method

In this method, notice the modifications to a couple of properties of the App object. The App object is a global, general-purpose object containing information about the current application. You can use the App object to change the application's title, to check to see if another instance is running, and more. In this application, we change two of its properties that affect the performance of OLE servers.

```
App.OleServerBusyTimeout = rtlOLEServerBusyDefault
App.OleRequestPendingTimeout = rtlOLERequestPendingDefault
```

Changing time-out values can determine whether your application runs or continuously bombs in a production environment.

The other actions that take place in *Main* are fairly straightforward. Notice the simple control of the splash screen (frmSplash).

Initialize method

This is the general startup routine called in *Main*. The *Initialize* method loads several general values (such as days of the week, months, and so on) and performs several other startup tasks. Here is also where we connect to the objects (Rental Connection, Rental Objects, and CallBackClass) that will perform all of our back-end processing. The connections are made in the *Set* statement near the end of this method.

```
Set goRental = New Connection
Set goCallBack = New CallBackClass
sCmd = Trim$(Command)
If Len(sCmd) > 0 Then
  ret% = goRental.Connect(goCallBack, sCmd)
Else
    ret% = goRental.Connect(goCallBack)
End If
Set goClerk = goRental.Clerk
```

One interesting thing this routine does is pick up any command line arguments and feed them to the *Connect* method of the Rental Connection object (goRental). The only legal command line argument this application accepts is a valid data source name. Passing it to the *Connect* method allows the application to validate it and skip the Data Source dialog box.

We use the *New* keyword in the *Set* lines because we are creating new instances of the objects, not setting references to existing instances of the objects. We did not use the *New* keyword when we declared the object variables in the Global module.

AddCustomer method

The *AddCustomer* method uses the *AddCustomer* method of the Rental Objects object to add the customer to the database. This occurs in the last line of the method. The rest of the code loads the garCustomer array with information from the form.

This simple routine illustrates the importance of using OLE objects because the entire work of updating the database is accomplished in one line: *goClerk.Add-Customer (garCustomer)*.

This line uses the *AddCustomer* method, which might be running locally or remotely on a server. The user does not know or care where that object is running. Now let's assume that you need a batch routine to load customers. Guess what? You can use *AddCustomer* for that also, as long as it is cleanly written and encapsulated, without any calls to other methods in other classes or back to the current application.

DoCalender method

The *DoCalender* method takes two parameters: the name of a grid control to use; and a variant containing the start date. This method builds the calendar in the grid control on the Trip tab. Before using this method for general purposes, add a parameter that will contain the name of the TextBox control to set, rather than setting the txtTripCalMonth control on frmMain directly.

GetAvailableVehicleList method

The *GetAvailableVehicleList* method retrieves a list of all vehicles that match the requested information. The list of vehicles is returned in the garVehicle array. The return value from *goClerk.GetAvailableVehicleList* is the number of vehicles in the list. A zero, of course, means there were no vehicles available that matched the request.

```
giVehicles = goClerk.GetAvailableVehicleList _
    (garVehicle, gsStartDate, gsEndDate, glClassID)
```

The *For* loop loads the vehicles in the lboCar Combo control. The ItemData property is also loaded into the Combo control with the vehicle ID (*garVehicle-(rtlAVehicleID, x%)*). ItemData is useful because it lets you assign your own number (such as a vehicle ID) to an item in a Combo or List control. Normally the value you assign to ItemData will be a key field. When you retrieve a clicked item from the list, you can use ItemData to retrieve the key field and directly load the corresponding record from the database.

GetClassList method

This method is almost identical to *GetAvailableVehicleList*, except that it returns a list of car classes.

```
giClasses = goClerk.GetClassList(garClass)
```

GetCustomerHistory method

This method is similar to the other *Get* methods. This time we retrieve the rental history for a customer. We pass the customer ID (custid) to the *GetCustomerHistory* method of the goClerk object, and the method returns the history for that customer in the garCustHist array.

```
giCustHists = goClerk.GetCustomerHistory (garCustHist, custid, 100)
```

A neat feature in this method is the use of a comment to show the column names for the grid. This is handy when using the *AddItem* method as you must pass the column values to the method in order, separated by a tab character (chr(9)).

After we retrieve the history, we clean out the current rows in the grid using the first *For* loop. Notice how the loop increments backward from the number of rows in the grid to 2. (It stops at 2 because row 0 is the grid header and row 1 is blank.)

Another quick way to reset a grid with less code is to reset the number of rows in the grid to 1 as in *frmMain!grdCarHistory.Rows = 1*. This just truncates the grid after the first row, which usually contains your header.

The second *For* loop loads the grid. After the grid is loaded, the code removes row number 1 (actually the second row) from the grid. This row was not removed in the first *For* loop.

GetCustomerList method

This method relies on the *GetCustomerList* method in the goClerk object to retrieve a list of customers that match the entry in the txtLicense control on frmMain. We could also call *GetCustomerList* and pass it either the first or last name or a combination of first, last, and license. This makes for a flexible retrieval method.

If the first *If* statement is successful, *GetCustomerList* returns a value greater than zero, indicating the number of customers returned. Then the second *If* checks to make sure the customer ID is greater than zero. If so, we load the form from the array.

```
If goClerk.GetCustomerList(garCustomer, frm.txtLicense.Text) > 0 Then
    If goClerk.GetCustomer(garCustomer, _
        garCustomer(rtlCustomerID, 0)) Then
```

GetDiscountList method

This method retrieves a list of discounts using the *GetDiscountList* method in the goClerk object. (By this time, you should be getting the idea that goClerk contains the retrieval engine for all the items we might want relating to the clerk function.)

```
giDiscounts = goClerk.GetDiscountList(garDiscount)
```

GetLocationList method

This method retrieves the trip locations using the *GetLocationList* method of the goClerk object.

```
giLocations = goClerk.GetLocationList(garLocation)
```

GetRateList method

This method retrieves the rates using the *GetRateList* method of the goClerk object.

```
giRates = goClerk.GetRateList(garRate, classid, ratetype)
```

GetSpecialList method

This method retrieves special information, such as any special rate, using the *GetSpecialList* method of the goClerk object.

```
giSpecials = goClerk.GetSpecialList(garSpecial)
```

SetTabImage and SetDriverImage methods

These methods change the image on various parts of frmMain.

SetDriverImages method

This method changes the colors on the Driver tab for each driver in the list. The image changes to reflect whether or not the driver is valid. Notice that whether a particular driver is flagged as good or bad depends on the length of the driver's license number. If the license has more than six characters, the license is good. (The real world usually requires a little more stringent verification process.)

RentalComplete method

This method checks the status of each tab by checking its image. If all are set to TAB_GREEN, the return value is *True*. Otherwise, the return value is *False*.

Rental Manager Application

The Rental Manager application allows you to retrieve lists of items from the database. It presents each list in the same format using a grid control. Figure 10-9 shows the Customers list, which you can display by selecting Customers from the View menu.

Figure 10-9. *The general interface of the Rental Manager application.*

Figure 10-10 shows tiled views for Customers, Vehicle Classes, Manager Specials, Rate Discounts, Rates, and Rentals. To show tiled views, choose Tile from the Window menu.

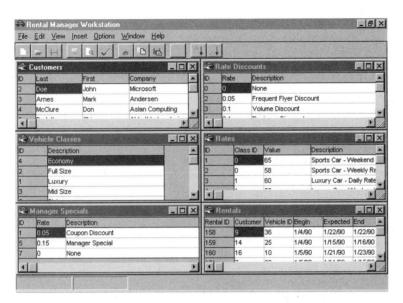

Figure 10-10. *The Rental Manager application with several views open.*

Most of the File, Edit, Insert, and Help menu options are not wired to perform any tasks in this sample application. The toolbar is also nonfunctional. They are included only for appearances.

The project file is Manager.vbp and is located in the Project – Manager directory.

frmMgr Form

This is an MDI form, which contains all the child forms when they are open.

MDIForm_Load event procedure

The *MDIForm_Load* event procedure performs lots of startup activities, such as redimensioning properties. Note that the third line creates eight instances of the View form in the View control array.

```
ReDim View(8)
```

This might be the first time you have run across a control array consisting of forms. If so, this application provides a practical example of how to use them.

The ViewInfo array contains information about each form, such as whether that form has been loaded or not. This is *very important* because trying to access a form in a control array that has not been loaded is not pretty.

```
ReDim ViewInfo(8)
```

The first *For* loop loads a control array of the menu object mnuViews.

```
For x% = 1 To 8
    Load mnuViews(x%)
Next x%
```

The balance of the method sets the Caption properties for the menus and the ViewInfo array, loads the mnuOptionsFontName control array, and loads the images for the toolbar from the ImageList control ImageList1.

mnuOptionsFontName_Click event procedure

We tried our best to leave this application in its original state, but, alas, we had to change something or we wouldn't be programmers! When we first used the Font command on the Options menu, it generated an error. The original code is commented out in the last line of this method (in the source file only).

With a little playing around, we got this to work. If the user changes a font, we loop through each form and check the Loaded property of the ViewInfo array. If the form is loaded, we change its font. Pretty simple.

```
Dim i As Integer
  For i = 0 To 8
    If ViewInfo(i).Loaded Then
      View(i)!grdMaint.Font.Name = mnuOptionsFontName(index).Caption
    End If
  Next i
```

mnuEditFind_Click and mnuEditFindNext_Click event procedures

Clicking Find on the Edit menu starts the search form (frmSearch). Clicking Find Next directly executes the *FindIt* method if the search string is filled in. Otherwise, it executes the *mnuEditFind_Click* method to initiate a new search.

mnuViews_Click event procedure

This event procedure opens a new View form when the user chooses the corresponding View menu option. The index value passed to the routine identifies the number of the menu option chosen. The *Select Case* statement uses the index to check the Loaded property of the ViewInfo array.

```
Select Case ViewInfo(index).Loaded
Case True
    View(index).Show
Case False
    Load View(index)
    View(index).Tag = index
    View(index).Caption = ViewInfo(index).Caption
    ViewInfo(index).Loaded = True
    FillView (index)
    View(index).Show
End Select
```

If the form is already loaded (Case True), we just show it. This will pop the form almost instantly. If the form is not loaded (Case False), we load it, set the appropriate values, fill the form with data using the *FillView* method, and show the form.

mnuWArrange_Click, mnuWCascade_Click, and *mnuWTile_Click* event procedures

■ On the Window menu, choosing the Arrange Icons command arranges the icons of the minimized views.

■ The Cascade command cascades the open View forms.

■ The Tile command tiles the open View forms horizontally.

Toolbar1_Click event procedure

This event procedure fires when the user clicks a tool on the toolbar. However don't forget that this code is disabled in this application. Remember, this is a demonstration application!

MgrCode Module

This is the code module for the application. Most of the core methods are contained here.

FillView method

This method loads the view indicated by the index value passed to the method when it is executed. Below are the first two Case options:

```
Select Case index
Case CUSTOMER
    GetCustomerList View(index).grdMaint
    View(index).Show
Case RENTAL
    GetRentalList View(index).grdMaint
    View(index).Show
```

This method works like pure magic. Each one of the methods used to retrieve a list is passed the handle to the Grid control: *View(index).grdMaint*. This allows the method to retrieve the information using the appropriate method in the OLE server (such as goClerk.GetCustomerList) and then directly update the grid. Once the grid is updated, *FillView* shows the form.

You can simplify this routine even more by deleting the line used to display the form. Why? Because we show it in mnuViews anyway!

FindIt method

This method searches the ActiveControl property on the frmMgr form for the search string. In its current form, it doesn't work. We suspect the problem is that the method searches the Text property of the Grid control. This doesn't work because the Text property of the Grid control only returns the current column and row value. To actually work on a Grid control, the method must loop through all the rows and columns, checking each one.

Get methods

The *Get* methods are all basically the same. The operation is as follows:

1. Retrieve the list of items from the goClerk object. (Remember these routines from the Rental Clerk application?)

2. Configure the Grid.

3. Load the Grid with data.

We will not go through the details for each method here, but we have included a list of the methods for completeness:

- *GetClassList*
- *GetCustomerList*
- *GetDiscountList*
- *GetRateList*
- *GetRentalList*
- *GetSpecialList*
- *GetVehicleList*

Initialize method

The *Initialize* method is the master setup method for the application as in the Rental Clerk application on page 261.

Main method

The *Main* method is the startup method. It fires the *Initialize* method and then creates the object references. It also executes the *Connect* method, passing it the CallBackClass reference.

```
Set goRental = New Connection
Set goCallBack = New CallBackClass
ret% = goRental.Connect(goCallBack)
Set goClerk = goRental.Clerk
Set goManager = goRental.Manager
```

Notice how the goClerk and goManager references are created. We are actually setting the reference through the Rental Connection object. Check out the Rental Connection class, and you will see a reference created to the Clerk and Manager objects. We are just setting a reference in Main to those references created in the other server. Notice the absence of the *New* keyword on the last two *Set* lines.

The last thing we do is load frmMgr and show it.

Global Module

This module is similar to the Global module (Clerk.glo) in the Rental Clerk application. The module contains the general declarations for the entire application.

Some of the declarations are exactly the same as those in the Rental Clerk application. In a real application, you would be far better off to move these common declarations to a common module, such as Rental Constants.

CallBackClass Class

The CallBackClass class is not used for functionality in the Rental Manager application, but it is included for completeness. Remember, when the application starts we must pass a reference to the *CallBack* method to the *Connect* method of the Connection class in the Rental Connection server. The asynchronous methods in the Rental Objects class use the *CallBack* method to let the calling application know when a task is completed.

Declarations

None.

CallBack method

This is a simple callback method, which checks the lContext parameter and verifies the driver or payment appropriately.

frmSearch Form

The methods in this search form are only used to set the options for the search. All of the functionality is in the *FindIt* method in the MgrCode module. Using a form to set options and placing all the action code in a global module or, even better, a class is a good programming practice and makes it easy to reuse your code.

cmdcancel_Click event procedure

This event procedure is supposed to cancel the search. Then why does it set the global search string (*gFindString*) and the case checking switch before it exits? To work correctly, the only thing this button should do is reset all values to their originals and unload the form.

frmMaint Form

The frmMaint form is used to create instances of our View forms.

Every View form is based on this form. When we declare the View control array in the Global module, we are declaring an instance of this form:

```
Global View() As New frmMaint
```

Each time we use the *Load* statement to create a new View form, the instance is created at that time.

Treating forms as objects in this manner opens up new possibilities for your application. You can now determine how many forms each user will need during the execution of the application. You can create forms on demand that are all replicas of the master form.

Form_QueryUnload event procedure

The *Form_QueryUnload* event procedure has some interesting code that looks like the beginning of a Save routine. This code checks the Dirty property of the ViewInfo array entry for a form to determine if the form has changed:

```
If ViewInfo(Me.Tag).Dirty Then
```

Your application needs to maintain the Dirty property, of course. This method stops short of actually saving the information to a file, but it does provide some ideas on how to implement this technology.

Form_Unload event procedure

This event procedure sets the Deleted property whenever a form is unloaded:

```
ViewInfo(Me.Tag).Deleted = True
```

This event procedure would be a nice place to encapsulate the following code:

```
ViewInfo(Me.Tag).Dirty = True
```

grdMaint_GotFocus **event procedure**

When the *grdMaint* grid gets the focus, this event procedure simply brings it to
the top of the visible forms in the application:

```
frmSearch.ZOrder 0
```

Using MDI Forms

The MDI form object supports the use of the *Arrange* method to automatically
arrange the children of the master MDI form. Below is the syntax for using the
method:

```
<MDIFormName>.Arrange <argument>
```

The following table shows the arguments for the method.

Visual Basic Constant	Value	Description
vbCascade	0	Cascades all child forms
VbTileHorizontal	1	Tiles all child forms horizontally
VbTileVertical	2	Tiles all child forms vertically
VbArrangeIcons	3	Arranges icons for minimized MDI child forms

The first three arguments (0 through 2) work on nonminimized child forms.
The last argument (3) works on minimized child forms.

You will notice in the Rental Car application that the old Visual Basic 3 syntax is
used. Constants are defined in the Global module for all MDI *Arrange* actions.
For instance, the TILE_HORIZONTAL constant equates to 1 just as the built-in
vbTileHorizontal constant does. You should use the built-in constants whenever possible.

Common Modules

There are several common modules in the Rental Car application that are used
by more than one subapplication. These modules provide consistency and
ease of maintenance for the entire application.

Rental Constants.bas   The Rental Car application contains one common module
named basRentalConstants, which includes some useful ideas. For instance,
check out the use of public constants to specify the location of a particular item
within a multidimensional array (for example, rtlAVehicleID).

Object Constants.bas Another constants module that is used by several applications is basObjectConstants.

RentLib.res This is the resource file used by the Rental Car application. You can build a resource file using tools that come with C++ compilers, including Microsoft Visual C++ and Borland C++. VBAssist from Sheridan Software can also be used to create resource files. This is a more convenient and less costly alternative for those who do not already own a C++ compiler. It is also worth noting that 32-bit Windows resource files are structurally different from 16-bit resource files, so make sure you use the right tool for the environment in which you design.

Rental Connection Application

The Rental Connection Application is used by the other subapplications to provide a single point of connection to the database and to provide many of the database-related methods. This module uses some neat tricks to provide the user with a list of ODBC data sources from which to choose. The module can also create a data source on the fly if necessary.

frmDSN Form

This form displays a list of valid data sources from the system running the Rental Connection server. The user must select a valid data source to use from the list.

Check out the use of the resource file in this form. The action takes place in the Form_Load event where the resource strings are used to set the form's title and various label captions.

Connection Class

This class includes the *Connect* method, which is used to make the connection to the database. The *Class_Initialize* and *Class_Terminate* event procedures are also used in this class.

Class_Initialize event procedure
This event procedure sets new instances of the Clerk and Manager objects. The instances are not actually created until the objects are referenced the first time.

Class_Terminate event procedure
This event procedure fires the *Disconnect* method to close everything before exiting.

Connect method
The *Connect* method makes the connection to the database. The method accepts several parameters:

- The first parameter (ocb) is the object reference to the CallBack object in the client application.

- The second parameter is optional and should contain a valid data source name.

- The third and fourth parameters are also optional and can contain a user name and password.

If only the required parameter is passed to the method, it will display the frmDSN form to allow the user to select a data source. It is interesting to note that the data sources presented to the user are running on the same system as the Rental Connection object, which might be on a remote system.

A valid list of data sources is retrieved with the following statement:

```
icount = Clerk.GetDataSourceList(grecDSN)
```

The *GetDataSourceList* method returns the number of data sources found and places the data source names in grecDSN.

Disconnect method
This method executes the *Disconnect* method on both the Clerk and Manager objects and then sets the object references to *Nothing*.

Module basRtlCMain

This module contains two methods for testing various parts of the server applications.

Rental Objects Application

The Rental Objects application contains most of the business rules for the Rental Car demo application. Rental Objects provides a good example of how to isolate the business rules from other parts of the application and to create reusable business objects.

frmObjectWatch Form

This form displays the status of the server as various actions take place. Displaying information like this on a remote server might not always be a good idea. It is helpful sometimes to have an updated status display, but it can also slow down the application. What happens if someone closes the application while a client is connected?

frmStatus1 and frmStatus2 Forms

These two forms display the status of an action. The action is actually simulated in the timer on either form. The use of the CallBackClass object is of interest.

The line in the *Timer1_Timer* event procedure in the frmStatus1 form executes the *CallBack* method in the client application:

```
basRentalServerMain.goCB.CallBack _
    CLng(rtlCBVerifyDriver), CLng(rtlCBReturnOK)
```

What is going on here? The goCB property of basRentalServerMain is set to the object reference for the CallBackClass (objCB) in the *Connect* method for either the Clerk or Manager class. Remember when we passed the reference to the CallBackClass to the *Connect* method of the Connection object in the Clerk application? The *Connect* method then cranked up the *Clerk.Connect* method and passed along the object reference as well as the data source, user name, and password.

Now that we have a reference to the CallBackClass object, we can execute its methods directly. Awesome.

Clerk Class

We will go into more detail in the Clerk and Manager classes. There are lots of database-related and OLE automation hooks in both of these classes that are worth exploring.

The Clerk class contains the functions required by the Rental Clerk application.

All the methods that start with *Get* return a list to the calling program. The list is returned in an array the calling method can use to manipulate the individual items.

Declarations

Here we declare the required RDO environment and connection objects. We also declare the ocb object to hold the reference to the CallBackClass in the client application.

```
Dim env As rdoEnvironment      'Global environment (workspace)
Dim cn As rdoConnection        'Global connection (db)
Dim ocb As Object
```

Class_Initialize event procedure

This event procedure creates a reference (env) to the RDO environment. It also displays the frmObjectWatch form and loads the two status forms (frmStatus1 and frmStatus2).

```
Private Sub Class_Initialize()
    Set env = rdoEnvironments(0)
    frmObjectWatch.Show
    WatchObject rtlObjClerk, rtlObjMsgInit
    Load frmStatus1
    Load frmStatus2
End Sub
```

Class_Terminate **event procedure**

This event procedure disconnects and cleans up.

```
Private Sub Class_Terminate()
    If bConnected Then Disconnect
End Sub
```

Connect **method**

The *Connect* method connects to the database using the sDSN and other parameters. The CallBack references are also created here.

```
Public Function Connect( _
    objCB As Object, _
    sDSN As String, _
    sUserID As String, _
    sPassword As String _
    ) As Boolean
    Dim sConnect As String
    Dim sDriver As String
    On Error GoTo ConnectError
    WatchMethod rtlMetConn
    'Build the DSN string from the parameters
    sConnect = ConcatDSN(sDSN, sUserID, sPassword)
    Set cn = env.OpenConnection("", rdDriverNoPrompt, _
        False, sConnect)
    Set ocb = objCB
    Set basRentalServerMain.goCB = objCB
    sDriver = GetODBCDriver(sDSN)
    SetODBCDriver sDriver
    Connect = True
    bConnected = True
    WatchObject rtlObjClerk, rtlObjMsgConnected
    Exit Function
ConnectError:
    On Error GoTo 0
    Select Case rdoErrors.Item(rdoErrors.Count - 1).Number
        Case 0
            'Assume ODBC error
            'Create the default data source and connect to that
            CreateDefaultDS sDSN
            sConnect = ConcatDSN(sDSN, sUserID, sPassword)
            Resume
        Case 40005
            'Invalid connection string (Error 40005)
            Debug.Print "Invalid connection string (Error 40005)"
            Debug.Print "sConnect = "; sConnect
```

(continued)

```
      Case 40054
          'Invalid parameter
          Debug.Print "Invalid parameter (Error 40054)"
          Debug.Print "sConnect = "; sConnect
    End Select
    WatchMethod rtlMetConn, rtlMetMsgError
    WatchObject rtlObjClerk, rtlObjMsgError
    Connect = False
    bConnected = False
End Function
```

Disconnect method

This is the *Disconnect* method that shuts down everything. Notice the *For* loop that runs the *Close* method on all open RDO connections. It's a nice trick to borrow for your own applications.

```
For i = env.rdoConnections.Count - 1 To 0 Step -1
    env.rdoConnections(i).Close
Next i
'Close the environment
env.Close
```

The *CallBack* method must be completed before the *Disconnect* method executes because the reference to the CallBackClass is destroyed near the end of the *Disconnect* method.

```
Set ocb = Nothing
Set basRentalServerMain.goCB = Nothing
```

GetDataSourceList method

Here is a good candidate for placement in CSUtilities. This method retrieves a list of the current data sources on a system.

The ODBC function *SQLDataSources* is used to retrieve the data sources. The list is placed in the Record parameter that is passed to the method.

```
If SQLAllocEnv(lHenv) <> -1 Then
    sDataSource = String(32, 32)
    sDescription = String(255, 32)
    'get the first DSN
    bDefaultDSN = False
    sDefaultDSN = LoadResString(rtlDefaultDSN + rtlLangOffset) _
        & Chr(0)
    sDefaultDSN = sDefaultDSN & Space$(32 - Len(sDefaultDSN))
    nRet = SQLDataSources(lHenv, 2, sDataSource, Len(sDataSource), _
        nDataSourceLen, sDescription, Len(sDescription), _
        nDescriptionLen)
```

```
Do While nRet = 0 Or nRet = 1
    Record(rtlDSName, icount) = sDataSource
    Record(rtlDSDescription, icount) = sDescription
    If Not bDefaultDSN And sDefaultDSN = sDataSource Then _
        bDefaultDSN = True
    sDataSource = String(32, 32)
    sDescription = String(255, 32)
    'get the next DSN
    nRet = SQLDataSources(lHenv, 1, sDataSource, _
        Len(sDataSource), nDataSourceLen, sDescription, _
        Len(sDescription), nDescriptionLen)
    icount = icount + 1
    ReDim Preserve Record(rtlDSLastField, icount)
Loop
```

CreateDefaultDS method

This is another useful method that creates a data source entry. The following lines build the data source definition string:

```
sDSOptions = "DBQ=" & App.Path & "\" _
    & LoadResString(rtlDefaultMDB + rtlLangOffset)
sDSOptions = sDSOptions & Chr(13) & "DefaultDir=" & App.Path
sDSDriver = LoadResString(rtlMDBDriver + rtlLangOffset)
```

The following line registers the data source:

```
rdoRegisterDataSource sDSName, sDSDriver, True, sDSOptions
```

ConcatDSN method

The *ConcatDSN* method builds the DSN string and returns it.

GetODBCDriver method

The *GetODBCDriver* method checks to see if the data source name (dsn) passed to the method exists on the current system. Notice that it uses the *GetDataSourceList* method from this class to retrieve the list of valid data source names.

```
GetDataSourceList dsnlist
```

Once we have the list, we can loop through it and check our data source name (dsn) against all the items in the list.

```
iubound = UBound(dsnlist, rtlDSName + 1)
For i = 0 To iubound
    If dsnlist(rtlDSName, i) = dsn Then
        GetODBCDriver = dsnlist(rtlDSDescription, i)
        Exit For
    End If
Next i
```

SetODBCDriver method

This method sets the ODBC driver options based on the driver used, either Access or SQL Server. Notice how it sets the global properties to handle the different wildcard characters for each driver.

Get methods

The *Get* methods in this class are all functionally similar. Each one retrieves a result set from the database and then returns it in an array passed to the method as a parameter. The number of items returned is set as the return value from each method.

The *GetCountryList* method is a good example of a method that retrieves a simple list. Other methods that return simple lists are *GetDiscountList, GetSpecialList, GetLocationList,* and *GetClassList.*

The *GetCountryList* method illustrates a new way to accomplish loading an array with data. First, we load the array (Record) with all the rows from the result set in one statement using the *GetRows* method against the result set (rs). *GetRows* returns multiple rows at once. You specify the number of rows to return as a parameter. The rows are placed into a two-dimensional array. In our example, the Record parameter is a variant that becomes an array when it is filled by *GetRows.* The next line uses the *Ubound* function to determine the number of rows in Record. We add 1 to the total because the array is zero-based.

Notice how the *If* statement just before these two lines checks both the EOF and BOF properties of the result set. This allows us to determine if any valid rows will be returned before we execute *GetRows.*

```
Public Function GetCountryList(Record As Variant) As Integer
    Dim icount As Integer
    Dim rs As rdoResultset
    WatchMethod rtlMetGetCountryL
    Set rs = cn.OpenResultset _
        ("Select CountryName from Country order by CountryName")
    'Set rs = cn.OpenResultset("{call spGetCountryList}")
    If Not rs.EOF And Not rs.BOF Then
        Record = rs.GetRows(rtlGetRowsMax)
        icount = UBound(Record, 2) + 1
    Else
        icount = 0
    End If
    rs.Close
    GetCountryList = icount
End Function
```

The other *Get* methods also return lists but take other parameters to select the items returned. For instance, in the next snippet of code from the *GetCustomer* method, we can see it takes a customer ID as an optional parameter. If the customer ID is present, the method will return only that customer. If the customer ID is not present, the method will return all customers but load only the first customer found. The return value of this method is also a Boolean value to indicate success or failure.

```
Public Function GetCustomer( _
    ByRef Record As Variant, _
    Optional ByVal CustomerID _
    ) As Boolean
```

Later in the method, we can check for the existence of the customer ID by using the *IsMissing* function and then build the *Where* statement appropriately:

```
If IsMissing(CustomerID) Then
    swhere = ""
Else
    swhere = " and CustomerID = " & Str$(CustomerID)
End If
```

The *GetCustomerList* method is a general-purpose routine to return a list of customers. The result set is based on the optional parameters passed to the method when it is executed.

```
Public Function GetCustomerList( _
    ByRef Record As Variant, _
    Optional ByVal DriversLicence As Variant, _
    Optional ByVal FirstName As Variant, _
    Optional ByVal LastName As Variant _
    ) As Long
```

Other than having more optional parameters to deal with, the method above is similar to the other *Get* methods.

UpdateCustomer method

This method updates a customer record and provides a good illustration of how to use the SQL *Update* command to update a result set.

First, we start a transaction on our connection, and then the sUpdate property is loaded with the entire SQL statement.

```
cn.BeginTrans
sUpdate = "Update Customer set FirstName='" & _
    Record(rtlCustomerFName, 0) & "'," & _
    "LastName='" & Record(rtlCustomerLName, 0) & _
```

(continued)

```
"',DriversLicense='" & Record(rtlCustomerDLicense, 0) & "'," & _
"AddressLinel='" & Record(rtlCustomerAdd1, 0) & _
"',AddressLine2='" & Record(rtlCustomerAdd2, 0) & "'," & _
"City='" & Record(rtlCustomerCity, 0) & "',Region='" & _
Record(rtlCustomerRegion, 0) & "'," & _
"Country='" & Record(rtlCustomerCountry, 0) & "',PostalCode='" _
& Record(rtlCustomerPCode, 0) & "'," & _
"Phone='" & Record(rtlCustomerPhone, 0) & "',CompanyName='" & _
Record(rtlCustomerCName, 0) & "'," & _
"DiscountID=" & Record(rtlCustomerDiscountID, 0) & _
" Where CustomerID = " & Record(rtlCustomerID, 0)
```

Then we execute the SQL statement with the *Execute* method.

```
cn.Execute sUpdate
```

The rest of the method closes the transaction. If the RowsAffected property returns *1*, we can commit the transaction. If RowsAffected does not return *1*, we roll back the transaction.

```
If cn.RowsAffected = 1 Then
    bReturn = True
    cn.CommitTrans
Else
    bReturn = False
    cn.RollbackTrans
End If
```

We also do a rollback if we hit the error handler.

AddCustomer method

This method adds a new customer record to the database, providing a good example of how to use the SQL *Insert* method to insert rows into a result set. Executing SQL commands directly is the fastest way to do something almost every time, but you have less control.

The main difference between this method and *UpdateCustomer* is that *AddCustomer* uses the SQL statement as a parameter to the *Execute* method, instead of using a property such as sUpdate. Notice the structural difference between the *Insert* statement and the *Update* statement.

```
cn.Execute "insert into customer (" & _
    "FirstName, LastName, DriversLicense, AddressLinel, _
    AddressLine2, " & _
    "City, Region, Country, PostalCode, Phone, CompanyName, _
    DiscountID) " & _
    "values ('" & Record(rtlCustomerFName, 0) & "', '" & _
    Record(rtlCustomerLName, 0) & "', '" & _
    Record(rtlCustomerDLicense, 0) & "', '" & _
```

```
Record(rtlCustomerAdd1, 0) & "', '" & _
Record(rtlCustomerAdd2, 0) & "', '" & _
Record(rtlCustomerCity, 0) & "', '" & _
Record(rtlCustomerRegion, 0) & "', '" & _
Record(rtlCustomerCountry, 0) & "', '" & _
Record(rtlCustomerPCode, 0) & "', '" & _
Record(rtlCustomerPhone, 0) & "', '" & _
Record(rtlCustomerCName, 0) & "', '" & _
Record(rtlCustomerDiscountID, 0) & ")"
```

Default methods

There are two general-purpose methods for setting default values in variants to use to hold records. The *DefaultCustomer* method initializes a variant as a customer array if the variant is empty. The *DefaultRental* method initializes a variant as a rental array if the variant is empty.

AddRental method

The *AddRental* method takes a different approach to adding a record from using the SQL *Insert* statement. This method opens the Rental table and adds a new record to the table for the current customer, which was passed to the method. The method also returns the RentalID from the new record in the record passed in.

This time, we create a result set from the Rental table. The *Select* statement below returns all the rows in a Keyset cursor. It would be better to either restrict the number of rows with a *Where* clause or use a prepared statement and set the MaxRows property to *1*.

```
cn.BeginTrans
Set rs = cn.OpenResultset("select * from rental", _
    rdOpenKeyset, rdConcurLock)
```

After we have the result set, we use the *AddNew* method to create a new record. After we set the CustomerID property to the current customer ID field from our incoming parameter, we can use the *Update* method to update the database.

```
With rs
    .AddNew
    !CustomerID = Record(rtlRentalCustomerID, 0)
    .Update
End With
```

After updating the database, we use the Bookmark property to set the current record to the one we just created. The LastModified property returns a bookmark to the record we created.

```
rs.Bookmark = rs.LastModified
```

Next we commit the transaction.

```
cn.CommitTrans
```

The next line in this code sample retrieves the RentalID from the new record and places it in the incoming parameter.

```
Record(rtlRentalID, 0) = rs("RentalID")
```

This approach is different from using the SQL *Insert* statement. It is useful in this example, where we want to add a new record and then retrieve a value from the record.

UpdateRental method

This method is similar to the *AddRental* method, except that it looks up a record by the RentalID column and performs an update.

The *Edit* method places the current record into update mode, so we can modify the record. The *Update* method at the end of the sequence updates the database.

```
If Not rs.BOF And Not rs.EOF Then
    With rs
        .Edit
        !CustomerID = Record(rtlRentalCustomerID, 0)
        !VehicleID = Record(rtlRentalVehicleID, 0)
        !RentalBegin = Record(rtlRentalBegin, 0)
        !ExpectedEnd = Record(rtlRentalExpected, 0)
        !RentalEnd = Record(rtlRentalEnd, 0)
        !Rate = Record(rtlRentalRate, 0)
        !Discount = Record(rtlRentalDiscount, 0)
        !Total = Record(rtlRentalTotal, 0)
        !Damage = Record(rtlRentaldamage, 0)
        .Update
    End With
    cn.CommitTrans
    UpdateRental = True
Else
    cn.RollbackTrans
    UpdateRental = False
End If
```

Manager Class

The Manager class is similar to the Clerk class in the techniques it uses. It uses *Connect* and *Disconnect* methods to perform the same functions as the methods with the same names in the Clerk class. The *Get* functions also work in the same manner, except that most of them are not as complicated as those in the Clerk class.

RemoveRental method

The *RemoveRental* method deletes a particular row from the Rental table. The row is identified by the RentalID parameter. Notice that we use the SQL *Delete* statement to perform this action.

```
Public Sub RemoveRental(ByVal RentalID As Long)
    WatchMethod rtlMetRemoveRental
    cn.Execute "Delete * from Rental where RentalID = " & _
        Str$(RentalID)
End Sub
```

AddRate method

The *AddRate* method has one interesting twist. The next line is used to determine if the result set can be updated:

```
If rs.Updatable Then
```

The Updatable property returns *True* if the record set can be updated or *False* if it cannot.

basRentalServerMain Module

Main method

This method is the startup method for the executable. It does not really do much, unless the TEST constant is *True*. TEST is a conditional compilation constant and is used only when the application compiles. If TEST is *True*, the included code causes a beep and executes the *TestClerk* method to test the functionality of the application.

```
#If TEST Then
    Beep
    TestClerk
#End If
```

11

Management of Databases and Applications

This chapter discusses a number of tips that should help you in the management of your client/server applications and databases. It is not an in-depth manual on Microsoft SQL Server, Microsoft Windows NT, or other tools but an overview of techniques that we have found useful.

This chapter discusses the following topics:

- Installing applications
- Managing databases at a high level
- Using SQL-DMO to manage SQL Server
- Handling database transaction log problems and related issues
- Dealing with transaction time-out errors
- Using the Jet database engine and how it can impact local disk space
- Monitoring SQL Server performance
- Using custom utilities for migrating legacy applications to client/server systems
- Trapping errors in client applications
- Understanding what some Visual Basic error codes really mean and how to look them up
- Using conditional compilation
- Using help files to reduce support calls

Installing Applications

Where do you install your nifty client/server applications? You can place the executable and support files (EXEs, DLLs, OCXs, and so forth) in a directory on the server, or you can place these files on the client's hard disk. Both approaches have advantages. Placing the files on the server makes updating them somewhat easier but can have a negative impact on performance. Placing them on the client will improve performance but might make managing them much more difficult.

The best approach for the 1990s is to place the files on the client and use a network management package, such as System Management Server, to manage them. The new application properties available in Microsoft Visual Basic when you create an EXE or a DLL also help. (Choose the Make EXE File or Make OLE DLL File command from the File menu, and then click Options.) To make management easier, these properties are retrievable by several methods. For instance, you can now embed version and other information in the files.

You must also face the issue of how to install your software. You can use a number of the listed options below:

- Third-party products (for example, Install Shield, Echelon, and so on)
- Visual Basic Setup Wizard
- Custom Visual Basic setup programs
- Custom setups in other languages
- Manual installation or BAT files
- Any or all of the above with a tool such as System Management Server

Whichever strategy you choose should be usable by your network management system, and it should be easily managed and reconfigured.

Database Management Tips

A number of tasks must be performed on your system to make sure it runs successfully all the time. Your users will not take kindly to the system going down at frequent intervals or to losing some of their valuable data. The following list contains several items that you should learn well.

- DBCC (database consistency checking)
- Backup chores
- Device management
- Database management

- Transaction log management

- Transact-SQL

SQL Enterprise Manager, ISQL/w, and other SQL Server tools will prove invaluable to you. The next section shows you a simple example (did we say simple?) of how to use the SQL-DMO (Distributed Management Objects) to automate many typical management tasks.

Using SQL-DMO to manage SQL Server

Client/server databases typically offer powerful features not found in desktop databases such as Microsoft Access, FoxPro, Paradox, or dBASE. These features provide not only powerful capabilities for use in developing applications but also facilitate management automation.

Some features, such as cursors, are performance related, while others, such as MAPI, add new functionality to applications. Many features turn out to be designed for one thing but can be used for something else. For instance, you can use MAPI to mail-enable an application, but MAPI is also useful as a transport for queries and results to and from remote systems.

In this section we introduce some of the features you are likely to use in managing a remote database. The optimal use of features is actually critical to the success of your applications. For example, cursors are important because they provide functionality and maximize performance. Using cursors in previous versions of Visual Basic was difficult at best, but with Visual Basic 4 you might be using cursors and not even know it. This implicit use of cursors might not be optimal for your particular application. Of course, explicit use of cursors isn't as simple as using them implicitly, but it is now far easier than before.

SQL-DMO, on the other hand, is a useful tool for managing your database. SQL-DMO allows you to quickly build lots of tools to automate many tasks that you are currently performing manually or by using Transact-SQL. SQL-DMO can be called from Visual Basic or any application, such as Excel, that can use OLE automation servers. This section shows you how to use SQL-DMO to add some effective database management tools to your applications.

Fundamentals of SQL-DMO SQL-DMO objects provide a 32-bit interface into the heart of SQL Server that every Visual Basic programmer can use. The utilities provided with SQL Server, including SQL Enterprise Manager, are based on these objects. In fact, SQL Server exposes every function available via this interface, which means that anything you can do with SQL Enterprise Manager, you can do programmatically using SQL-DMO.

In order to use SQL-DMO you must include the SQL-DMO type library in your Visual Basic project. To do so, choose References from the Visual Basic Tools menu and select Microsoft SQLOLE Object Library. If this entry doesn't appear in the list, click the Browse button and select SQLOLE32.TLB from the SQL60\DLL directory. (This directory is on the server where you installed SQL Server.)

Some of the supporting files for programming SQL-DMO via Visual Basic are as follows:

- SQLOLE32.TLB—the type library
- SQLOLE32.DLL—the in-process server
- SQLOLE.REG—the SQL-DMO Registry file
- SQLOLE.HLP—the help file for SQL-DMO

Some useful documentation on the functionality of SQL-DMO is contained in the help file. All of these files are located in the SQL60\DLL directory (assuming a default installation of SQL Server).

Of course, programming OLE automation objects is easy because of their object models, and SQL-DMO is no exception. Figure 11-1 shows the SQL-DMO object model. If you will be developing applications around this model, make sure you keep a copy handy. SQL Server is a powerful and complex product. As a result, the object model is extensive, especially when all the properties and methods are taken into account.

Handling errors Error handling can be particularly problematic with SQL-DMO. For example, if you use an error handler and an error occurs, execution branches to the error handler. In an effort to correct a problem, you want to execute another SQL-DMO method or alter a SQL-DMO property within the handler. However, doing either of these precludes the ability to handle errors arising from execution while in the handler.

The simplest way around this dilemma is to do error checking in line. When a SQL-DMO operation fails, it sets the Err object's Number property. By checking this property immediately after each call, you can determine whether the call was successful and, if not, what went wrong. To enable inline error handling, place the following statement at the beginning of each procedure in which you want to implement it:

```
On Error Resume Next
```

This version of the *On Error* statement instructs Visual Basic to ignore all errors in the procedure and continue execution with the next line. Since you have error-handling code in the next line, all is well, if you handle all possible errors. We strongly recommend using the *Select Case* structure with an obligatory *Case Else* clause for inline error handling. This way, even if you miss a specific error number in your *Select Case*, the *Case Else* will catch anything you missed.

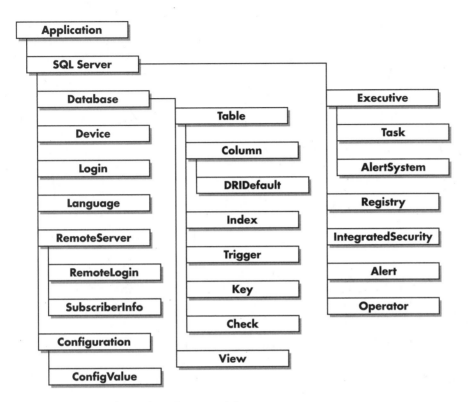

Figure 11-1. *The SQL-DMO object model.*

Errors can come from one of three sources when dealing with SQL-DMO:

- sysmessages table
- DB-Library
- SQL-DMO

SQL-DMO errors are most frequently encountered and, fortunately, have error constants that make tracking them much easier. Using these constants instead of hard-coding error numbers will also make your code infinitely more readable. Error constants are contained in the Microsoft SQLOLE Object Library and can be found by selecting SQLOLE_ERROR_TYPE from the Object Browser.

SQL-DMO error numbers are grouped by category. With about 10 categories, it is a simple process to determine to which category a returned error belongs. Just use the *And* operator between the SQL-DMO error number and the SQLOLE_ECAT_MASK constant. The result, best determined through a Select Case structure, will be equal in value to one of the categories.

You should note that SQL-DMO runtime errors are fatal, so if you don't handle them Visual Basic will—by terminating the application. For more information on error handling when using SQL-DMO, refer to the SQL-DMO help file named Sqlole.hlp and search for *Error Handling*. You can find this file in the Sql60\Dll directory.

Declaring SQL-DMO objects Visual Basic 4 supports early binding (or vtable binding) of OLE objects. This is what enables the use of the *New* keyword when declaring an instance of an object. Using the *New* keyword is faster than the alternative generic declaration of an Object or use of the *CreateObject* function. To take advantage of this additional speed boost, simply declare your object instances using the *New* keyword as in `Dim OMySQLServer As New SQLOLE.SQLServer`.

Connecting to a SQL Server Before you can use SQL-DMO, you must connect to a SQL Server in your application. You need three pieces of information to connect to a SQL Server: the server's name, a login ID, and a password. Certain methods and properties, such as those associated with replication and task management, are available only to a user with Administrative privileges. Make sure the login ID provided is sufficient for the tasks to be performed.

After connecting successfully (the specified SQL Server exists and is running and both the ID and password are verified), the SQLServer object and all of its sibling objects are valid and available for use.

It is possible to execute methods that disconnect the SQLServer object from the server (for example, the *Disconnect* method of the SQLServer object). If you execute one of these methods, you will have to reconnect to SQL Server before you can use the SQLServer object again.

Working with collections SQL-DMO makes considerable use of collections, and it is through these collections that much of the useful work can be done. A database, a table, a field, or an index is added using the appropriate collection.

To add an object, create a new instance of that object and set any properties you want to have specific values. Next, use the *Add* method to add the object to the appropriate collection using the following syntax:

```
ObjectCollection.Add NewObject
```

Deleting an object from a collection is even simpler—just use the *Remove* method and specify the object's name or its ordinal (the position the object occupies within the collection). If you opt to use the ordinal, note that collections are 1-based so numbering begins with 1, not 0. Use one of the following formats:

```
ObjectCollection.Remove ObjectName
ObjectCollection.Remove ObjectOrdinal
```

If you prefer, you can remove the object directly:

```
Object.Remove
```

As with other Visual Basic collections, SQL-DMO collections permit the use of the *For Each...Next* structure, which facilitates easy iteration through a collection, as shown in the following code:

```
For Each ODatabase in OMySQLServer.Database
  lstInfo.AddItem ODatabase.Name
Next ODatabase
```

Updating cached information The information for the SQL-DMO hierarchy is kept in a local cache on the client system and can become out-of-date if another user (or stored procedure) alters it. For this reason, the *Refresh* method exists to update the local information.

When you look up the *Refresh* method for a SQL-DMO collection, you will find that unlike most other Visual Basic *Refresh* methods it accepts a Boolean parameter. (You can find this information in *Programming SQL-DMO* in the Microsoft SQL Server Programmer's Toolkit.) If True, this parameter instructs Visual Basic to reinitialize the entire hierarchy. After a *Refresh*, any references to underlying objects are invalid. The upside is that the hierarchy will be up-to-date. If False, Visual Basic releases only objects in the hierarchy that have been dropped (and would therefore be unusable anyway). It refreshes the SQLServer object but not underlying objects in the hierarchy. In other words, any object references to underlying objects remain valid (providing the object has not been dropped), but they might not be up-to-date.

Cleaning up When you are finished with a SQLServer object, you should release the memory associated with it by setting the object variable equal to *Nothing*:

```
Set OMySQLServer = Nothing
```

In the resource-scarce world of Windows, releasing everything you no longer need is a good practice.

Sample Program: Using SQL-DMO

You can find the SqlDmo application in the SqlDmoManager directory on the companion CD. This application emulates the behavior of the SQL Service Manager application provided with SQL Server, as shown in Figure 11-2 on the next page, and shows how to programmatically control SQL Server using SQL-DMO. (See Figure 11-3 on the next page.)

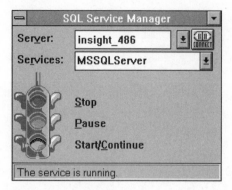

Figure 11-2. *The SQL Service Manager application provided with SQL Server.*

Figure 11-3. *Our emulation of the SQL Service Manager using SQL-DMO.*

To build or run this application (which you must run on the server where you installed SQL Server), you must make sure that the project contains a valid reference to the Microsoft SQLOLE Object Library, as described in "Fundamentals of SQL-DMO" on page 297.

Module1 Module

This module contains global declarations.

Declarations

The second line in the code below instructs Visual Basic to use early binding (the fastest possible method) to create an instance of the SQLOLE object. The object is declared globally so that it can be used throughout the application.

```
Option Explicit
Global OMySQLServer As New SQLOLE.SQLServer
Global DefDir As String

Global Const None As Integer = 0
Global Const Stopped As Integer = 3
Global Const Paused As Integer = 2
Global Const Running As Integer = 1
Global Const Starting As Integer = 4
Global Const Stopping As Integer = 5
Global Const Color As Integer = 1
Global Const Gray As Integer = 2
Global Const Depressed As Integer = 3
```

Form1 Form

Form1 is the application's startup form. It contains all the code except for the global declarations in Module1.

cmdConnect_Click event procedure

After specifying a server name and SQL Server login ID and password, the user clicks the Connect command button to establish a connection to SQL Server. This procedure uses the information entered to request a SQL Server connection.

```
Private Sub cmdConnect_Click()

' Inform Visual Basic that error handling will be done in-line.
' Without in-line or another form of error handling, an error
' causes the application to terminate because all
' SQLOLE errors are fatal.
  On Error Resume Next

  cmdConnect.Enabled = False
  MousePointer = vbHourglass
  Dim sServerName As String
  Dim sLogin As String
  Dim sPassword As String
  lblStatus = "Attempting to connect to SQL Server..."
  lblStatus.Refresh
  sServerName = txtServer
  sLogin = txtLogin
  sPassword = txtPassword

' Connect to the server.
  OMySQLServer.Connect ServerName:=sServerName, _
    Login:=sLogin, Password:=sPassword
```

(continued)

```
    If Err <> 0 Then
      Select Case Err

' The server is already running, so
' we can ignore the error and proceed.
        Case -2147211500

' The user ID or the password is invalid.
        Case -2147217502
          MsgBox "Login Failed"
          cmdConnect.Enabled = True
          Exit Sub

' We got some other error.
        Case Else
          MsgBox "Unknown Error"
          Exit Sub

      End Select
    End If

' After successfully connecting, it is safe to fire
' the timer without fear of generating errors.
    Timer1.Enabled = True
    MousePointer = vbDefault

End Sub
```

Combo2_Change event procedure

The following event procedure updates the status every time the Combo control data changes.

```
Private Sub Combo2_Change()
  UpdateStatus
End Sub
```

Form_Load event procedure

The *Form_Load* event procedure sets the default directory property (DefDir) and loads the Combo control.

```
Private Sub Form_Load()

  DefDir = App.Path

' If the application is started from the root,
' we don't append a "\" to App.Path.
  If Right(DefDir, 1) <> "\" Then
    DefDir = DefDir & "\"
  End If
```

```
   Combo2.AddItem "SQLExecutive"
   Combo2.AddItem "SQLServer"
   Combo2.ListIndex = 1

End Sub
```

Form_Unload event procedure

This event procedure closes the SQL Server object and releases it.

```
Private Sub Form_Unload(Cancel As Integer)
  OMySQLServer.Close
End Sub
```

lblStop_DblClick, lblPause_DblClick, and lblStart_DblClick event procedures

Because either a double-click on the Label control or a click on the stoplight can initiate the same activity, the StopServer, PauseServer, and StartServer subroutines are more efficient than having the code appear twice.

```
Private Sub lblStop_DblClick()
  StopServer
End Sub

Private Sub lblPause_DblClick()
  PauseServer
End Sub

Private Sub lblStart_DblClick()
  StartServer
End Sub
```

StopServer method

The *StopServer* method shuts down SQL Server.

```
Sub StopServer()

  On Error Resume Next

  MousePointer = vbHourglass

' Determine the type of service.
  Select Case Combo2
    Case "SQLServer"

' The Status method returns the current state of SQL Server.
' (It is also available for the Executive object.)
' The server can be stopped only if it is paused or running.
```

(continued)

```
        Select Case OMySQLServer.Status
          Case Paused
            OMySQLServer.Shutdown
          Case Running
            OMySQLServer.Shutdown
          Case Else
            MsgBox "SQL Server must be paused or " & _
               "running to be stopped", , "SQL Server"
        End Select

' Only an administrator can stop SQL Server. If you provide
' login information without adequate privileges to shut down
' SQL Server, you will receive this error. The same is not
' true for pausing SQL Server--any user can do it.
        If Err = -2147215500 Then
          MsgBox Err.Description
          MousePointer = vbDefault
          Exit Sub
        End If

' Executive can be stopped only if it is running.
      Case "SQLExecutive"
        Select Case OMySQLServer.Executive.Status
          Case Running
            OMySQLServer.Executive.Stop
          Case Else
            MsgBox "SQL Executive must be running to be stopped", , _
               "SQL Server"
        End Select

  End Select

  MousePointer = vbDefault

End Sub
```

PauseServer method

This method pauses SQL Server.

```
Sub PauseServer()

  MousePointer = vbHourglass

  Select Case Combo2

' SQL Server can be paused only if it is running.
    Case "SQLServer"
      Select Case OMySQLServer.Status
```

```
      Case Running
         OMySQLServer.Pause
      Case Else
         MsgBox "SQL Server must be running to be paused", , _
            "SQL Server"
      End Select

    Case "SQLExecutive"
      MsgBox "SQL Executive cannot be paused", , "SQL Server"

  End Select

  MousePointer = vbDefault

End Sub
```

StartServer method

The *StartServer* method starts SQL Server. (All of these methods have looked pretty similar, haven't they?)

```
Sub StartServer()

  MousePointer = vbHourglass

  Select Case Combo2
    Case "SQLServer"
      Select Case OMySQLServer.Status
        Case Stopped
          OMySQLServer.Start
        Case Paused
          OMySQLServer.Continue
        Case Else
          MsgBox "SQL Server must be stopped or paused " & _
            "to be started or continued", , "SQL Server"
      End Select

    Case "SQLExecutive"
      Select Case OMySQLServer.Executive.Status
        Case Stopped
          OMySQLServer.Executive.Start
        Case Else
          MsgBox "SQL Executive must be stopped to be started", , _
            "SQL Server"
      End Select
  End Select

  MousePointer = vbDefault

End Sub
```

Picture1_MouseDown event procedure

Now we sneak in a little example of how to use some graphics in our applications. Many of the applications available these days use hot graphics that you can click to initiate actions. How do these graphics work?

Most of these applications use graphics with *hot spots* on them. A hot spot is basically an area you've defined that the user can click to trigger an action. This event procedure uses the *Select Case* statement to check the *Y* location of the mouse when the user clicks anywhere on Picture1.

```
Private Sub Picture1_MouseDown(Button As Integer, _
  Shift As Integer, X As Single, Y As Single)

' Depending on where the user clicks on the
' stoplight, execute one of the procedures.
  Select Case Y
    Case 405 To 588
      StopServer
    Case 576 To 900
      PauseServer
    Case 1030 To 1236
      StartServer
  End Select

End Sub
```

Timer1_Timer event procedure

Rather than placing the code directly in the timer routine, a separate subroutine is called as it is also called from the *Combo2_Change* event procedure.

```
Private Sub Timer1_Timer()
  UpdateStatus
End Sub
```

UpdateStatus method

SQL-DMO provides for the programmatic control of both SQL Server and SQL Executive. SQL Server and SQL Executive are separate NT services and can be started and stopped independently. The following procedure reflects the current status of the selected service.

```
Sub UpdateStatus()

  On Error Resume Next

  Static LastServerStatus As Integer
  Static LastExecutiveStatus As Integer
  Static sServiceStatus As String
```

```
' The If statements are included in the following
' Select Case statement so the overhead of loading
' an already loaded bitmap is not incurred.
  Select Case Combo2

    Case "SQLServer"
      Select Case OMySQLServer.Status
        Case Stopped
          If LastServerStatus <> Stopped Then
            Picture1 = LoadPicture(DefDir & "red.bmp")
            LastServerStatus = Stopped
            sServiceStatus = "stopped"
          End If
        Case Starting
          If LastServerStatus <> Starting Then
            Picture1 = LoadPicture(DefDir & "green.bmp")
            LastServerStatus = Starting
            sServiceStatus = "starting..."
          End If
        Case Stopping
          If LastServerStatus <> Stopping Then
            Picture1 = LoadPicture(DefDir & "red.bmp")
            LastServerStatus = Stopping
            sServiceStatus = "stopping..."
          End If
        Case Paused
          If LastServerStatus <> Paused Then
            Picture1 = LoadPicture(DefDir & "yellow.bmp")
            LastServerStatus = Paused
            sServiceStatus = "paused"
          End If
        Case Running
          If LastServerStatus <> Running Then
            Picture1 = LoadPicture(DefDir & "green.bmp")
            LastServerStatus = Running
            sServiceStatus = "running"
          End If
        Case Else
          If LastServerStatus <> None Then
            Picture1 = LoadPicture(DefDir & "none.bmp")
            LastServerStatus = None
            sServiceStatus = ""
          End If
      End Select

    Case "SQLExecutive"
      Dim vTempVar As Variant
      vTempVar = OMySQLServer.Executive.Status
```

(continued)

```
      If Err = -2147201022 Then
        MsgBox "You must have a valid connection to a " & _
          "SQL Server before manipulating its SQLExecutive", , _
          "SQL Server"
        Combo2.ListIndex = 1
        Exit Sub
      End If


' There's no need for a Paused case as SQLExecutive
' can only be stopped or running.
      Select Case vTempVar
        Case Stopped
          If LastExecutiveStatus <> Stopped Then
            Picture1 = LoadPicture(DefDir & "red.bmp")
            LastExecutiveStatus = Stopped
            sServiceStatus = "stopped"
          End If

        Case Running
          If LastExecutiveStatus <> Running Then
            Picture1 = LoadPicture(DefDir & "green.bmp")
            LastExecutiveStatus = Running
            sServiceStatus = "running"
          End If

        Case Starting
          If LastExecutiveStatus <> Starting Then
            Picture1 = LoadPicture(DefDir & "green.bmp")
            LastExecutiveStatus = Starting
            sServiceStatus = "starting..."
          End If

        Case Stopping
          If LastExecutiveStatus <> Stopping Then
            Picture1 = LoadPicture(DefDir & "red.bmp")
            LastExecutiveStatus = Stopping
            sServiceStatus = "stopping..."
          End If

        Case Else
          If LastExecutiveStatus <> None Then
            Picture1 = LoadPicture(DefDir & "none.bmp")
            LastExecutiveStatus = None
            sServiceStatus = ""
          End If

      End Select

    End Select
```

```
' Display the status of SQL Server in the label.
  If sServiceStatus <> "" Then
    lblStatus = "The service is " & sServiceStatus
  Else
    lblStatus = ""
  End If

End Sub
```

Database transaction logs and related problems

What happens when a database transaction log fills up? You or your users will most likely receive an error message such as *Failed to allocate disk space for a work table in database 'tempdb'*. The tempdb database is used to store temporary tables that are generated during normal operations. When this database or its transaction log fills up, your users will see an error when the application they are using issues a SQL statement that uses tempdb.

Users might also see such errors when the transaction log for the database they are using fills up. These errors raise two issues:

■ How do we try to anticipate this problem and prevent its occurrence?

■ How do we fix it when it occurs?

Both of these issues are fairly easy to handle. Performance Monitor on Windows NT can watch the size of the database and its log devices. Set an alert on both of these values to alert the database administrator whenever the devices are approaching full. You can also use Performance Monitor to actually run the command to clear the log or expand the database.

Another approach would be to use the new SQL Server Executive scheduling feature to routinely run a program that checks the size of the logs and takes appropriate action.

Fixing a full transaction log is also fairly simple. The *DUMP TRANSACTION* Transact-SQL command has a number of options that you should understand before you use it. For details on these options, refer to the Transact-SQL Reference Help file, which can be accessed by choosing Transact-SQL Help from the Help menu in ISQL/w. (Search for *DUMP*.)

Transaction time-outs

Another error you might receive is number 40002, which reads: S1T00: [Microsoft][ODBC SQL Server Driver]Timeout expired.

The time-out error usually occurs when something has caused a result set to pause too long between operations and exceed the time-out value setting. A variety of possible causes for this error includes overloading the database engine, network errors, server errors, and so on, and all of them are sure to cause you grief.

The solution to the problem is not necessarily to increase the time-out value but to discover the actual cause of the problem and repair it. Increasing the time-out will usually mask the real problem and lead to further problems.

Jet and Disk Space

Dynaset-type Recordsets build the keyset on the client workstation executing the application. If you're not careful, this can overflow the Temp directory on your hard disk. Snapshot-type Recordsets also build the keyset on the client and download the data to the client's Temp directory. You can minimize the impact on the client by always managing the scope of your queries and never allowing someone to request a query of an entire table unless the table is very small.

It is a good idea to set a standard for a minimum amount of free disk space on client workstations and then monitor free disk space regularly. Using System Management Server or another tool, you can accomplish this task daily and take appropriate action.

Monitoring SQL Server Performance

Performance Monitor is a powerful Windows NT tool for tracking the performance of systems running on Windows NT. Performance Monitor is based on an open architecture that allows vendors and corporate developers to place their own objects in its database. SQL Server includes a Performance Monitor configuration file for some of its own objects. You can access the preconfigured settings by clicking the SQL Performance Monitor icon in the Microsoft SQL Server group in Program Manager.

Performance Monitor is also a remote access tool that can work from any Windows NT–based system on the network or that connects to the network using Remote Access Service (RAS) or another remote access method. Performance Monitor can monitor more than one SQL Server at a time, providing a system manager the ability to track several critical performance criteria on multiple systems simultaneously.

Performance Monitor can also display its statistics in a graphical or report view, monitor alert values and trigger certain actions when they occur, and store values in a log file. Performance Monitor must be running to perform any of its actions, including the log and alert functions.

For more information on Performance Monitor, refer to the Windows NT documentation, the *Windows NT Resource Kit,* and *NT Server: Management and Control* by Ken Spencer (Prentice-Hall, 1996).

Homegrown Utilities for Migration

One topic that is frequently overlooked during the move from legacy systems to client/server systems (or during development of a client/server system) is the variety of tasks that must be performed, ranging from filtering existing data files to migrating data from the old system to the new. Most people resort to batch languages or other familiar methods to accomplish these tasks without giving much thought to Visual Basic.

Visual Basic frequently turns out to be the best and most flexible way of creating tools for these tasks, as the following examples illustrate. Each of these tools has actually been used during different projects. Some of them were created in a few minutes, while others took a couple of hours. The All-In-1 converter took 10 days to develop.

Building an Access database from a PowerHouse dictionary

Our DBBuilder program grew out of a client/server project that involved migrating existing flat files (Record Management System, or RMS, format) from a VAX to SQL Server. The concept was to mirror the existing flat-file system in a relational format. This would allow us to do sophisticated reporting early in the project and provide a stable foundation to migrate data to the new system. This seemed at first to be a difficult task until we considered what we could do with Visual Basic.

The first step was to build a structure in SQL Server that matched the file structure on the VAX. Typically, this involves manually creating tables and columns and so on, which with 100 files or more quickly becomes a nightmare. Our solution was to build a database generator in Visual Basic that read the existing format and built an Access database, which we could move to SQL Server using the Upsizing Wizard from Microsoft.

This tool took less than a week to build. Using it and the Upsizing Wizard, we performed the migration of the data structure in about two weeks. Now you might say, "We could have manually built the structure in that time," which is true. But what happens when someone changes the structure of the RMS file system? With our approach, we simply ran DBBuilder again and then used the Upsizing Wizard again. Besides that, the next application that calls for such a conversion is a no-brainer (and a no-timer) with this utility in place.

Automatically transferring data (RunFiles)

What about getting data from your legacy system to the new database? This task is not even mentioned in most client/server books, but it's a necessary one.

RunFiles is a neat little program originally written in Visual Basic 3 and later migrated to Visual Basic 4. It doesn't make significant use of any of Visual Basic

4's new features, but it is essential to moving data from a VAX/VMS system to Windows NT and SQL Server. We used Pathworks 4.1 on the VAX/VMS system to provide a network interface for Windows NT to access its shared disk system. RunFiles is not shown in this book but is included in the RunFiles directory on the companion CD.

As we were putting together this application, we ran into a small problem: the legacy files were stored in RMS files on the VAX/VMS system. To copy the files to Windows NT, we used PowerHouse (from Cognos) to export the data to simple delimited text files on the VMS system. Some records in the output files exceeded the 250-character-per-line limit of PowerHouse, so we had to split the records across multiple lines using the sequence : / for the end of the logical record delimiter. Now how would we put these records back together to import them to SQL Server? We created a little program called SplitFix that reads a file and outputs a new file, putting all the rows back together.

To indicate to the RunFiles program which files need to be run through SplitFix, we built a little text file (Copyindx.txt) that contains the source filename and the word *Split*.

The RunFiles program reads Copyindx.txt and builds an array to use for checking the split status of each file and for building the error log file. The overall operation of RunFiles is listed in the following steps:

1. Initialize stuff.

2. Check for any TBL*.FLG files on the VAX share directory.

3. If any flag files exist, copy the text file for each to Windows NT.

4. Run SplitFix on the file, if required.

5. Start the batch procedure to load SQL Server.

6. Loop back to Step 2 and continue.

7. After all files are copied, delete the flag files used in this run.

Benefits of the RunFiles approach You might be wondering why we wanted to create a database that contained the same file structure as the legacy data since we were going to reengineer all business applications anyway. We had several reasons for using this process:

■ The data was refreshed every night, leaving us with a fresh database every morning.

■ All input errors were trapped, providing a nice way to begin cleaning up the legacy data even as we designed the new system. For instance, we were able to find bad date values, clean up the various client master files, and correct numerous other data issues.

- We could easily move the data into the new database structure and create procedures to automate the move. This let us easily move the old data to the new system when it came online, even moving parts of the data while the old system was still in use.

- Reports that were difficult or impossible to generate with the old format became easy to generate using reporting tools, such as Access.

- The staff could begin using the new tools immediately.

SplitFix is the handy little program we created to put the multiple record files back together. It is run by RunFiles on specific files.

You might think this program would be slow, but this program screams. The code for SplitFix is not shown in this book, but it is included in the SplitFix directory on the companion CD.

Fixing OLE Server Problems

When creating OLE servers in Visual Basic, you might from time to time run into problems that occur with both in-process and out-of-process servers. One such problem is encountered most frequently when the OLE server has been modified in a way that makes it incompatible with the client application. You will usually discover the incompatibility when you try to use the OLE server in an application.

This problem occurs when you modify a method or property in a manner that makes it incompatible with the older version—for example, changing the project name. Changing a class name can also cause you lots of grief. The incompatibility can also occur when you enter a Compatible OLE Server entry in the Project tab in the Options dialog box (accessed from the Tools menu).

Incompatibilities are bad enough when they occur while you are testing a server. Imagine what happens when 1000 users run an application that relies on the OLE server and you compile it over the top of the production server. Now let's further complicate the situation by saying you are working late and make an incompatible server that compiles cleanly. Users come in the next morning, and nothing works. You might have to deal with from 100 to 1000 users calling the help desk.

There are many possible causes and solutions and a number of steps that you can take to prevent the problems from occurring:

1. Do not change the parameters or return values of any public method or Property procedure. Instead, create a new method with an extension added to the name.

2. Do not change the Project Name or Application Description of an existing OLE server.

3. Create a *StartApplication* method in every OLE server. Make sure this method requires the name of the client application and writes it to a master log file. This would be a good place to use the utilities in our CSUtilities sample application.

4. Test, test, test any changes to an OLE server before putting it into production.

5. Use SourceSafe or another source code management package to track your program versions.

6. Make a backup copy of the original server executable before replacing it.

You should take further precautions if you experience any problems with a server. If the server compiles cleanly, the problems will usually appear when you try to access properties or methods in the server from a client application. You can get one of several error messages that indicate some type of OLE error. Here are a few potential solutions to try:

- Check the reference to the server from the client application by choosing References from the Tools menu.

- Unregister the original server by executing the server with the */Unregserver* command option. Then register the new server by executing the server with the */Regserver* command option. In Visual Basic, load the client application and choose References from the Tools menu to set a reference to the server.

- Remove the Compatible OLE Server entry on the Project tab in the Options dialog box. (Choose Options from the Tools menu.) Recompile the server application, and test the client application again.

- You might find that you must resort to ugly methods to correct an OLE problem. For instance, if all of the preceding steps failed, you might need to edit the client application's VBP file and manually delete the reference to the OLE server. This requires resetting the reference in the client.

Except for the first item, all the solutions listed above require that you recompile *all* client applications using the OLE server. This is no trivial task and should not be undertaken lightly. If you used the CSUtilities approach described on page 140, you could use Visual Basic's automatic compile option with a list generated from the PerformanceLog database to recompile the applications. But, of course, you must then use a tool such as System Management Server to update the applications. You must also test the applications thoroughly before deploying them.

Trapping Client Application Errors

The default behavior of Visual Basic when it encounters an error is to display an error number without a description of the error and then abruptly terminate the application. Not only is this behavior a shock to the end user, but it can also be a shock to the system. Files can be left open, and database transactions can be left in an indeterminate state—neither committed nor rolled back.

While many errors are introduced during the development of the system, not all are. Even if you could write perfect code, some errors are unavoidable. For example, if your application allows the user to save files to a floppy disk drive, the user might forget to insert a floppy disk, which produces a runtime error. Errors will occur in your applications. What do you do about them?

Some programming languages have what is known as a global error handler. The lack of a global error-handling system within Visual Basic 4 presents a development challenge. To protect against runtime errors, it is necessary to add error handling in every event procedure and code module of any significance. This can become quite a chore because a typical client/server application might contain hundreds of code modules and event procedures. The amount of time it takes to insert and test good error-handling code can approach the amount of time necessary for coding the rest of the application.

Figure 11-4 illustrates the standard Visual Basic error dialog box. When the user clicks the OK button, the application terminates.

Figure 11-4. *The Visual Basic default error dialog box.*

Error Handling Made Easy

Placing error-handling code in each procedure of a Visual Basic application is such a time-consuming task that far too many applications are released without adequate error handling. Wouldn't it be nice if there were some way to insert error-handling procedures automatically? Well, there is a way, using VB/Rig from Avanti Software. Using VB/Rig doesn't mean that you won't have to write any error-handling code, but VB/Rig reduces much of the tedium.

The error-handling routines that VB/Rig inserts are well documented and, when the appropriate option is selected, even contain a *Select Case* shell for you to fill in with your own error-handling code. Using VB/Rig will affect both the size and execution speed of your application, but its effect is no different from writing the same error-handling capability yourself. Considering the gain in reliable performance, it's a good trade-off.

Figure 11-5 shows the standard VB/Rig error dialog box.

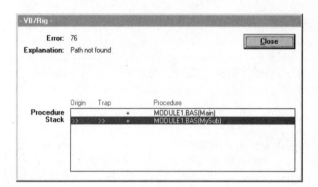

Figure 11-5. *The VB/Rig error dialog box shows considerably more information than the default message Visual Basic shows under the same error condition.*

Selective debugging

Not all error handling is created equally, and VB/Rig knows this. It allows you to select which routines will be rigged (which routines will have error-handling code added) and to what extent they will be rigged, and then it lets you make your own modifications. VB/Rig is available in standard and professional versions, but both versions allow you to choose not to install error handling in a particular routine.

Selectively choosing specific routines is easier in the professional version, which allows you to pick and choose routines individually from a list box. In the standard version, you will need to place the following comment on the first line of any procedure you don't want to be rigged:

```
'+++ VB/Rig Skip +++
```

Recording errors

One of the most useful features of VB/Rig is its ability to log errors to a disk file. The name of the file can be specified in the application's INI file, or you can simply let VB/Rig log to its default file, Errorlog.err. The error file is a comma-delimited ASCII file that contains a listing of the time the error occurred, the routine that was executing at the time, and a snapshot of Visual Basic's procedure stack. This is an especially useful feature if your application will be in the hands of users who report problems simply as "it broke" and don't copy any information the application offers about what went wrong.

Limitations

There are two drawbacks to using VB/Rig. The first is specific to the product, and the second is specific to error handling in Visual Basic:

■ Once a Visual Basic project has been rigged with a certain set of options, these options cannot be changed without removing the rigging (an automatic operation) and then rerigging the project with the new options. This can be especially frustrating after you have added your own error-handling code to that of VB/Rig.

■ The second drawback is not an issue with VB/Rig but rather an issue with the way Visual Basic implements error handling. All of that error-handling code can really bloat your project code, sometimes as much as 30 to 40 percent. Unfortunately, a lot of that additional code is executed during the normal operation of your application, so VB/Rig does slow the execution down a bit.

How does VB/Rig work? VB/Rig adds one code module and one form to your application. The code module contains support functions for the runtime features of VB/Rig. The form is VB/Rig's error dialog box, which replaces the default Visual Basic message box should an unhandled error occur. The VB/Rig dialog box provides additional information, such as a verbal description of the error and the procedure in which the error occurred, instead of just a number. Also, after the error is reported the application continues to run—a definite plus if the error wasn't fatal.

VB/Rig then opens the files contained in your Visual Basic project and writes its rigging code directly to them. Finally, VB/Rig tracks your application's execution flow by maintaining a procedure call stack. VB/Rig places an identifier for each procedure at the beginning of that procedure, and when the procedure is called, the identifier is pushed onto VB/Rig's stack. When execution returns from the called procedure, its name is popped off VB/Rig's procedure call stack. This is where some of the additional processing time is consumed.

What does a rigged application look like? The code below is an example of original code.

```
Sub MySub()
  Dir "d:"
End Sub
```

The code that follows is the same code after VB/Rig is done rigging it.

```
Sub MySub()
'+++ VB/Rig Begin Push +++
Const VBRIG_PROC_ID_STRING = "+MySub"
```

(continued)

```
Dim VBRigErr As Long, VBRigErrMsg As String
On Error GoTo MySub_VBRigErr
Call VBRig_Error(VBRIG_PUSH_PROC_STACK, 0, "", _
  VBRIG_MODULE_ID_STRING, VBRIG_PROC_ID_STRING)
'+++ VB/Rig End +++
  Dir "d:"
'+++ VB/Rig Begin Pop +++
Call VBRig_Error(VBRIG_POP_PROC_STACK, 0, "", _
  VBRIG_MODULE_ID_STRING, VBRIG_PROC_ID_STRING)
Exit Sub


'==============
MySub_VBRigErr:
'==============
VBRigErr = Err
VBRigErrMsg = Error$
Call VBRig_Error(VBRIG_SHOWLOG_ERROR, VBRigErr, _
    VBRigErrMsg, VBRIG_MODULE_ID_STRING, VBRIG_PROC_ID_STRING)
Call VBRig_Error(VBRIG_POP_PROC_STACK, 0, "", _
    VBRIG_MODULE_ID_STRING, VBRIG_PROC_ID_STRING)
Exit Sub
'+++ VB/Rig End +++
End Sub
```

It should be mentioned here that VB/Rig doesn't do anything you couldn't do on your own. In fact, on a wager that it was not possible to provide global error handling in Visual Basic, one of the authors developed a similar, less thorough, approach to demonstrate the feasibility of global error handling in Visual Basic. As with many third-party commercial Visual Basic products, VB/Rig is priced to make development of your own version a less-than-economical undertaking. However, VB/Rig is an excellent product that will save you an enormous amount of time and will result in the construction of better applications.

Untrappable errors

Some errors such as Error 28, "Out of stack space," are not trappable. You should rigorously test for this type of error, or your applications might crash for unexplained reasons. You can prevent many of these types of errors by using good programming practices. For instance, to prevent Error 28, don't use recursion and minimize other actions such as deeply nested procedures that can use up all the stack space in your system.

General application errors

Figure 11-6 shows a typical error that can creep into your application. This particular error is likely to occur after thorough testing—when you allow your users to enter data, such as a column name, that you incorporate into a SQL statement. These types of errors are difficult to test for and demand that you use extremely thorough error handling.

Figure 11-6. *This error resulted from using an invalid column name (Author) in a SQL query.*

You will see errors like the one shown in Figure 11-7 for many reasons.

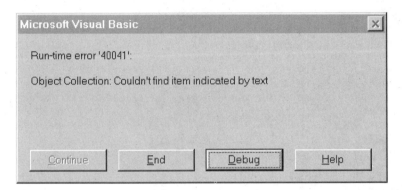

Figure 11-7. *This error resulted from some type of problem using a collection.*

Your error-handling code must do an extremely good job of preventing or catching all errors. These include the typical Visual Basic errors like the one shown in Figure 11-4, the ODBC-specific errors like the one shown in Figure 11-6, and others such as those tied to a specific object such as the one shown in Figure 11-7.

Error numbers and Visual Basic

Some aspects of error handling don't encourage its use. The relationship between the error values you will see if you examine the numeric value of the Err object and the constants you will find in the Object Browser provide a good example of the inconsistency that makes error handling problematic.

For example, we check for the SQLOLE_E_ALREADYCONN error in one of our sample applications. While designing the application, error number -2147201024 occurred. Here's what we saw in the debug window after a little probing:

```
debug.print err
-2147201024
debug.print err.description
This server object is already connected.
```

We started searching for the appropriate constant to put in the error handler for this error number by looking in the Microsoft SQLOLE Object Library using the Object Browser. We found the SQLOLE_ERROR_TYPE class, which looked like a good candidate. Based on the description of the error message, you can find the constant SQLOLE_E_ALREADYCONN as shown in Figure 11-8.

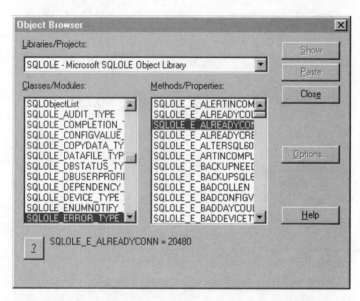

Figure 11-8. *Object Browser showing the SQLOLE_ERROR_TYPE class.*

Notice the value of the SQLOLE_E_ALREADYCONN error constant. The Object Browser shows a value of 20480, yet the Err object reported a value of -2147201024. For the purposes of error handling within Visual Basic, -2147201024 is equal to 20480. Why?

To fully understand what's going on behind the scenes in Visual Basic, a brief expedition into the world of binary and hexadecimal arithmetic is necessary. This isn't as bad a trip as it might first sound since using the Windows Calculator in Scientific mode (found in the View menu) greatly simplifies the process. In Calculator, enter *-2147201024* and select the Bin option. The display shows the 32-bit binary value 10000000000001000101000000000000. As Visual Basic's Err object stores values as long integers and because long integers are signed values in Visual Basic, that leftmost *1* results in the value being interpreted as a negative number.

Now select the Hex option to display the same number as a hexadecimal value: 80045000.

Notice that when you select Hex, word size options appear and Dword is selected. If you select Word, thereby displaying the value as a 16-bit value instead of a 32-bit value, the display will show only the four least significant hex digits, or 5000. But 5000 base 16 is exactly equal to 20480 base 10. Hence, for purposes of error resolution, we can conclude that Visual Basic uses only the least significant 16 bits of the Err object's number and that is how -2147201024 is equal to 20480 in Visual Basic.

Where did the minus sign go? Here's the value 20480 in binary: 0101000000000000. We've added a leading *0* so that 16 digits are shown. Visual Basic's integers are also signed values, but because the leading digit is not a *1,* the number is interpreted as being positive.

Conditional Compilation

Conditional compilation is one of Visual Basic 4's new features that developers who have migrated from compiled languages such as C will appreciate. Conditional compilation works by providing constructs that allow decisions to be made at compile time, such as whether to use 16-bit or 32-bit API declarations.

The traditional example of using conditional compilation demonstrates how to differentiate between 16-bit and 32-bit platforms using the appropriate API calls. In addition to managing the difference in Win16 and Win32 applications, you can use conditional compilation to turn debug code on and off. This reduces the size of your application's EXE file and the debug code overhead. You can also use conditional compilation to handle any decisions that must be made at compile time. Another real-world example is provided by VB/Rig.

VB/Rig provides the ability to log errors to a file through the use of Windows API calls. These calls are declared in the code module that VB/Rig adds to your application. But because Visual Basic could be running on either a 16-bit platform or a 32-bit platform and because the API declarations are different for each platform, we must have a way to determine for which system we are compiling and then use the appropriate API. The determination is made using the intrinsic variable Win32. Win32 is a Boolean constant that is *True* if the Visual Basic development environment is 32-bit and *False* if not. It's probably worth mentioning that a Win16 intrinsic variable also exists that always has the opposite value of Win32.

The ability to change compiler flow is accomplished through the *#If…Then…#Else…#End If* construct. The pound sign (#) preceding the keywords is an indication that what follows is a compiler directive. This is necessary in order for Visual Basic to distinguish the construct from a regular *If…Then…Else…End If* statement.

The code shown below comes from VB/Rig and provides a good demonstration of using conditional compilation to separate 16-bit and 32-bit sections of code.

```
' =====================
' Windows API functions
' =====================
#If Win32 Then
Const LB_SETTABSTOPS = &H192
Const LB_SETHORIZONTALEXTENT = &H194
Const EM_SETTABSTOPS = &HCB

Declare Function vbrig_GetProfileString Lib "kernel32" _
   Alias "GetProfileStringA" (ByVal lpAppName As String, _
   ByVal lpKeyName As String, ByVal lpDefault As String, _
   ByVal lpReturnedString As String, ByVal nSize As Long) _
   As Long
Declare Function vbrig_GetPrivateProfileString Lib "kernel32" _
   Alias "GetPrivateProfileStringA" (ByVal lpAppName As String, _
   ByVal lpKeyName As String, ByVal lpDefault As String, _
   ByVal lpReturnedString As String, ByVal nSize As Long, _
   ByVal lpFileName As String) _
   As Long
Declare Function vbrig_SetTabstops Lib "user32" _
   Alias "SendMessageA" (ByVal hwnd As Long, _
   ByVal wMsg As Long, ByVal wParam As Long, _
   lParam As Long) _
   As Long
Declare Function vbrig_SetHorizScrollBar Lib "user32" _
   Alias "SendMessageA" (ByVal hwnd As Long, _
   ByVal wMsg As Integer, ByVal wParam As Long, _
   lParam As Long) _
   As Long
#Else
Const WM_USER = 1024
Const LB_SETTABSTOPS = WM_USER + 19
Const LB_SETHORIZONTALEXTENT = WM_USER + 21
Const EM_SETTABSTOPS = WM_USER + 27

Declare Function vbrig_GetProfileString Lib "kernel" _
   Alias "GetProfileString" (ByVal lpAppName As String, _
   ByVal lpKeyName As String, ByVal lpDefault As String, _
   ByVal lpReturnedString As String, ByVal nSize As Integer) _
   As Integer
Declare Function vbrig_GetPrivateProfileString Lib "kernel" _
   Alias "GetPrivateProfileString" (ByVal lpAppName As String, _
   ByVal lpKeyName As String, ByVal lpDefault As String, _
   ByVal lpReturnedString As String, ByVal nSize As Integer, _
```

```
  ByVal lpFileName As String) _
  As Integer
Declare Function vbrig_SetTabstops Lib "user" _
  Alias "SendMessage" (ByVal hwnd As Integer, _
  ByVal wMsg As Integer, ByVal wParam As Integer, _
  lParam As Any) _
  As Long
Declare Function vbrig_SetHorizScrollBar Lib "user" _
  Alias "SendMessage" (ByVal hwnd As Integer, _
  ByVal wMsg As Integer, ByVal wParam As Integer, _
  lParam As Any) _
  As Long
#End If
```

When the preceding code is compiled on a 32-bit platform, the kernel32 and user32 API calls are declared, but when compiled on a 16-bit platform, the kernel and user API calls are declared.

Another good use of conditional compilation is for building applications that handle different number formats, such as regular vs. international phone numbers. Sometimes it is handy to store all the data in a text field and use conditional compilation to select the appropriate code to use to display the data.

Using Help Files

Certain features of a product are so useful that they become expected. For example, many people buy a car expecting that it will come with an automatic transmission. When the users of your applications need assistance, the first place they will turn to is the online, context-sensitive Windows help file that you will naturally be providing.

There are many ways to create Windows help files. They range from the most fundamental—embedding codes directly into an RTF document (akin to programming in Assembler) and manually running the result through the Help compiler—to using a $1,000 package in which you click on the type of item you want and enter your text and the software does the rest of the work. We're going to take a look at both of these options and an alternative in the middle.

The full manual help transmission

The Windows Help compiler is widely available, shipping with virtually every development tool, including Visual Basic. The only complications in the manual process for creating a Windows help file are the number of steps required and the level of detail you must deal with. Type your text into any word processor capable of saving in Rich Text Format (RTF). Ultimately, this is the file that will be imported into the Help compiler. To tell the Help compiler what to do with the file, you embed codes, such as *$#K+*, at the beginning of a line that starts a new topic. Help files have a lot of options and a lot of these little codes, so they are not fun to work with in full manual mode. Here's what the codes just mentioned represent:

$ Title
# Topic
K Keyword
+ Browse

In addition to an RTF file, you will need a help project file (HPJ), which instructs the Help compiler about particulars such as the title of the help file, copyright information, which navigation buttons to display, whether to compress the help file, and what RTF files to roll into the help file. The HPJ file is a standard ANSI text file.

Once you have created an HPJ file and at least one RTF file containing your help text and Help compiler codes, you invoke the Help compiler and pass it the name of the HPJ:

```
C:\VB\HC\HC31 C:\OurHelpFiles\First.hpj
```

The Help compiler then obtains more information about the help file to be constructed from the information contained in the HPJ file. A simple HPJ file might look something like the following:

```
[Options]
Root = C:\OurHelpFiles
TITLE = Our First Help Project
Compress = 0          ; 0 = Do not compress
Warning = 3           ; 3 = Report all errors
Report = 1            ; 1 = Report progress of compile
ERRORLOG = First.Log  ; store errors in this text file
copyright = Copyright (c) 1996 by Ken Miller, Inc.
Contents = Contents

[Files]
First.rtf

[Config]
BrowseButtons()       ; Permit browsing

[Map]
Contents 0
First Topic 5
Second Topic 10
Third Topic 15
```

You place the map values in the *HelpContextID* property of Visual Basic controls to provide a direct path to a topic for context-sensitive help.

Tired of shifting manually? You think there must be a better way? There is.

The basic automatic three-speed help transmission

The family sedan comes with a basic automatic transmission that is a reasonable compromise between functionality, cost, and performance. So it is with the *Microsoft Windows 95 Help Authoring Kit* (Microsoft Press, 1995). The first thing to say about this book and accompanying CD is that they aren't just for Windows 95. You can use the tools provided to create help files for all versions of Windows, including Windows 3.1, Windows 95, and Windows NT.

You'd have to be a techno-nerd to take the manual approach when this tool is available at that price. In fact, even if you opt for a more full-featured help generator, this book is worth having for the concise explanation and simple examples of the technical details behind Windows help files and how to take advantage of the new features of WinHelp 4.0. The CD contains Microsoft Help Workshop, shown in Figure 11-9, which is the latest incarnation of the Windows Help compiler with a GUI interface.

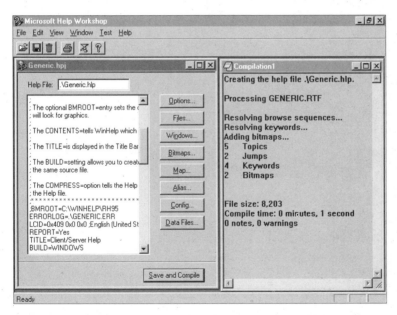

Figure 11-9. *Microsoft Help Workshop's graphical interface greatly simplifies pulling together the disparate components of full-featured help files.*

Rather than go into further details about the *Microsoft Windows 95 Help Authoring Kit,* we offer this simple advice, regardless of the approach you ultimately take in the construction of your help files: buy it!

The automatic five-speed help transmission with overdrive

Considering the complexity of the Windows help files that can be constructed with RoboHELP, its manufacturer, Blue Sky, has done an absolutely wonderful job of making it easy to use. The WinHelp Office Suite even comes with a video that demonstrates the fundamentals of creating help files using RoboHELP.

Figure 11-10 shows how RoboHELP makes creating help files so easy. This opening dialog box eliminates any possible confusion about what will happen when you make a selection.

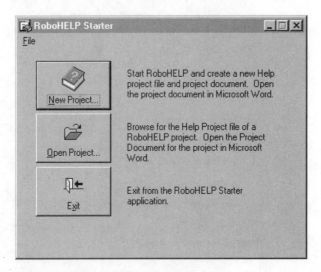

Figure 11-10. *Clicking New Project starts an instance of Microsoft Word, which gathers text for the help file.*

You can see from Figure 11-11 how simple it is to select your target environment for the help file.

While additions to the menus in Word let you perform activities such as creating hot spots and adding topics, the rollup toolbar in RoboHELP is a lot handier. Just right-click the toolbar's title bar and voilà!—the toolbar rolls up out of the way. A second right-click and the toolbar is back and ready to use.

We've seen some help tools that get bogged down with the large help files needed for a client/server application. They can take so long to compile (hours) that we get tired of waiting and give up. Not only is RoboHELP easier to use, but it is also significantly faster than macro-based help generators.

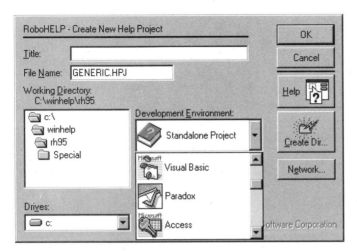

Figure 11-11. *Selecting a Development Environment lets RoboHELP add product-specific features.*

One of the benefits of using Visual Basic is that RoboHELP can automatically create a file named <project>.ghc, which contains global constant declarations for the integer mapping of the topic ideas. This makes programmatic reference to a specific topic a snap. The GHC file is created in addition to the standard <appname>.hh file containing the topic mappings. The contents of either file can be used to set the property on any control for context-sensitive help.

Before concluding, we'll mention one innovation in RoboHELP that's especially interesting to Visual Basic programmers—an OLE Custom Control that makes providing context-sensitive help in your Visual Basic projects very easy.

You must make RoboHELP's SmartHelp OLE control available to your Visual Basic project by choosing Custom Controls from the Tools menu. If you accept the default setup parameters, Smthlp32.ocx can be found in the WinHelp\Rh95 directory.

After adding the control to the project, place a Help command button directly on each form for which you want to provide context-sensitive help. RoboHELP considerately provides a dialog box (see Figure 11-12 on the next page) that you can use to browse for an associated help file and then select the topic to display. A Preview command button is also provided, so you can take a quick look at the topic to make sure it is what you want. When the user clicks the Help button, the selected topic is displayed.

RoboHELP is so feature-packed that it would take an entire book to cover it in any detail. WinHelp Office comes with several well-written volumes.

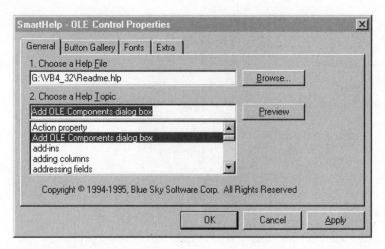

Figure 11-12. *The SmartHelp OLE Control Properties dialog box, which can be opened by double-clicking the Custom item in the Visual Basic Properties window.*

Appendix

Vendor Contact Information and Additional Tools

Vendor Contact Information

The following table includes contact information for vendors that make the tools we used in this book.

Company	Product	Description
Avanti Software 800-329-8889	VB/Rig Pro and PinPoint	Debugging and performance tuning tools
Logic Works, Inc. 800-78-ERWIN	ERwin	Database development tool, which uses entity relationship diagrams
Blue Sky Software 619-459-6365	WinHelp Office RoboHELP	Windows help file development tools
Visual Components 913-599-6500	First Impression and Formula One OCXs	Graphics and grid ActiveX controls

Additional Tools

We would like to mention several products that time did not permit us to include in the book. We will definitely be including them in the update for Visual Basic 5. We've worked with these tools and found them to be extremely valuable. Choose your tools with care, and your applications will sing and dance.

Company	Product	Description
Lead Technologies 704-332-5532	LeadToolsOCX32	A powerful set of graphics functions that allows you to manipulate images.
Desaware 408-371-3530	Storage Tools	Allows you to read and write to the OLE file format (the same file structure used in Microsoft Office and other products). It also includes a set of tools to manipulate the Registry in Windows 95 and Windows NT.
Sheridan Software Systems, Inc. 516-753-0985	sp_Assist	Useful for creating and managing SQL queries and stored procedures.

INDEX

Note: italic page numbers indicate figures and tables.

Kenneth L. Spencer has over 20 years of experience with computer software, including experience with mainframe and personal computer databases dating back to the early 1980s. He first started developing Microsoft Visual Basic and client/server applications with Visual Basic 1.0 using Digital's RDB on the server side and has since moved on to using Microsoft Access, Microsoft SQL Server, and numerous other tools in building state-of-the-art solutions. He also provides consulting assistance to organizations for reengineering and downsizing, specializing in the development of client/server solutions. He has made numerous presentations and has written articles and books, including *NT Server: Management and Control* (Prentice Hall, 1995) and *OLE Remote Automation with Visual Basic* (Prentice Hall, 1995). Ken has two children and has been married for 25 years. He enjoys playing guitar, snorkeling, and hiking and is a certified scuba diver.

Ken Miller has been designing and building computer hardware and software since 1975. For the past four years, he has concentrated on solving real-world client/server issues for Fortune 1000 companies and for the United States government. Ken is a Microsoft-certified Visual Basic instructor.

The manuscript for this book was prepared using Microsoft Word 6.0 for Windows and submitted to Microsoft Press in electronic form. Galleys were prepared using Microsoft Word 7.0 for Windows. Pages were composed by ArtSource using Adobe PageMaker 6.01 for Windows, with text type in Garamond and display type in Futura Medium Bold. Composed pages were delivered to the printer as electronic prepress files.

Cover Graphic Designers
Robin Hjellen

Greg Erickson

Cover Illustrator
Glenn Mitsui

Interior Graphic Designer
Kim Eggleston

Interior Graphic Artist
Michael Victor

Principal Proofreader
Deborah Long

Composition and Layout
ArtSource, Inc.

Indexer
Richard Evans

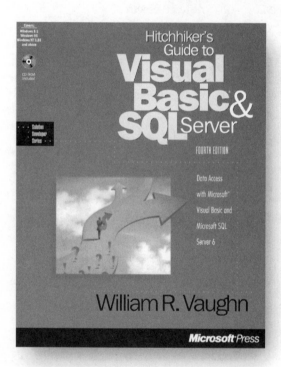

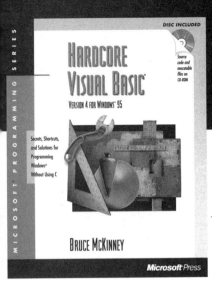

Unleash the power of
Microsoft® Visual Basic® with
HARDCORE VISUAL BASIC!

Visual Basic wizard Bruce McKinney shows how to blast through the so-called limits of Visual Basic and reach the powerful object-oriented development tool that lurks within. The result: applications with better performance and more functionality.

Valuable Information Included on CD!

- Thousands of lines of code that illustrate advanced programming techniques with the Windows API and the new object-oriented features of Visual Basic 4

- The Windows API type library and other useful tools, such as Property Shop, Bug Wizard, Time It, and the VBUTIL dynamic-link library

HARDCORE VISUAL BASIC provides developers and programmers with detailed coverage of such topics as:

- **Exploring the Spirit of Basic**—Language purification, the Basic Hungarian naming convention, efficient code versus correct code, and Basic wrappers for un-Basic hacks

- **Taking Control of Windows®**—Calling the Windows API, understanding C in Basic, and mastering messages and processes

- **Programming Objects, Basic Style**—Classes and objects, the form class, collecting objects, and creating new controls by delegating to classes

- **Painting Pictures**—The Basic way of drawing, painting, and animating

- **Reusing Code**—Modular packages for sorting, shuffling, searching, and parsing; reusable Search, Replace, About, and Color Select forms; and classes for editing, animating, managing the keyboard, handling menus, and sharing memory between programs

- **Programming in Different Environments**—Code for MS-DOS®, Windows 3.1, Windows 95, Windows NT®, and OLE

If you want to push Visual Basic to the max, HARDCORE VISUAL BASIC is your guide—it's essential for any serious Visual Basic programmer's library.

"HARDCORE VISUAL BASIC is a book for people who like Basic but don't like limits. It's for people who won't take no for an answer. If you're willing to go the extra mile for better performance and more functionality, you'll have fun with this book."

—Bruce McKinney

Microsoft Press® books are available wherever quality books are sold and through CompuServe's Electronic Mall—**GO MSP**—or our Web page, http://www.microsoft.com/mspress/. Call **1-800-MSPRESS** for more information or to place a credit card order.* Please refer to **BBK** when placing your order. Prices subject to change.

*In Canada, contact Macmillan Canada, Attn: Microsoft Press Dept., 164 Commander Blvd., Agincourt, Ontario, Canada M1S 3C7, or call 1-800-667-1115. Outside the U.S. and Canada, write to International Coordinator, Microsoft Press, One Microsoft Way, Redmond, WA 98052-6399, or fax +1-206-936-7329.

ISBN 1-55615-667-7
664 pages, one CD-ROM
$39.95 ($53.95 Canada)

Microsoft Press

IMPORTANT—READ CAREFULLY BEFORE OPENING SOFTWARE PACKET(S). By opening the sealed packet(s) containing the software, you indicate your acceptance of the following Microsoft License Agreement.

MICROSOFT LICENSE AGREEMENT
(Book Companion CD)

This is a legal agreement between you (either an individual or an entity) and Microsoft Corporation. By opening the sealed software packet(s) you are agreeing to be bound by the terms of this agreement. If you do not agree to the terms of this agreement, promptly return the unopened software packet(s) and any accompanying written materials to the place you obtained them for a full refund.

MICROSOFT SOFTWARE LICENSE

1. GRANT OF LICENSE. Microsoft grants to you the right to use one copy of the Microsoft software program included with this book (the "SOFTWARE") on a single terminal connected to a single computer. The SOFTWARE is in "use" on a computer when it is loaded into the temporary memory (i.e., RAM) or installed into the permanent memory (e.g., hard disk, CD-ROM, or other storage device) of that computer. You may not network the SOFTWARE or otherwise use it on more than one computer or computer terminal at the same time.

2. COPYRIGHT. The SOFTWARE is owned by Microsoft or its suppliers and is protected by United States copyright laws and international treaty provisions. Therefore, you must treat the SOFTWARE like any other copyrighted material (e.g., a book or musical recording) except that you may either (a) make one copy of the SOFTWARE solely for backup or archival purposes, or (b) transfer the SOFTWARE to a single hard disk provided you keep the original solely for backup or archival purposes. You may not copy the written materials accompanying the SOFTWARE.

3. OTHER RESTRICTIONS. You may not rent or lease the SOFTWARE, but you may transfer the SOFTWARE and accompanying written materials on a permanent basis provided you retain no copies and the recipient agrees to the terms of this Agreement. You may not reverse engineer, decompile, or disassemble the SOFTWARE. If the SOFTWARE is an update or has been updated, any transfer must include the most recent update and all prior versions.

4. DUAL MEDIA SOFTWARE. If the SOFTWARE package contains more than one kind of disk (3.5", 5.25", and CD-ROM), then you may use only the disks appropriate for your single-user computer. You may not use the other disks on another computer or loan, rent, lease, or transfer them to another user except as part of the permanent transfer (as provided above) of all SOFTWARE and written materials.

5. SAMPLE CODE. If the SOFTWARE includes Sample Code, then Microsoft grants you a royalty-free right to reproduce and distribute the sample code of the SOFTWARE provided that you: (a) distribute the sample code only in conjunction with and as a part of your software product; (b) do not use Microsoft's or its authors' names, logos, or trademarks to market your software product; (c) include the copyright notice that appears on the SOFTWARE on your product label and as a part of the sign-on message for your software product; and (d) agree to indemnify, hold harmless, and defend Microsoft and its authors from and against any claims or lawsuits, including attorneys' fees, that arise or result from the use or distribution of your software product.

DISCLAIMER OF WARRANTY

The SOFTWARE (including instructions for its use) is provided "AS IS" WITHOUT WARRANTY OF ANY KIND. MICROSOFT FURTHER DISCLAIMS ALL IMPLIED WARRANTIES INCLUDING WITHOUT LIMITATION ANY IMPLIED WARRANTIES OF MERCHANTABILITY OR OF FITNESS FOR A PARTICULAR PURPOSE. THE ENTIRE RISK ARISING OUT OF THE USE OR PERFORMANCE OF THE SOFTWARE AND DOCUMENTATION REMAINS WITH YOU.

IN NO EVENT SHALL MICROSOFT, ITS AUTHORS, OR ANYONE ELSE INVOLVED IN THE CREATION, PRODUCTION, OR DELIVERY OF THE SOFTWARE BE LIABLE FOR ANY DAMAGES WHATSOEVER (INCLUDING, WITHOUT LIMITA-TION, DAMAGES FOR LOSS OF BUSINESS PROFITS, BUSINESS INTERRUPTION, LOSS OF BUSINESS INFORMATION, OR OTHER PECUNIARY LOSS) ARISING OUT OF THE USE OF OR INABILITY TO USE THE SOFTWARE OR DOCUMENTATION, EVEN IF MICROSOFT HAS BEEN ADVISED OF THE POSSIBILITY OF SUCH DAMAGES. BECAUSE SOME STATES/COUNTRIES DO NOT ALLOW THE EXCLUSION OR LIMITATION OF LIABILITY FOR CONSEQUENTIAL OR INCIDENTAL DAMAGES, THE ABOVE LIMITATION MAY NOT APPLY TO YOU.

U.S. GOVERNMENT RESTRICTED RIGHTS

The SOFTWARE and documentation are provided with RESTRICTED RIGHTS. Use, duplication, or disclosure by the Government is subject to restrictions as set forth in subparagraph (c)(1)(ii) of The Rights in Technical Data and Computer Software clause at DFARS 252.227-7013 or subparagraphs (c)(1) and (2) of the Commercial Computer Software — Restricted Rights 48 CFR 52.227-19, as applicable. Manufacturer is Microsoft Corporation, One Microsoft Way, Redmond, WA 98052-6399.

If you acquired this product in the United States, this Agreement is governed by the laws of the State of Washington.

Should you have any questions concerning this Agreement, or if you desire to contact Microsoft Press for any reason, please write: Microsoft Press, One Microsoft Way, Redmond, WA 98052-6399.

Register Today!

Return this
*Client/Server Programming
with Microsoft® Visual Basic®*
registration card for a Microsoft Press® catalog

U.S. and Canada addresses only. Fill in information below and mail postage-free. Please mail only the bottom half of this page.

1-57231-232-7A   ***CLIENT/SERVER PROGRAMMING
WITH MICROSOFT® VISUAL BASIC®***   *Owner Registration Card*

_____

NAME

_____

INSTITUTION OR COMPANY NAME

_____

ADDRESS

_____

_____

CITY   STATE   ZIP

Microsoft®Press
Quality Computer Books

**For a free catalog of
Microsoft Press® products, call
1-800-MSPRESS**